D1567900

A Rift in the Clouds

A Rift in the Clouds

RACE AND THE
SOUTHERN FEDERAL JUDICIARY,
1900–1910

Brent J. Aucoin

The University of Arkansas Press
Fayetteville • 2007

Library of Congress Cataloging-in-Publication Data

Aucoin, Brent J. (Brent Jude)
   "A rift in the clouds" : race and the southern federal judiciary, 1900–1910 /
Brent J. Aucoin.
      p. cm.
   Includes bibliographical references and index.
   ISBN-13: 978-1-55728-849-3 (hardcover : alk. paper)
   ISBN-10: 1-55728-849-6 (hardcover : alk. paper)
   1. African Americans—Civil rights—History—20th century. 2. African Americans
—Civil rights—Southern States—History—20th century. 3. Race discrimination—
Law and legislation—United States—History—20th century. 4. Civil rights movement
—United States—History—20th century. 5. Trieber, Jacob, 1853–1927. 6. Speer,
Emory. 7. Jones, Thomas Goode, 1844–1914. 8. Judges—United States. I. Title.
   KF4757.A953 2007
   342.7308'73—dc22
                                                                 2007019049

For my parents, Richard and Clelia Aucoin

Look! The wages you failed to pay the workmen who mowed your fields are crying out against you. The cries of the harvesters have reached the ears of the Lord Almighty. You have lived on earth in luxury and self-indulgence. You have fattened yourself in the day of slaughter.
—James 5:4–5

Contents

Acknowledgments   xi

Chapter One: Dark Clouds   1

Chapter Two: Judge Jacob Trieber   17

Chapter Three: Judge Emory Speer   37

Chapter Four: Judge Thomas Goode Jones   53

Chapter Five: Conclusion   81

Appendix A: Revised Statutes, U.S. Compiled
Statutes 1901   91

Appendix B: Judge Jacob Trieber's Charge to the
Jury, Helena, Arkansas, October 6, 1903   93

Appendix C: Judge Jacob Trieber's "A Rift in the Clouds"
Letter to Judge Thomas Goode Jones, October 14, 1904   97

Appendix D: Judge Jacob Trieber to President
Theodore Roosevelt, February 27, 1905   101

Appendix E: Opinion of Judge Emory Speer in the
Case of *United States v. Thomas McClellan and William F. Crawley,*
March 15, 1904   105

Appendix F: Judge Thomas Goode Jones's "Suggestions
in the Bailey Case"   117

Notes   127

Bibliography   149

Index   165

Acknowledgments

Because this book could not have been written without the support and sacrifices of my wife, Amanda, and my grandmother, Genevieve Buras, I would be remiss if I did not acknowledge my deep indebtedness to them first and foremost.

Most of this book was researched and written while I was a PhD student at the University of Arkansas, where I received much assistance and encouragement from the faculty, staff, and my fellow students. The generous support of both the Mary D. Hudgins Research Grant and the Mary D. Hudgins Fellowship helped to make my studies and scholarly endeavors at Arkansas possible. I received indispensable guidance and encouragement from my mentor, Willard B. Gatewood Jr. I also received invaluable assistance from Beth Juhl, Andrea E. Cantrell, and the entire staff at the David W. Mullins Library as well as from Jeannie Whayne, Randall Woods, Daniel Sutherland, David Chappell, James Chase, David Sloan, Lori Bogle, Joseph Carruth, and William Atto.

So many people helped me at so many libraries and archives that I hesitate to attempt to try identifying them. I nevertheless would like to thank Norwood Kerr, Rickie Brunner, and the rest of the staff at the Alabama Department of Archives and History for their generous assistance. Likewise, Mary Ann Hawkins and other staff members at the National Archives, Southeast Region (Atlanta) deserve special mention, as do Paul Pruitt at the Bounds Library at the University of Alabama Law School and Marilyn Goodwin and Debbie James of the Felix Goodson Library at Williams Baptist College. I also received much assistance from staff members at the National Archives in Washington, D.C., the National Archives, Southwest Region (Ft. Worth, Texas), the Manuscript Division of the Library of Congress, the Arkansas History Commission and State Archives, the Federal Judicial History Office, and the libraries of the University of Arkansas Law School, Arkansas State University, Southeastern Baptist Theological Seminary, the University of North Carolina, Chapel Hill, Duke University, Auburn University, the University of Alabama, the University of Alabama Law School, Samford University, Emory University, and Mercer University.

I owe a special debt of gratitude to Kenneth Moore Startup, Michael Travers, and the anonymous readers for the University of Arkansas Press who read through the manuscript and provided me with suggestions that greatly improved the finished product. They alerted me to numerous flaws and errors and bear no responsibility for those that invariably passed unde-tected. I also wish to thank Larry Malley and the editors at the University of Arkansas Press for their guidance and hard work.

Throughout the process of writing this book I benefited greatly from the support and encouragement of numerous colleagues and students. I am grateful to everyone at Williams Baptist College, but must single out Jerry Gibbens, Todd Ewing, Chris Lawrey, Jerol Swaim, Heather Prater, Bekah Lockhart, and Lisa Mamula, in particular, for their assistance. I am grateful for the collegial and scholarly atmosphere that exists at Southeastern College at Wake Forest and am especially thankful for the assistance provided by Peggy Loafman, James Alexander, Bryan Huff, Lew Ayotte, Billy Shaw, Dougald McLaurin III, and Donald Jamison, and the support of Pete Schemm and Daniel Akin.

I owe a special thanks to James and Clelia Fargason, Ross and Mary LaDart, John and Lynn Briggs, Sheppard and Angie Nance, and Wes and Kathy Burgess for their kindness and hospitality. I also appreciate the encour-agement I have received over the years from John Ailie, Rick Vis, Jimmy DeMoss, Jerry Watson, Marilyn Briggs, Charles F. DeVane Jr., Gerald James, David Wells, Carrie Wells, and the members of the Texarkana Reformed Baptist Church in Texarkana, Arkansas; Covenant Presbyterian Church in Fayetteville, Arkansas; and Grace Baptist Church in Paragould, Arkansas.

I am also deeply indebted to my family for all that they have done. I have been inspired by my fond memories of Wallace and Genevieve Buras, Lydia Buras, and Edward and Lillian Aucoin, and have received much encouragement from my brothers, Brian and Steven Aucoin. My in-laws, Henry and Melba Wood and Genevieve Wood, have gone out of their way over the years to help facilitate my research and writing and never ceased to inquire about the progress (or lack thereof) of my various scholarly projects. Finally, I wish to thank my three sons, Addison, Andrew, and Aaron, who (thankfully) never failed in their daily efforts to liberate me from the con-fines of southern legal history so that I might experience the refreshing joys and pleasures of their company in their world.

- CHAPTER ONE -

Dark Clouds

AT THE DAWN of the twentieth century the future looked bright for the citizens of the United States of America. The patriotic fervor surrounding America's entry into the Spanish-American War in 1898 helped to heal the sectional wounds of the Civil War and propelled the country into the twentieth century unified and victorious. Likewise, the Industrial Revolution in America, which came in the wake of the Civil War, transformed the country during the last quarter of the nineteenth century and enabled it to enter the new century as one of the most modern, prosperous, and powerful nations in the entire world. And as the country stepped confidently into the 1900s, many Americans considered the transition as the beginning of a Progressive era for the nation. But for some Americans, particularly black Americans, there was much darkness at the dawning. From their vantage point dark clouds obscured the rising sun and clear skies that so many other Americans saw when they peered into the "American century." As blacks moved into the new century, the vast majority of them did so on a segregated basis, without access to the ballot box and haunted by the specter of racial violence and prejudice. For them, the turning of the century did not usher in an era of progress but rather a descent into the nadir.

Unfortunately for blacks, the situation that many of them faced around the turn of the century had been made possible by the rulings of the American judiciary—the branch of the United States government that more than any other is expected to safeguard a minority from the tyranny of the majority. But during the late nineteenth and early twentieth centuries the judicial branch, led by the U.S. Supreme Court, did much to encourage (and little to prevent) oppression of blacks by the majority under the banner of white supremacy.[1] Although the Court had historically been no friend to the Negro, this turn of events was nevertheless a bit perplexing to blacks because their closest white allies—northern Republicans—dominated the Court at the time.[2] Betrayed by their white "friends" on the bench, and with the formation of the National Association for the Advancement of Colored People still years away, it appeared that blacks had few advocates in the American legal community at the turn of the century. Nevertheless, there were some in the bar who raised their voices on behalf of blacks at this time, and they originated from a surprising source—the southern federal judiciary. At the dawn of the new century at least three white, southern federal judges sought to protect blacks from hostile southern governments and individuals. These three southern federal judges—Jacob Trieber (1853–1927) of Arkansas, Emory Speer (1848–1918) of Georgia, and Thomas Goode Jones (1844–1914) of Alabama—and their forgotten struggle for racial justice and civil rights is the focus of this book.

During the first years of the twentieth century, when these three men sat on the federal bench, the white South, led by the Democratic Party, was completing its counterrevolution to Reconstruction. When congressional Republicans had taken control of the Reconstruction process decades earlier in 1867, it appeared that a revolution was then at hand. The party of Lincoln had, in swift succession, passed the Thirteenth, Fourteenth, and Fifteenth amendments to the U.S. Constitution, and in doing so had seemingly transformed over four million ex-slaves into free and equal citizens of the United States. Men who just years earlier were slaves, viewed by most whites (and the U.S. Supreme Court) as "property" with no legal rights, were now guaranteed the equal protection of the law and armed with the right to vote and hold office. These and other actions on the part of the Republican Party threatened to turn southern society upside down and transform the numerous ex-slaves and their descendants into the South's most influential bloc of voters.

White southern Democrats who opposed such a revolutionary transformation of society responded to congressional Reconstruction with election fraud and violence as they attempted to oust Republicans from elective office. The use of such tactics, and the acquiescence of the federal government and the northern public, meant that by 1877 the Democratic Party, self described as the "party of white supremacy," had reclaimed its status as the dominant party in Dixie. Upon winning political control of all of the ex-Confederate states, white southern Democrats sought to re-establish, as closely as possible, the conditions that had prevailed in the *antebellum* South. This meant not only that whites would control the region economically, socially, and politically, but also that African Americans would form the basis of a stable, cheap, and subservient agricultural work force.[3]

One method used by southern Democrats to replicate the conditions of the antebellum South involved the utilization and abuse of the convict leasing system. This system consisted of state authorities leasing the state's prisoners to landowners and business owners to be used as laborers. The state typically relinquished oversight of the leased convicts, leaving them to the mercy of the profit-minded farmer or business owner. The ranks of the convicts were frequently replenished through the efforts of unscrupulous local law enforcement officials who funneled black men into the system by imposing excessive sentences for minor crimes and even leveling false charges against innocent blacks. Possessing contracts which obligated the state to provide him with a stipulated number of laborers, the lessee had little incentive to adequately house, clothe, and feed those in his charge. This situation led to conditions that have been described as worse than slavery.[4]

In addition to utilizing the convict leasing system, southern Democratic leaders also passed laws that compelled African Americans to remain on the farms of white landowners. The contract-labor laws passed by some Democratic-controlled southern legislatures stipulated that if a laborer broke a contract with his employer, then he could be arrested and either returned to his employer or sent to work on the state chain gang.[5] Likewise, southern state legislatures also passed legislation making it a criminal offense for a laborer to leave the premises of his landlord when he owed the landlord money. This system of "debt peonage" spread throughout the post-Reconstruction South. In light of the agricultural labor system that existed in the South during the late nineteenth century, it was not uncommon for poor black (and white) farmers to become debt peons. After the Civil War, most freedmen and many whites became sharecroppers. Due to a lack of money, they rented land by agreeing to give their landlord half of everything they harvested. The shortage of money that prevented sharecroppers from simply paying rent also caused them to seek credit for items needed before the crop was harvested. The primary source of credit for sharecroppers was their landlord. They purchased clothes, food, seed, tools, and other items from their landlord, with the intention of paying for these goods with the money earned from the proceeds of their half of the crop. Low crop prices, usurious interest rates, and shamelessly fraudulent bookkeeping made it impossible for many sharecroppers to pay their debts at the end of the year. Consequently, those sharecroppers became indebted to their landlords and fell into debt peonage.[6]

The entire apparatus of unfree labor in the postbellum South, although often sanctioned by law, was dependent upon the use of force. This was evident even in the years immediately following the Civil War when officials with the Freedman's Bureau oversaw the development of the South's labor system. Throughout Reconstruction, Herbert Shapiro explained, "the freedmen were intimidated, whipped, and beaten to compel them to agree to onerous labor contracts with landlords."[7] Only by terrorizing blacks could the South's economic elite keep them from moving on in search of better conditions. The numerous letters that black peons sent to federal officials demonstrate that it was not legislation that kept them on their landlord's land, but rather it was the fear that came with looking into the barrel of the landlord's gun that prevented them from fleeing. For instance, one black peon in Georgia wrote to the Department of Justice and complained: "I am in no contract with Mr Price he only taken his gun in his hand and say negroes let me have the work [sic]."[8] Likewise, a black Mississippi peon wrote that his landlord and other whites "took a colored man out last night and tied him to a tree and blindfolded him and they beat him until the blood run down on the ground and they shot they guns till the people thought war had began and the people went today and looked at where the blood soked in the ground, and I am afraid my time next I cant sleep at night when I go to bed so do Some thing at once and get me away from this place [sic]."[9] Unfortunately, the "peons customarily found no champion."[10] Local, state, and even federal officials generally ignored the pleas of those men and women, black and white, who were being held in a state of involuntary servitude. Debt peonage represented the South's most blatant defiance of the Thirteenth Amendment, and by the turn of the century, according to Daniel Novak, "a majority of the black population of the South" had fallen prey to this attempt to reinstitute slavery.[11]

When white southerners were not using force or the threat of force to compel blacks to stay on a particular piece of land, they used force to drive them away from certain areas. Landowners and business owners viewed blacks as potential laborers, but for poor whites they were economic competitors. Consequently, white farmers and laborers frequently sought to displace blacks who threatened their economic security. Although there was no set standard for such an undertaking, it typically consisted of a group of whites on horseback visiting blacks in the middle of the night to deliver the message to them that they were not welcome. This activity was commonly referred to as "nightriding" or "whitecapping." The latter term implies a similarity to the tactics utilized by members of the notorious Ku Klux Klan, who dressed in white caps and sheets when terrorizing the local black population.

Whitecapping in the rural South became most severe during the 1890s and the first decade of the twentieth century. One of the primary reasons for the timing of this epidemic is that many southern farmers, by 1890, began to suffer economically from low crop prices and severe downturns in the nation's economy. Black laborers made convenient scapegoats for the depressed conditions, and poor whites frequently took out their frustrations by attacking their black neighbors. In addition, whitecappers realized that they could gain access to desirable lands and jobs occupied by blacks by scaring them away. The practice became so effective that "even after the return of prosperity white farmers continued into the twentieth century attempts to drive blacks away" from communities and jobs.[12] This led one historian to conclude that "attacks on blacks by whitecappers" were "almost commonplace in the South in the late nineteenth and early twentieth centuries."[13]

Even though the southern counterrevolution had, by the late 1880s, succeeded in severely restricting the economic mobility of African Americans, white southern Democrats did not rest content. Starting in the 1890s, the South entered a more radical phase of racism, and the turn of the century came to be known as the "nadir" of the postbellum African American experience.[14] Even though the voting booth was already off-limits to many African Americans as a result of intimidation, southern white Democrats began to pass legislation disenfranchising blacks. Mississippi led the way when it denied blacks of the right to vote in 1890. Over the course of the next decade, the "Mississippi Plan" became the American way—or at least the Southern way.[15] By 1908, every southern state had in place some disfranchising device designed to prevent blacks and, in many cases, poor whites from exercising the right to vote.[16]

The 1890s ushered in not only a period of disfranchisement, but also an unprecedented era of racial lynchings. It is estimated that during the 1890s, on average, one person was lynched in the South every other day, and two out of three of the victims were black.[17] Rather than denouncing the use of extralegal violence against African Americans, many white southern leaders instead publicly encouraged such action, arguing that it was necessary to maintain white supremacy and to protect white southern women from black rapists. Rather than being ostracized for taking such a position, the defenders of lynching rode a wave of white southern support into high political offices. Men such as James K. Vardaman of Mississippi, Jeff Davis of Arkansas, and Ben Tillman of South Carolina were elected as governors and U.S. senators in part because of their public support of lynching African Americans.[18]

Those few southerners who did dare to question lynching and whitecapping found themselves stigmatized and harshly criticized. "Ready with acerbic pens and race-baiting oratory, the radicals [extreme southern

racists]," according to W. Fitzhugh Brundage, "savaged any southerners who
dared to criticize mob violence." Professor Andrew Sledd of Emory College
found this out the hard way after writing an article in the July 1902 issue of
the *Atlantic Monthly* that moderately criticized lynching. Even though he
asserted that blacks belonged to an "inferior race," his denunciation of lynching caused a public outcry that led to his forced removal from Emory.[19]

A year later, Professor John Spencer Bassett of Trinity College (now
Duke University) published a similar article in the *South Atlantic Quarterly*.
By criticizing southern politicians for demagoguing the race issue (and by
calling Booker T. Washington the greatest southerner since Robert E. Lee),
"he created a storm that very nearly consumed him." Josephus Daniels, a
leading journalist and Democratic leader of North Carolina, led the attack
on Bassett. As for the issue of lynching, Daniels said, "What Prof. Bassett
enumerates as evidence of hostility [to blacks] is the growing glory of
Southern manhood and Southern chivalry."[20]

In light of the treatment afforded Sledd and Bassett, it is no surprise that
when one historian set out to identify turn-of-the-century southern liberals, he had to conclude that "the ranks of these men were thin."[21] Charles
Wynes said that it was "physically dangerous" for southern whites to stand
up for the rights of blacks, and at "no time in the South's history has this
been more true than in the period of roughly 1885–1917."[22] Likewise,
when Timothy Huebner surveyed the racial climate during those same
decades he concluded that the "sectional orthodoxy on racial issues" was so
pervasive that if anyone "stepped outside of the white convention on such
matters, they invited the wrath of the region's power structure." In particular, he asserted that the racial climate of the time in the South explained
why state "judges [in the South] ensured that the Reconstruction Amendments and civil rights measures remained ineffective and guaranteed that
new forms of racial oppression—debt peonage and lynching, for example—
continued unabated."[23] Although this may have been true for most state
judges in the South, there were at least three southern judges on the federal
bench—Judges Jacob Trieber, Emory Speer, and Thomas Goode Jones—
who actually called upon the federal government to take a more active role
in protecting African Americans from hostile, exploitative white southerners,
and to do so on the basis of the Reconstruction-era amendments.

But as early as 1873 the U.S. Supreme Court began to narrowly interpret the Thirteenth, Fourteenth, and Fifteenth Amendments, thus essentially
aiding and abetting the southern counterrevolution. When the Court
handed down its decision in the famous *Slaughterhouse Cases* in 1873, it con-

stituted the "first great judicial setback suffered by blacks in their quest for effective constitutional protection of their liberties."[24] Although unrelated to the issue of black civil rights on the surface, this case provided the Court with its first opportunity to interpret the meaning of the Fourteenth Amendment. At issue in the case was a Louisiana law providing a privately owned company with a monopoly of the slaughtering business in New Orleans. Ostensibly, the Louisiana legislature had created this monopoly to prevent further contamination of the city's drinking water by butchers who slaughtered their animals on the riverfront just north of the city's water intake valves. The law passed by the legislature mandated that all butchering be done in one location, south of the city. New Orleans butchers, unhappy with the law that forced them to relocate and pay fees to the monopoly company, sued the state in an attempt to have the law declared unconstitutional.[25]

The lawyer for the disaffected butchers, John A. Campbell, contended that the Louisiana law violated the Thirteenth and Fourteenth Amendments.[26] The law, he asserted, placed the butchers in a position of involuntary servitude, as the term was used in the Thirteenth Amendment. In addition, the law transgressed the Fourteenth Amendment by abridging the privileges and immunities of citizens, denying the plaintiffs of equal protection of the laws, and depriving them of their property without due process of the law.[27] The Supreme Court, in a five to four decision, rejected these arguments. Justice Samuel Miller, speaking for the majority, said that to "withdraw the mind" from the true intent of the amendment and to believe that people are forced into involuntary servitude by a law limiting where they can engage in certain business practices "requires an effort, to say the least of it."[28] He then rejected Campbell's view of the privileges and immunities clause by ingeniously separating state and federal citizenship and specifying, to a certain extent, the characteristics of both. With the Fourteenth Amendment, Americans became both citizens of their respective states and citizens of the United States. But most of the rights of citizenship, the Court said, still stem from a person's state citizenship. With national citizenship Americans won relatively insignificant rights, such as the right to receive protection abroad, to have access to the District of Columbia, and to engage in interstate and foreign commerce. Those were the "privileges and immunities" of national citizenship according to the Court. Consequently, the privilege of earning a living or running a legitimate business, the Court concluded, rested with one's state citizenship. All those seeking such security needed to look for it from their state government. In summarizing the *Slaughterhouse* decision, one Republican commented that it "allowed the nation to protect American citizens anywhere in the world except in the states."[29]

Justice Miller concluded the decision by dismissing, with very little comment, Campbell's arguments regarding the "due process" and "equal protection" clauses. He then addressed those "who believe in the necessity of a strong National government." He told them that "the existence of the States with powers for domestic and local government, including the regulation of civil rights—the rights of person and property—was essential to the perfect working of our complex form of government." The Court, he said, did not see in the Reconstruction-era amendments "any purpose to destroy the main features of" America's federal system. In what was meant to be a statement of reassurance to the American people, he pledged that the Court would continue to uphold "the balance between State and Federal power."[30]

It is generally believed that the Court's decision in *Slaughterhouse* constituted the opening salvo of the judicial counterrevolution in the area of black civil rights. Some scholars assert that the framers of Reconstruction-era civil rights legislation intended to revolutionize federalism and constitutional law. It is further asserted that the justices of the Supreme Court chose to ignore the intentions of these lawmakers and, in the process, minimized the changes they had sought to establish. For instance, legal scholar Donald Lively insists that the framers of the Fourteenth Amendment intended "to transfer at least the guarantees of the Civil Rights Act of 1866 to the privileges and immunities clause."[31] They intended for the federal government to protect the rights of citizens, especially blacks, even if it was limited to times when states failed to do so themselves. But with *Slaughterhouse,* the Court took a giant step toward establishing the legal doctrine that the state alone was responsible for protecting citizens and that the federal government had no authority to intervene under any circumstances. In evaluating the affect of *Slaughterhouse,* Lively concluded that it "so eviscerated the meaning of the privileges and immunities clause that it remains an insignificant factor in Fourteenth Amendment jurisprudence."[32]

The line of logic followed in the *Slaughterhouse* decision led the Court in 1883 to rule that the Reconstruction-era amendments did not empower the federal government to prosecute members of lynch mobs—even when the state failed to act. The case *U.S. v. Harris* stemmed from an incident in which an armed mob of Tennessee whites forcefully removed several African Americans from their jail cells, killing one and severely beating the others. Federal authorities in Tennessee indicted some of the mob members under section two of the 1871 Ku Klux Act, which outlawed two or more people conspiring together to deprive someone of their constitutional rights. The Court declared this important part of the act unconstitutional. Section two authorized the federal government to intervene in instances of private injustice even in the absence of any evidence that the state had failed to take appropriate action. In addition, the Court asserted that none of the recent amendments had granted Congress the power to prosecute individuals for committing "regular" crimes such as murder or assault.[33]

During that same year, the Court dealt a blow to another important piece of civil rights legislation, again using *Slaughterhouse* as its starting point. This time the Court gutted the 1875 Civil Rights Act in a decision known as the *Civil Rights Cases*. Justice Joseph P. Bradley, speaking for the eight to one majority, argued that the act did not fall within the limits of the Fourteenth Amendment because it prohibited individuals, such as the owners of inns and theaters, from discriminating against other individuals. The amendment, Justice Bradley said, only authorized Congress to regulate the states, not individuals.[34]

Although handing down a decision that led to the infamous *Plessy v. Ferguson* decision and over a half-century of legalized racial segregation, the Court actually evidenced in this decision a willingness (for the time being) to broadly interpret the Thirteenth Amendment. Justice Bradley asserted that the amendment established and decreed "universal civil and political freedom throughout the United States" and that it provided "Congress with power to pass all laws necessary and proper for abolishing all badges and incidents of slavery in the United States." In addition, such legislation "may be direct and primary, operating upon the acts of individuals whether sanctioned by State legislation or not."[35] But according to the Court, denying blacks the right to use public accommodations did not constitute a badge or incident of slavery. So, although the Court implied that Congress could prosecute individuals as a result of its obligation to abolish badges of slavery, it stipulated that the Thirteenth Amendment could not be used to support legislation outlawing racial segregation.

While the Court proceeded to strike down Reconstruction-era legislation, it also appeared determined to thwart the efforts of federal officials to punish whites who violated the civil rights of African Americans. For instance, in its first decision regarding the 1870 Civil Rights Act, the Court dismissed the charges against two white election officials (Hiram Reese and Matthew Foushee) in Lexington, Kentucky, who refused to count the vote of a black citizen named William Garner.[36] In the decision known as *U.S. v.*

Reese (1876), the Court declared unconstitutional sections three and four of the 1870 act.[37] The Court reasoned that the Fifteenth Amendment only authorized Congress to intervene when a state denied someone of the right to vote on account of race. The section of the act in question, the Court said, made it illegal to deny a qualified person the suffrage, but did not specifically stipulate that such denial must be based on race. In other words, the Court claimed that the sections were too broad. They included, allegedly, all instances of denial, not just those in which race was the deciding factor.

Justice Ward Hunt dissented, arguing that his colleagues ignored the clear fact that the entire act was geared toward denials based on race. Sections one and two, he pointed out, state this explicitly. The sections in question contain the words "as aforesaid," which obviously refer to the sections containing the reference to race. The Court easily could have read racial motivation into the two sections in question, but refused to do so. So, although the decision did not alter the federal government's ability to prevent states from discriminating on the basis of race in qualifying people to vote, it allowed two racist election officials to escape punishment and sent a message to those concerned with black civil rights that the Court seemed determined to find ways to avoid sanctioning the spirit of the Reconstruction amendments and laws.[38]

The notion that the Court was hostile to the rights of blacks appeared to be confirmed when, on the same day that it handed down its *Reese* decision, it also freed the white men who had been indicted in Louisiana for killing at least 105 blacks and three whites on Easter Sunday, 1873. This incident, known as the Colfax Riot or the Grant Parish Massacre, occurred when black Republicans (along with a few whites) occupied the Grant Parish Courthouse in an effort to claim the offices they felt they had won in a disputed election. White Democrats in the community, seeking to claim the offices for their candidates, besieged the courthouse, set it on fire, and shot the occupants as they fled the burning building. Although federal officials secured ninety-six indictments, they succeeded in arresting only nine of the accused participants. The Court, through its decision in *U.S. v. Cruikshank* (1876), reversed the conviction of William Cruikshank and the eight other white Louisianians who had been indicted for the massacre. The Court, once again, appeared almost desperate to justify freeing the defendants. This time the Court faulted the indictments for not claiming that the actions of the defendants were motivated by race. Had the indictments stated this explicitly, the Court said, then the convictions may have been upheld under the 1870 Civil Rights Act. As for the assertion that Cruikshank and his cohorts had denied the victims of their federal right to assemble peacefully, the Court utilized its *Slaughterhouse* ruling to its advantage. They ruled that the Louisiana Republicans had gathered in response to local and state affairs—not national. As such, their gathering fell under state jurisdiction, not federal. Had they assembled, for instance, to petition Congress, then they would have been exercising a right associated with national citizenship, and Cruikshank and the others could have been convicted on those grounds.[39] In light of this and previous decisions, it is no wonder that the editor of the *Voice of the Negro* concluded in 1904 that "The United States Supreme Court has always either decided openly against the Negro in this country or avoided the contentions of the colored people by the most artful dodges behind hair-splitting technicalities."[40] The end result, according to one historian, was that "practically all the relevant decisions of the United States Supreme Court during Reconstruction and to the end of the century nullified or curtailed those rights of Negroes which the Reconstruction 'Radicals' thought they had written into law and into the Constitution."[41]

The natural question that arises when one considers the Supreme Court's evisceration of the Reconstruction-era amendments and the racial climate of the time is, Why did Judges Trieber, Speer, and Jones challenge the reigning orthodoxy, both legal and racial? If confronted with this question themselves, the judges, who generally embraced the dominant legal philosophy of the day (legal formalism), would most likely have responded by asserting that they reached their decisions on the basis of interpreting legal sources. While it is evident that as legal formalists they, indeed, embraced an originalist approach to the Constitution and gave great weight to precedent, it is also apparent that their political beliefs and social values played an important role in their judicial conduct. While their decisions seem to indicate an adherence to precedence and original intent, their personal correspondence betrays the role that their political and social views played in their jurisprudence.

In her study of the jurisprudence of Supreme Court Justice John Marshall Harlan, Linda Przybyszewski demonstrates the importance of examining non-legal sources in the course of doing judicial biographies. In particular, she uses Harlan's unpublished lecture notes and his wife's memoirs (among other sources) to show that paternalism, orthodox Christianity, and constitutional nationalism shaped his worldview and, therefore, guided his responses to the legal issues he faced as a judge.[42] Likewise, it is beneficial to look beyond the legal writings (case opinions, charges to juries, etc.)

of Judges Trieber, Speer, and Jones to flesh out the various influences and concepts that shaped, as Benjamin Cardozo put it, their "underlying philosophy of life" and their actions on the bench.[43] Judges Trieber, Speer, and Jones were kind enough to leave behind an ample supply of such sources, namely, the personal letters they wrote to one another discussing the civil rights cases being heard in their courts. These letters provide us not only with further insight into their thoughts and motivations, but also with an extraordinary glimpse into the decision-making process of federal judges around the turn of the century. It is apparent from that correspondence that the judges were very much aware of the racial situation in the South at the time and of the possible effect that their decisions might have on relations between the races. For instance, when Judge Jones called upon federal authorities to punish the members of lynch mobs in the South, Judge Trieber of Arkansas wrote him, "I see a rift in the clouds when men like yourself, Judge Speer of Georgia, and Judge [John H.] Rogers of this state, all natives of the South and ex-Confederates, lead in this patriotic movement to awaken the conscience of our people" and solve the race problems plaguing the South.[44]

The fact that the judges of this era considered the ramifications of the decisions they handed down, particularly in the area of race relations, is one of the key points that Michael J. Klarman makes in his monumental book *From Jim Crow to Civil Rights*.[45] But in making this point, Klarman asserts that before the civil rights movement, judges almost universally ruled against the rights of blacks because it was popular to do so.[46] Judges, he argued, almost inevitably reflect the broader social and political context of the times and thus rule in accordance with the prevalent racial views of the day.[47] He therefore asserts that the Supreme Court ruled in favor of segregation in *Plessy* because doing so reflected popular opinion. Likewise, the Court ruled against segregation in *Brown v. Board of Education* because, by the 1950s, public opinion had shifted in opposition to segregation. As such, he concluded, judges should be viewed neither as heroes nor villains. The Warren Court should not be praised for its progressive views on race when in actuality they merely reflected the views of most whites (outside of the South). Similarly, the Fuller Court should not be villainized for sanctioning segregation because it, too, was merely reflecting the majority view on the subject.[48] In fact, Klarman even seems to assert that had the Fuller Court wanted to strike down segregation in the 1890s, it could not have done so because the Court could not rely on lower court judges to support and enforce such a decision when confronted by the violent white opposition such judges would inevitably face.[49] But the actions of Judges Trieber, Speer, and Jones do not conform to Klarman's thesis. It was during the very nadir of race relations in America that these judges contravened the popular racism of the day and called for the recognition and protection of black civil rights. They were obviously capable of resisting both popular opinion and the threat of violence, and presumably were not the only judges in America who possessed the ability to do so.

Klarman does acknowledge that some judges (namely, the justices on the Supreme Court) did occasionally rule on behalf of African American civil rights in the decades before *Brown,* but dismisses such actions as rare exceptions to the rule. In such instances, Klarman explains, the issue at hand was such an egregious violation of the law that the Court could not but rule against it. Examples of this, he says, can be found in the Court's willingness to rule against the grandfather clause and debt peonage laws because they "were transparent evasions of constitutional constraints."[50] The other exception to the rule that Klarman identifies is when judges contravene public opinion on the basis of the "culturally elite values" they embrace.[51] Even though most Americans support prayer in school and are opposed to desecrating the American flag, the Supreme Court has taken the opposite position on both matters because such views conform with the views of the majority of the cultural elite in America—a group to which most Supreme Court justices belong, apparently.[52] These exceptions to the rule may very well explain why Judges Trieber, Speer, and Jones cut against the grain of racial and legal thinking in their day, but it begs the question of why other judges throughout the American judicial system did not act accordingly. Were Trieber, Speer, and Jones the only members of a cultural elite who subscribed to the notion that lynchings, whitecapping, and debt peonage were legally (and morally) questionable activities that may have a detrimental effect on society? Were they the only judges who considered such activities, particularly when sanctioned either directly or indirectly by the authority of the state, to be transparent evasions of the intent of the Reconstruction-era amendments? One could and should assume that the answer to both questions is "no." It is reasonable to assume that other judges were capable of viewing these matters the same way these southern federal judges did. The question, then, is why they did not. Klarman would answer by saying that the judges could not rule as Judges Trieber, Speer, and Jones because they reflected popular opinion. This, indeed, appears to be true. Most judges, both northern and southern, seem to have reflected popular white opinion regarding blacks around the turn of the century. But this does not mean they were destined to do so or incapable of doing otherwise.[53] Trieber, Speer, and Jones demonstrate that it could be done, and done on a sound legal and moral basis. All judges of the era had the freedom and the means to act heroically or not.

So the question remains, How and why did Judges Trieber, Speer, and Jones act heroically with regard to black civil rights? It is apparent from their correspondence and other sources that Trieber, Speer, and Jones subscribed to what historians have called the "New South Creed"—the belief that the postbellum South could experience peace and prosperity by following the northern model of economic and agricultural diversification.[54] Advocates of this view, including the judges, believed that such an economic transformation, and the northern capital necessary for it to take place, would not materialize until the racial situation in the region stabilized. This belief provided the judges with an incentive to seek justice for African Americans; in their view there could be no true social harmony in the South as long as racial injustice continued to breed discord, violence, mutual resentment, and suspicion. While it is true that proponents of the New South Creed advocated the fair treatment of African Americans, it did not mean that they sought true equality for African Americans. Most New South advocates—who were white, relatively well-educated, and usually from an urban middle-class background—typically embraced the paternalistic views that are so often associated with their socioeconomic class.[55] For such paternalists, the solution to the South's "race problem" was for whites to treat blacks as parents treat their children, and for blacks to relate to whites as a child does a father. In such a scenario, whites would be mindful of the welfare of African Americans, but in turn African Americans were to respectfully and dutifully acknowledge the authority and superiority of whites.

Although the paternalistic racial ideology conformed to primary tenets of white supremacy, it did clash and in some ways fundamentally contradict the "radical" racism of the 1890s. To be sure, the so-called radical racists of the South, like the advocates of the New South Creed, were also attempting to stabilize the racial situation in Dixie. But in contrast to the New South approach, the radicals believed that racial peace in the region could only be accomplished by completely subjugating blacks. Alarmed by such a view and fearful of its success, New South advocates attempted to blunt the radical racism of the turn of the century. This helps to explain why the three white southern federal judges who are the subjects of this book handed down pro–African American decisions at a time when it seemed unusual for them to do so. It was not that they were racial egalitarians, but rather that they were paternalists who believed that radical racists were pushing their extreme version of white supremacy too far and leading the South away from the path chartered for the region by advocates of the New South Creed.

This is not to say that the decisions handed down by Trieber, Speer, and Jones were purely political or economically inspired. That is clearly not the case. It is apparent that they took their responsibilities as federal judges seriously and believed it was their duty to abide by the U.S. Constitution. It is also apparent that in reaching decisions in which they called for greater federal protection of African Americans and their civil rights, these judges sincerely believed that they were simply being faithful to the federal laws that they had pledged to uphold as members of the federal judiciary. But it must be kept in mind that most, if not all, federal judges (then and now) believe they are faithfully interpreting the law. Yet, in the case of Trieber, Speer, and Jones, their view of the law, particularly the Reconstruction-era amendments, differed greatly from that of their colleagues on the federal bench. In seeking to explain how individuals can read the same amendments, statutes, and precedents and yet reach such wildly divergent conclusions, one must consider the judges' backgrounds and views and seek to understand how these factors may have colored their interpretation of the law. Therefore, chapters 2, 3, and 4 will attempt to explain the backgrounds and views of Judges Trieber, Speer, and Jones, respectively, and examine the decisions that they handed down relating to black civil rights. The concluding chapter then focuses on explaining in greater detail why they handed down such decisions and demonstrates that their actions were the result of some immeasurable fusion of their societal, legal, and political philosophies.

Jacob Trieber, U.S. District Judge,
Eastern District of Arkansas, 1900–1927, circa 1910.

Photo by Shrader Photo, courtesy of the Library of Congress.

- CHAPTER TWO -

Judge Jacob Trieber

N JULY 26, 1900, President William McKinley appointed Jacob Trieber (1853–1927) to the federal bench as U.S. district judge for the Eastern District of Arkansas. At the time of his appointment, Trieber was serving as the U.S. attorney for the district and had established himself as one of the leaders of the Arkansas state Republican Party. Such accomplishments were no small feat considering that he was a Jewish immigrant who had only been an American citizen for thirteen years when McKinley appointed him to the bench (thus making him the first Jew to be appointed to the U.S. federal judiciary). In 1866, when he was thirteen years old, he and his parents escaped the growing anti-Semitism in Prussia by moving to St. Louis, Missouri. A few years later the Trieber family moved down the Mississippi River to open a dry-goods store in the Arkansas delta town of Helena, which boasted a small but growing Jewish community.[1]

Living in the Arkansas delta in the midst of the turmoil of Reconstruction, young Jacob Trieber jumped headlong into politics, aligning himself with the much-maligned Republican Party. At the same time, he began to read law under the tutelage of an ousted Republican member of the Arkansas State Supreme Court, Marshall L. Stephenson. After rising through the meager ranks of the Republican Party in Phillips County, Arkansas, he moved into the statewide arena by allying himself with Powell Clayton, the leader of the Arkansas state Republican Party. While establishing himself as one of Clayton's most trusted lieutenants, he pursued several elective positions. In 1884, 1891, 1892, and 1896, he lost races, respectively, for Arkansas attorney general, the U.S. Senate, the U.S. Congress, and chief justice of the Arkansas State Supreme Court. Despite these electoral failures, he enjoyed great success as a lawyer and a businessman in his adopted—and very southern —community. All the while he continued to work diligently on behalf of the Republican Party.[2]

Trieber frequently represented Arkansas as a delegate to Republican National Conventions (including as a McKinley delegate in 1896). After campaigning tirelessly for William McKinley in 1896, the president rewarded Trieber by appointing him to be a U.S. attorney in 1897. When Judge John A. Williams of the Eastern District of Arkansas died on July 3, 1900, Powell Clayton reminded McKinley of Trieber's dedication to the president and to the party and succeeded in convincing him to nominate Trieber for the position.[3] Garnering the support of "substantially the entire bar of the Eastern District of Arkansas," Trieber's nomination was easily confirmed by the U.S. Senate.[4]

As a federal district judge, Trieber embraced a broad interpretation of the Reconstruction-era constitutional amendments. This is particularly true with regard to the Thirteenth Amendment. His view of that amendment prompted him to advance the first significant challenge to the widespread debt peonage system in the Arkansas delta. It was during the first years of the twentieth century that this system first came under attack in the South as a whole, and officials in the southern federal judiciary played a vital role in this movement to free African Americans and poor whites from this form of forced labor.

In the spring of 1905, eight white men and one African American were brought before Judge Trieber on the charge of holding African Americans in a state of debt peonage.[5] In his charge to the federal grand jury, which was considering an indictment of the nine men, Judge Trieber expressed firm opposition to the system of debt peonage. He declared that "peonage was more dangerous to the safety of our republican institutions than slavery was."[6] He based this on the fact that peons, unlike slaves, could vote. Therefore, a peon master, unlike a slave owner, could use his position over individuals to force them to vote a certain way. Consequently, some peon masters had "a sufficient voice in the selection of the officials to determine the result of an election." This was especially true of wealthy individuals who could potentially control "thousands of people." It is no surprise then that he called the anti-peonage law "one of the most salutary statutes in existence."[7]

Judge Trieber implored the grand jury to indict the nine men. He made it clear to the jury members that it was illegal for one person to hold another person to labor for the purpose of liquidating a debt. Even if the debtor willingly volunteered to enter into such an agreement, Trieber said, such a contract or understanding was in violation of the Thirteenth Amendment. The jurors, he said, should not allow any personal disagreement with the law itself to influence their decision. The duty of the jurors, rather, was to enforce the law, even if they deemed it unwise. He concluded by urging the jurors to cast their votes "without fear, . . . bias or prejudice." The grand jury, in response to Judge Trieber's charge and the evidence presented, indicted all nine defendants.[8]

The *Arkansas Gazette* reported that two of the men indicted, Thomas and Joseph Pugh, were "prominent merchants and planters of Portland" in Ashley County. The Pugh brothers and their cohorts were accused of enticing African Americans to travel from Texas to Ashley County, where they were put to work and told that they could not leave until they had paid debts that they allegedly owed to their employers. When the black Texans attempted to flee to their home state, they were arrested and returned to their Arkansas employers.[9] On April 8, 1905, seven of the men who were indicted by the federal grand jury pled guilty. Judge Trieber responded by imposing upon the Pugh brothers the minimum punishment allowable by law: the payment of a thousand-dollar fine. As for the other five defendants, he delayed sentencing until a later date.[10]

Two of the men who were indicted for holding blacks in a state of peonage, but who pled not guilty, went to trial on April 17, 1905. One of the defendants, Robert Hill, was a "wealthy negro planter" from Lincoln County, according to the *Arkansas Gazette*. John McElwee (white), the other defendant, served as justice of the peace for Lincoln County. During the first day of the trial, two of the black men who were allegedly kept in a state of peonage by the defendants were allowed to testify. The black laborers, William Armstrong and Henry Davis, both recounted that they attempted to leave Hill's farm, even though they owed him money, and were arrested three different times on warrants issued by McElwee. Davis also stated that Hill threatened to kill him if he attempted to leave a fourth time.[11] The trial of Hill and McElwee ended after just one day. On April 19, 1905, McElwee's lawyer filed a demurrer, asserting that the evidence demonstrated that his client acted within the law and merely fulfilled his duties as justice of the peace. When Judge Trieber sustained the demurrer, thus freeing McElwee, Robert Hill changed his plea to guilty. Trieber then sentenced Hill to pay a thousand-dollar fine and court costs within sixty days.[12]

Despite the guilty pleas, the peonage cases ended in a disappointing manner. Although the federal authorities in the Eastern District of Arkansas can be credited with organizing the first prosecution of peon masters in Arkansas, it is apparent that Judge Trieber's actions did not eradicate the practice. Peonage persisted in the Arkansas delta after 1905. Walter White of the National Association for the Advancement of Colored People (NAACP), for instance, stated in 1919 that in Phillips County, Arkansas, "thousands of Negroes are held in the bonds of debt-slavery and peonage of the most flagrant sort."[13] In fact, debt peonage was cited as one of the primary causes of the infamous Elaine Race Riot of that year.[14] When African Americans in Trieber's own Phillips County, Arkansas, attempted to organize a union in opposition to oppressive white landowners, the white community took up arms and incited a race war. When it was over, at least five whites and an untold number of blacks had been killed. No whites were arrested in connection with the riot, but hundreds of blacks were. In rigged trials and under pressure from of a white mob surrounding the courthouse, six African Americans were ultimately sentenced to death for their involvement in the riot. Judge Trieber intervened in the matter to the degree that his granting of a habeas corpus petition stopped the state from executing the six; he then recused himself on the basis that the riot had taken place in his hometown. Ultimately, all of the African Americans sentenced to death were released, but not before spending years in jail.[15]

Judge Trieber's attempt to eradicate peonage in Arkansas resembles similar efforts made by other southern federal judges. For instance, Judge Thomas Goode Jones of Alabama, who challenged the legality of debt peonage a few years before Trieber, also dealt with peon masters leniently. Despite the leniency, Judge Jones believed that his publicized efforts against peon masters had effectively destroyed the system in Alabama. In addition, his desire to improve race relations motivated him to deal with the white offenders in such a manner as to reduce the anger and resentfulness of the white community, which sympathized with those who had been convicted in Jones's court. This policy, he believed, would keep those whites from seeking vengeance against African Americans. A lack of similar primary sources makes it impossible to determine why Judge Trieber was so lenient with the Arkansas peon masters. Perhaps he also believed that peonage would disappear once its illegality was made known and it was demonstrated that federal authorities were willing to prosecute offenders. Nevertheless, one can not avoid concluding that his efforts against peonage were a failure.

It is useful, nevertheless, to assess his actions within the context of what others in the legal community were doing about the problem; moreover, it is equally useful to consider his other efforts to protect the civil rights of African Americans. If nothing else, Trieber's jurisprudence clarifies the larger cultural and political context, regionally and nationally, that mitigated against elemental justice for black southerners.

It is certainly worth considering that two years before the peonage cases, Trieber had made a significant effort to punish "whitecappers." In 1903, W. G. Whipple, the U.S. attorney for the Eastern District of Arkansas, prosecuted twenty-seven Arkansans for violating statutes contained in the Civil Rights Act of 1866 by engaging in whitecapping. Twelve of the alleged whitecappers were accused of posting notices on the homes of African Americans, demanding that they leave Cross County, Arkansas. The other men were accused of converging upon Davis and Hodges's newly opened sawmill in Poinsett County, brandishing torches and guns, and demanding that the owners replace their African American employees with white ones.[16] According to the *Arkansas Gazette,* one of the owners, James A. Davis, "went to see John Harrison, [the] justice of the peace, who, it is alleged, not only refused to help keep the peace, but joined the mob, which told the negroes they must leave. Acting on Davis' advice, the negroes obeyed."[17]

The actions of the individuals, according to U.S. Attorney Whipple, violated section 1 of the 1866 Civil Rights Act, which became section 1978 in the Revised Statutes of 1874. Section 1978, as it will be referred to throughout this chapter, stipulated that all Americans, including blacks, have the same right to make contracts and to buy, sell, and rent property.[18] Whipple also accused the whitecappers of violating portions of the 1870 Civil Rights Act, including what became sections 5508 and 5510 of the Revised Statutes of 1874. Sections 5508 and 5510 made it illegal for two or more people to "conspire to injure, oppress, threaten, or intimidate any citizen in the free exercise or enjoyment" of his or her rights as a citizen or to deprive a citizen of those right "by reason of his color or race."[19]

The alleged whitecappers were brought before a federal grand jury to determine whether or not they could be tried under the above-mentioned statutes. On October 6, 1903, Judge Trieber delivered his charge to the federal grand jury, which consisted of twenty males—seventeen whites and three blacks. He began by quoting section 5508 to inform the jury that it was illegal for two or more people to deny, or attempt to deny, citizens of rights and privileges secured to them by the U.S. Constitution. Therefore, since the Thirteenth Amendment to the Constitution outlawed involuntary servitude, he said, the federal government, under section 5508, had the authority to punish those who conspire to enslave a citizen of the United States. The amendment, of course, had been added to the Constitution in order to destroy the system of chattel slavery that existed in the southern states prior to the Civil War. But in asserting that the government could prosecute those who enslaved others, he was not referring solely to southern whites buying and selling African Americans, or for that matter, any person literally owning another. Judge Trieber, instead, proposed an extraordinary definition of slavery in which a person can be considered "enslaved" whenever he or she is *not free*. In order for someone to be "free," Trieber argued, he or she must be able to exercise and enjoy the rights and privileges inherent in every human being.[20] Consequently, the Thirteenth Amendment made it so that "every citizen is entitled to enjoy those rights which are inherent in every free man." Thus, by refusing to define slavery in a negative manner (in which citizens are prohibited from enslaving others) and, instead, giving it a positive application (such as, all citizens are to be free), Judge Trieber attempted to use the amendment as a vehicle by which Congress could prevent someone from denying a citizen of the natural rights belonging to all men. Judge Trieber declined to enumerate all of the rights of a free man, but asserted that "it is sufficient to say that among them are, in the language of the Declaration of Independence, the cornerstone of our republican form of government, the following: 'That all men are created equal; that they are endowed by their Creator with certain inalienable rights; that among these are life, liberty and the pursuit of happiness.'"[21] He argued, in sum, that the federal government, through section 5508 and the Thirteenth Amendment, had the authority to prosecute any group of people who conspire to deny a citizen of his inalienable rights.

After asserting this extraordinary interpretation of the Thirteenth Amendment, he proceeded to relate these alleged powers of the federal government to the matter at hand. He told the jury that the right to own, lease, or rent property and to work to support one's family "are natural rights belonging to every free man, without any statute or written law." "Deprive a man of these rights," he asserted, "and he ceases to be a free man." In other words, deny a man these rights and he becomes a slave. After establishing, in his mind at least, that the Thirteenth Amendment empowered Congress to legislate against conspiracies designed to deprive individuals of their right to acquire land or to work, he quoted section 1978 to demonstrate that Congress had already passed such legislation.[22]

If the defendants attempted to intimidate black citizens of Arkansas because of their race, he insisted, then the jury was obligated to indict the alleged whitecappers. He left little doubt as to his opinion on whether or not the cases being considered met the criteria established by the law. He stated that "so far as this court is concerned, the cause of these lawless acts must have been the fact that the parties against whom they were directed were colored persons or negroes." He warned the jury not to be swayed by racial prejudice because "nothing tends more to bring the courts into disrepute and lead to mob rule than a failure of the courts and juries to enforce the laws of the country." In concluding the charge, Judge Trieber informed the jury that the court wishes "to see to it that those who are guilty of these acts should be punished."[23]

The jury indicted all twenty-seven of the defendants. The lawyers for the alleged whitecappers responded by filing a demurrer asserting that the federal statutes under which the men were indicted (sections 1978 and 5508) were unconstitutional.[24] On the next day, Judge Trieber overruled the demurrer to indictment, publishing his opinion under the case name of *United States v. Morris, et al.*[25]

In the opinion, Judge Trieber quickly dismissed the argument that section 5508 of the revised statutes was unconstitutional by pointing out that its validity had already been determined and upheld by the U.S. Supreme Court in *Ex parte Yarbrough* (110 U.S. 651) and in several other cases. In turning to the issue of section 1978's constitutionality, he first focused on congressional prerogatives for prosecuting individuals who denied African Americans of their civil rights. "Nothing in the Constitution of the United States as originally adopted, or in any of the first twelve amendments," he said, "would warrant the enactment of this act [section 1978] by Congress." In addition, he said, "neither the fourteenth nor the fifteenth amendment can be relied upon as an authority for" the statute because the statute applied to the actions of individuals as well as to the official actions of the state. Judge Trieber pointed out that "it is now well settled that these two amendments have reference solely to actions of the state, and *not* to any action of private individuals." In the *Civil Rights Cases, United States v. Cruikshank,* and numerous other cases—all of which Judge Trieber cited—the Supreme Court had narrowly interpreted the Fourteenth and Fifteenth Amendments so as to prevent either of them from applying to individuals who prevented blacks from enjoying the equal protection of the laws or from exercising their right to vote, even though the framers of the amendments intended for them to grant blacks these rights.[26]

If the federal government was to have the constitutional right to prosecute racist individuals, such as the alleged whitecappers, he said, then that authority must be found in the Thirteenth Amendment to the Constitution. In order to prove that Congress did indeed have this authority, he had to demonstrate that the Thirteenth Amendment applied to individuals as well as states. Fortunately for him, he could use the words of the Supreme Court to support this assertion. In the *Civil Rights Cases,* Justice Joseph P. Bradley, speaking for the Court, explained:

We must not forget that the province and scope of the thirteenth and fourteenth amendments are different. The former simply abolished slavery. The latter prohibited the states from abridging the privileges or immunities of citizens of the United States. . . . Under the thirteenth amendment, the legislation [passed by Congress], so far as necessary or proper to eradicate all forms and incidents of slavery and involuntary servitude, may be direct and primary, operating upon the acts of individuals, whether sanctioned by state legislation or not. Under the fourteenth, as we have already shown, it must necessarily be and can only be corrective in its character, addressed to counteract and afford relief against state regulations or proceedings.[27]

As a result of the Court's interpretation of the amendment, he concluded that "Congress is, therefore, authorized by the provisions of the thirteenth amendment to legislate against acts of individuals, as well as of the states, in all matters necessary for the protection of the rights granted by that amendment."[28]

After demonstrating that Congress possessed the authority to punish individuals who enslaved others, he proceeded to provide a brief history of the 1866 Civil Rights Act. After the Civil War many southern states passed legislation "which practically established a system of peonage but little removed from that of slavery." In addition, he said, "irresponsible persons" in those states "would prevent Negroes from working or cultivating lands, and the courts of the states were powerless to protect them." In order to prevent these "unjust discriminations against the Negroes" Congress enacted the Civil Rights Act of 1866.[29]

Contrary to the assertions of the defendants' counsel, Trieber said, Congress possessed the authority to pass the 1866 act. He pointed out that although the Supreme Court had never directly considered the constitutionality of the act, it had been affirmed by the lower federal courts on two separate occasions. One of these occasions was when the Circuit Court in the District of Louisiana heard the *Cruikshank* case. Trieber quoted generously from the majority opinion in that case written by Justice Bradley. "It was supposed," Justice Bradley wrote, "that the eradication of slavery and involuntary servitude of every form and description required that the slave should be made a citizen and placed on an entire equality before the law with the white citizen, and, therefore, that congress had the power, under the [Thirteenth] amendment, to declare and effectuate these objects." Consequently, "Congress then had the right to go further and to enforce its declaration by passing laws for the prosecution and punishment of those who should deprive, or attempt to deprive, any person of the rights thus conferred upon him. Without having this power, Congress could not enforce the amendment."[30] Justice Bradley made it clear, though, that the amendment did not authorize Congress to punish those who commit "ordinary crimes" against citizens, be they black or white. By "ordinary," he meant crimes committed for reasons other than racial prejudice. In other words, the federal government could only impose punishment upon those who deprive or attempt to deprive a citizen of his constitutional rights because of that citizen's race, color, or previous condition of servitude.[31]

Justice Bradley then provided an illustration to help explain when Congress could and could not, through its legislative powers, punish individuals for civil rights violations. Because Bradley's illustration was, ironically enough, quite similar to the Poinsett County whitecapping incident, Judge Trieber quoted it in full and italicized it for emphasis. Justice Bradley, in his illustration, said that if a black citizen acquired or attempted to acquire a farm in a white community and was prevented from getting or keeping the farm by a group of whites because he was black or because of his previous condition of servitude, then "this would be a case within the power of Congress to remedy and redress."[32] He added that this view was "approved by the Supreme Court in *United States v. Harris.*" In addition, he made sure to mention that "the allegations in this indictment expressly charge that these acts of the defendants were on account of the parties against whom they were directed being Negroes."[33]

To counter the objection that Congress had exceeded its authority in enacting the 1866 Civil Rights Act, Judge Trieber actually utilized the Supreme Court's decision *upholding* the notorious Fugitive Slave law. In the Supreme Court decision in *Prigg v. Pennsylvania,* Justice Joseph Story discredited and rejected a "limited" or strict interpretation of the Constitution, saying that such a view "has never yet been adopted as correct."[34] A limited construction of the Constitution, he asserted, would cause it to "fail to attain many of its avowed and positive objects, as a security of rights and a recognition of duties." In particular, it would hinder Congress's ability to enforce the rights and provide the privileges that are mandated by the Constitution. Recognizing this fact, Congress has been allowed, on occasion, to exercise powers not explicitly granted to it but "which were necessary and proper" in order for it to meet a constitutional mandate. Therefore, Story said, "The end being required, it has been deemed a just and necessary implication that the means to accomplish it are given also; or, in other words, that the power flows as a necessary means to accomplish the end." In response to Justice Story's justification for granting Congress the power to prosecute those who assisted fugitive slaves, Judge Trieber asked, "Shall the courts be less liberal in construing constitutional provisions in favor of freedom than those in favor of slavery?"[35]

In concluding his denial of the defendant's demurrer, Judge Trieber ruled that Congress, through the Thirteenth Amendment, has to power to protect the fundamental rights of African Americans because "the denial of such privileges is an element of servitude within the meaning of that amendment."[36] It was indisputable, he said, that the right to lease land and to accept employment was inherent and fundamental to every free citizen. As such, a conspiracy to deprive African Americans of these rights, because of their race, violated the Thirteenth Amendment and section 5508. Consequently, Congress possessed the authority to prosecute those who are guilty of such violations. After denying the demurrer, Judge Trieber scheduled the trials for the spring of 1904.

Trieber's opinion in *U.S. v. Morris* captured the attention of southern attorneys and federal judges. For instance, Thomas Goode Jones, the U.S. district judge for the Northern and Middle Districts of Alabama, wrote Judge David D. Shelby of the U.S. Court of Appeals for the Fifth Circuit in New Orleans to get his opinion on whether or not Jones could prosecute several white Alabamians who had set fire to a jail. The jail happened to contain federal prisoners. It was torched to capture and lynch a recently imprisoned African American, Horace Maples. In response to Judge Jones's inquiry, Judge Shelby cited Trieber's opinion in *Morris* as evidence "that the Federal court may have jurisdiction" due to the fact that the victim "was deprived of the right of trial on account of race." He reassured Judge Jones by saying that Judge Trieber's decision was "sustained by many citations of authority, including expression of Judges of the Supreme Court." He concluded his letter by saying that if Judge Trieber's interpretation of the law prevailed, then "the federal courts can stop the lynching of Negroes if juries will hold they are lynched because they are Negroes."[37]

Judge Jones also sought advice about the Maples lynching from Thomas Roulhac, the U.S. attorney for the Northern District of Alabama. Like Judge Shelby, Roulhac also cited Trieber's opinion in *Morris* in his response. Attorney Roulhac rejected the assertion that sections 1978 and 5508 were dependent upon demonstrating that the victims were targeted because of their race. In a letter to Judge Jones, Roulhac stated that as "distasteful as it may be to us of states' rights antecedents and instruction," I am inclined to believe "that any conspiracy to deprive any citizen, white, black, or otherwise, of any of his rights, natural or conferred, is an offense, as a conspiracy against the federal statutes." Roulhac's interpretation, then, proved to be even more radical than Judge Trieber's in asserting that the federal government possessed the authority to prosecute individuals who conspired to deprive anyone of their constitutional or inherent rights. He told Jones that "he could reach no other conclusion [regarding the extent of the statutes] from the consideration of Judge Trieber's opinion and the authorities cited therein, in *United States v. Morris*." Of the decision, he said: "It seems to me a very forceful and logical opinion. It was evidently prepared with great care after a thorough research and examination of the authorities and the result of the opinion appears irresistible." He urged Jones to proceed against the lynch mob. He asserted that if Judge Trieber's interpretation was correct, then "there can be no doubt that an indictment against the members of the mob formed to deprive Maples of his life could be sustained in the Federal Courts."[38]

Judge Trieber's actions in the whitecapping cases may have won the support of other southern federal authorities, but the southern press and Arkansas politicians failed to respond in kind. Although L. C. Going originally served as the lawyer for the defendants, one of Arkansas's representatives in the U.S. Senate, James P. Clarke, jumped at the chance to join the whitecappers' legal team after Trieber handed down his *Morris* decision. Clarke had a long and distinguished political career. In addition to representing Arkansas in the U.S. House of Representatives, he also served as governor of the state from 1895 to 1897. In campaigning for the governorship, he "touted white supremacy as the 'keystone of the Democratic party.'" In 1903, Clarke won a seat in the U.S. Senate after aligning with Jeff Davis, the popular race-baiting governor of Arkansas. Clarke kept his seat in the Senate until 1914.[39] His serving as counsel for alleged whitecappers obviously did not hurt his political career.

As for the press, the *Arkansas Gazette* kept its readers updated on Judge Trieber and the whitecapping cases throughout the entire ordeal. In an editorial pertaining to Judge Trieber's charge to the grand jury, the paper criticized him and called for a colorblind application of the law. Such a stance represented a significant, yet merely temporary, transformation of the *Gazette's* legal philosophy. The paper could usually be counted on to support color-conscious laws that benefited whites, such as those that mandating racial segregation and disfranchisement. The editors of the *Gazette* asserted that Trieber's interpretation of the law made it beneficial only to African Americans. Only those who conspired against ex-slaves, they complained, could be prosecuted under the laws based on the Thirteenth Amendment.

The editors argued that the law cited by Judge Trieber "might stand if its object were to prevent injuries from being inflicted on white men, black men, yellow men, red men, any men," but since it stipulates only "that it shall be unlawful to inflict certain injuries on a negro because he is a negro, then its validity is doubtful."[40] Apparently suffering from a rare infection of egalitarianism, the *Gazette* asked, "Is federal law to contradict itself? Is it to say that every citizen shall be equal with every other citizen and then that it shall be unlawful to injure certain men, not because they are citizens or men, but because their color is black?"[41] The editors made it clear that the answer to their own question was "no." They argued that cases consisting of citizens harming or intimidating others should be dealt with solely by local and state officials. "Our laws are adequate and sufficient," they asserted. But, as they conveniently forgot to mention, those laws were not (usually) enforced, especially when the victims happened to be black. And due to circumstances in the South, it was African Americans who needed laws in order to be protected from those in the region determined to re-establish white supremacy. The *Gazette,* nevertheless, saw no reason for the federal government's intervention in the matter and cited Judge Trieber's actions as an example of "overpowering federalism."[42]

In a later editorial responding to the decision in *U.S. v. Morris,* the *Gazette* reiterated its assertion that the whitecapping cases should be left to local and state officials, and it questioned the foundation of Trieber's argument. The editorial correctly pointed out that the cases, according to the judge, fell within the scope of the Thirteenth Amendment "on the principle that the right to lease land is an inherent and inalienable right, and therefore a necessary incident of citizenship." Such a principle, the *Gazette* asserted, could result in the federal government prosecuting any two white men who push a black man off a narrow sidewalk because "they don't want to be shouldered by a negro." "Certainly," the editorial said, "the right to walk the streets is an inherent right," just like the right to lease land.

The *Gazette* also questioned Judge Trieber's definition of slavery, as the term was used in the Thirteenth Amendment. As mentioned above, he had provided an extraordinary interpretation of the amendment so as to apply it to the cases at hand. This, of course, was obvious to most people, including the editors, who asked, "Is running a negro off a farm inflicting on him what the Thirteenth Amendment prohibits—slavery or involuntary servitude?" The editors obviously did not think that it did. They argued that if the alleged whitecappers had literally tried to enslave the black victims, "as was done in the recent peonage practices in Alabama," then the Thirteenth

Amendment could justifiably be applied. But if the matter was limited to intimidating blacks and not literally enslaving them, then federal officials had no basis for intervening "so long as the state court is moving to do its duty."[43]

The *Gazette*'s assertion that the whitecapping incidents should be handled by state rather than federal authorities did not prevent the trial of the Poinsett County defendants from starting as scheduled. After one day of testimony, Judge Trieber instructed the all-white male jury, on the morning of March 17, 1904, to convict the defendants. He told the jurors that they had several questions to consider. First, they had to determine "whether a man shall be permitted to employ whom he pleases to employ, or whether he shall be compelled to employ those whom others with whom he has no relations wish him to employ." Secondly, the jurors had to decide whether or not men will be allowed to deny others "of the right of every citizen, be he white or black, to work for a living, and to engage in the pursuit of happiness and a livelihood." In addition, they needed to establish "whether law and right shall prevail, or the unlicensed mob."[44]

After listening to Judge Trieber's strong yet brief charge, the jury deliberated for four hours before reaching a verdict. The jury found twelve of the defendants to be innocent of the charges, but convicted three "ringleaders" of the mob, including its "spokesman," Reuben Hodges. The Arkansas press reported that the jury asked Judge Trieber to be merciful on the three men and that it was widely believed that he would heed their plea because the men were "ignorant rather than vicious."[45] Judge Trieber's punishment was neither excessive, nor just a slap on the wrist. He sentenced Hodges and William R. Clampitt to serve a year and a day in the Atlanta penitentiary and to pay a fine of one hundred dollars. As for the third defendant, he had to pay the same fine but received a prison sentence of only sixty days.[46]

L. C. Going, one of the attorneys for the three men, immediately entered a motion for an appeal to the U.S. Supreme Court. Judge Trieber granted the motion. Going told reporters that the conviction should be overturned because "the federal court has no jurisdiction since the case is recognizable before the state courts" and because the statutes upon which the convictions are based are unconstitutional. Under the statutes, he complained, "a negro is given protection in federal courts not granted to white citizens."[47]

On the same day that the jury convicted Hodges and his two cohorts, Judge Trieber empaneled a jury to hear the case against the Cross County whitecappers. These eleven defendants were charged with not only intimidating blacks, but also conspiring to obstruct the investigation of whitecapping

by murdering a white detective, J. F. Brown, who had been hired by concerned white landowners. While guarding the cabin of a black family that
had been told to expect a visit from whitecappers if they did not leave Cross
county, detective Brown was shot several times through a cabin window by
masked men.[48]

Soon after the trial began U.S. Attorney Whipple dismissed the charges
against four of the alleged whitecappers because "the evidence adduced by
the government was clearly insufficient." The attorney for the remaining
seven defendants then demurred, claiming a similar insufficiency of evidence
against his clients. Judge Trieber overruled the demurer and ordered
Attorney Whipple to continue the case. Citing the difficulty of positively
identifying the masked culprits, Attorney Whipple soon thereafter dismissed
the charges against the seven men, even though "he believed the men were
guilty beyond a reasonable doubt." The *Gazette* reported that "Judge Trieber
also expressed it was his opinion that the case made out against the men was
not strong enough to warrant their conviction."[49]

The results of the two cases appear to be quite disappointing. Out of
the twenty-seven defendants, only three were convicted. In addition, the
men who murdered detective Brown went unpunished. One could easily
imagine that Judge Trieber would also be disappointed with the results. He
had taken a strong stance against the whitecappers both in his charges to the
jury and in his dismissal of the demurrer to indictment. Yet it is evident that
he supported and even boasted of the verdicts. In a letter to Judge Jones of
Alabama, he proudly stated that "the jury which convicted the parties [of
the Poinsett county whitecapping] was composed exclusively of natives of
the South" and that they had handed down "a righteous verdict."[50]

Judge Trieber not only approved of the results of the two trials, but also
considered the cases as being the deathblow of whitecapping in Arkansas.
He informed Judge Jones in a letter that his colleague on the federal bench
for the Western District of Arkansas, John H. Rogers, had also convicted
some whitecappers shortly after Hodges and his co-defendants had been
found guilty. Judge Trieber confidently told Jones that the decisions handed
down by himself and Judge Rogers would put an end to whitecapping in
Arkansas. Although the threat of federal prosecution undoubtedly would
have decreased the incidence of whitecapping, it was naive of him to assert
that the rulings handed down by the courts would bring the practice to an
end. Nevertheless, he told Jones that he was "satisfied that negro labor will
not be interfered with any more in this State, unless the Supreme Court
should hold that I was wrong and that the law [the 1866 Civil Rights Act]
is unconstitutional."[51]

On May 28, 1906, the U.S. Supreme Court did exactly that. In a case known as *Hodges v. United States,* the Supreme Court ruled that Trieber was wrong and declared the 1866 act unconstitutional.[52] Justice David J. Brewer wrote the majority opinion for the Court. He rejected the view that the Thirteenth Amendment was designed to protect blacks from those whites who would try to deny them from enjoying their newly won freedom. Justice Brewer asserted that the amendment was "not an attempt to commit that race to the care of the nation. It is the denunciation of a condition, and not a declaration in favor of a particular people."[53] Judge Trieber, in contrast, argued that the amendment had been passed in favor of a particular people; its purpose was to transform the ex-slaves into equal citizens of the United States.

Justice Brewer also rejected Judge Trieber's definition of the "slavery." According to Trieber, Justice Brewer said, "one of the *indicia* of [slavery's] existence . . . was a lack of power to make or perform contracts." Therefore, the defendants reduced the victims to a condition of slavery by intimidating them and preventing them from performing their contract. The Court agreed that the defendants had acted unlawfully, but they had not literally enslaved the black men. Justice Brewer and the Court failed to explicitly define "slavery," but it is clear that they subscribed to a strict construction of the term when they argued that "no mere personal assault or trespass or appropriation operates to reduce the individual to a condition of slavery."[54] Consequently, the Thirteenth Amendment, according to the Court, merely protected citizens from literally being owned by other persons. Enslavement, therefore, did not include the "incidents of slavery"—to use Justice Bradley's phrase from the *Civil Rights Cases*—which would include the inability to testify in court, own property, make a contract, or rent land, just to name a few.

Justices John Marshall Harlan and William R. Day dissented from the Court's opinion, arguing, as Judge Trieber had, that the Thirteenth Amendment destroyed "slavery and all its incidents and badges" and thereby "conferred upon every" American "the right, without discrimination against them on account of their race, to enjoy all the privileges that inhere in freedom." Likewise, Justice Harlan agreed with Judge Trieber that the second section of the amendment invested Congress with the power not only to prevent the re-establishment of slavery, but also to "make it impossible that any of its incidents or badges should exist or be enforced in any state or territory of the United States."[55] Justice Harlan provided a partial list of the "incidents and badges of slavery," saying, "The long existence of African slavery in this country gave us very distinct notions of what it was and what were its necessary incidents. Compulsory service of the slave for the benefit of the master, restraint of his movements except by the master's will, disability to hold property, to *make contracts,* to have standing in court, to be a witness against a white person, and such like burdens and incapacities, *were the inseparable incidents of the institution.*"[56]

Justice Harlan supported his position by citing the Court's recent decision in the peonage case of *Clyatt v. United States.*[57] Justice Brewer, who wrote the opinion in the *Clyatt* case, argued that the Thirteenth Amendment empowered Congress to prosecute individuals who subjected others to involuntary servitude. If Congress can punish peonage masters, Justice Harlan asked, then could it not also prosecute whitecappers? To Harlan, the two conditions differed little, if at all, from one another. "One who is shut up by superior or overpowering force . . . from earning his living in a lawful way of his own choosing," he argued, "is as much in a condition of involuntary servitude as if he were forcibly held in a condition of peonage."[58]

Justice Harlan concluded his dissent by calling the Court's interpretation of the Thirteenth Amendment "entirely too narrow" and asserting that it ran counter to the objective of the Reconstruction-era amendments: "to secure to people theretofore in servitude, the free enjoyment, without discrimination merely on account of their race, of the essential rights that appertain to American citizenship and to freedom."[59]

One of the immediate results of the Court's decision in *Hodges* was the release of those who had been convicted of whitecapping and the nolle prosequi of those cases still pending in the Courts. Judge Trieber had convicted three men—Lee Bromley, Joe Bromley, and Wash Morgan—of violating sections 1978 and 5508 on April 17, 1906, just over a month before the Court handed down *Hodges.* The three men had posted notices to the black employees of the Arkansas Lumber Company in Bradley County, demanding that they quit their jobs. On February 15, 1905, the three men finally compelled the African Americans workers to leave their employment by threatening to shoot them. Judge Trieber had sentenced the whitecappers to serve half a year in the Pulaski County jail and to pay a fine of five hundred dollars.[60] In addition, at the time of the decision, several people were "awaiting a hearing before the Federal Grand Jury at Helena on charges of whitecapping."[61] The same was true in Texarkana, Texas, where several men had been charged with conspiracy to intimidate. In the wake of *Hodges,* the charges were dismissed.[62]

The Court's rejection of Trieber's and Harlan's interpretation of the Thirteenth Amendment forced blacks in the South to look to local and state authorities for protection against intimidation and employment discrimination. This left African Americans at the mercy of the Democratic Party, which touted itself as the "white man's party." The eagerness of local Democratic authorities to protect the rights of African Americans was demonstrated when the sawmill owners sought help from the justice of the peace, only to watch as he joined the ranks of the very people they were complaining about. In addition, the fact that a sitting U.S. senator represented whitecappers in federal court could not be very reassuring to African Americans. If African Americans had any fears as to what would happen as a result of the *Hodges* decision, those fears were confirmed when the Arkansas State Legislature, on May 13, 1907, repealed a state law, passed by Republicans in 1873, protecting blacks from employment discrimination.[63]

By 1906, the country had already diminished the rights that had been granted to blacks by the Republicans during Reconstruction. But with the *Hodges* decision, the Court eliminated the Thirteenth Amendment as a means of making African Americans truly free. By this point the Supreme Court had already interpreted the other two Reconstruction-era amendments in such a way as to keep them from applying to the actions of individuals. Federal officials no longer possessed the constitutional means of protecting the civil rights of African Americans from hostile whites.

Legal scholars and historians have recognized the importance of the *Hodges* decision. Harold Hyman and William Wiecek described the *Hodges* decision as being even more harmful to the cause of African Americans than the infamous *Plessy* decision. They wrote that "*Plessy* was outdistanced in 1906 by the even more constraining Supreme Court decision in *Hodges v. United States*" which "all but completed the federal judiciary's dilution of Reconstruction."[64] Mary Frances Berry, in her book *Black Resistance, White Law*, observed, "For almost fifty years . . . the *Hodges* case . . . became the rod and staff of those who denied that the federal government had the authority to intervene in race relations."[65] Jeannie M. Whayne called the *Hodges* decision "a final capitulation to the forces of redemption in the South." By emasculating the Thirteenth Amendment, she argues, the Supreme Court struck down "the only possible legal argument remaining for those who wished to protect the rights of black citizens."[66]

Half a century after the Court had rejected Justice Harlan's (and Trieber's) interpretation of the Thirteenth Amendment, African Americans found themselves without an effective legal remedy against private discrimination and intimidation. Whites in America, for instance, could refuse to sell or rent land to blacks or refuse to hire them as employees without fear of legal repercussions. In the mid-1960s, Joseph Lee Jones, a black resident of Missouri, found this out the hard way when he attempted to buy a home in a St. Louis subdivision. Jones believed that his offer for a home had been rejected because of racial prejudice and sued the owners of the subdivision for violating his civil rights. The lower courts rejected Jones's assertion, but he appealed the case to the U.S. Supreme Court. In preparation for presenting the case to the Court, Jones's lawyer, Samuel H. Liberman, came across the case of *U.S. v. Morris*. Liberman made Judge Trieber's reasoning in that case the cornerstone of his argument before the Court. On June 17, 1968, the Supreme Court, in a seven to two vote, ruled on behalf of Joseph Lee Jones.[67]

It is evident that Judge Trieber's reasoning influenced the Court's decision in the *Jones* case. Writing for the Court, Justice Potter Stewart specifically referred to Judge Trieber's decision while covering the legal history of the 1866 Civil Rights Act. Justice Stewart pointed out that *U.S. v. Morris* constituted the only case that squarely confronted the question of whether or not purely private discrimination violated section 1978.[68] Although the Court ruled in *Hodges* that the statute did not reach such discrimination, Justice Stewart declared that the *Hodges* decision "rested upon a concept of congressional power under the Thirteenth Amendment" that was "incompatible with the history and purpose of the Amendment itself." Consequently, the Court declared that *"Hodges* . . . is hereby overruled."[69]

The Court overturned this precedent that reigned for half a century by re-examining the original intentions of the men who framed the Thirteenth Amendment and the 1866 Civil Rights Act. After devoting one-third of his opinion to excerpts from congressional debates on these bills, Justice Stewart concluded that the amendment established "universal freedom" by abolishing slavery and its "badges and incidents."[70] This, therefore, gave Congress the authority to pass legislation, such as the 1866 act, prohibiting states and individuals from denying citizens of this universal freedom. Justice Stewart pointed out that the representatives of the Alfred Mayer Company, in their brief to the Court, argued that if section 1978 "means what it says" then it prohibits practically every racially motivated refusal to sell or rent to blacks. They said Congress could not have possibly intended for the act to have such revolutionary implications. Justice Stewart responded to this assertion by saying that the Court's "examination of the relevant history, however, persuades us that Congress meant exactly what it said."[71]

The Supreme Court's 1968 interpretation of the Thirteenth Amendment was revolutionary. By adopting Judge Trieber's expansive view of the amendment, the Court transformed it into a potentially effective legal weapon against racial discrimination. Justice Stewart correctly pointed out that white southerners refused to recognize the freedom of the ex-slaves and had resorted to various tactics to keep blacks from fully enjoying their freedom. The white South, he said, appeared determined to develop "substitutes for the slave system."[72] The Court and country had allowed white southern Democrats to create such substitutes by altering the scope and original meaning of the Thirteenth Amendment. This development fueled the southern counterrevolution and made the re-establishment of white supremacy in the South possible. Had Judge Trieber's interpretation of the amendment not been rejected, the federal government would at least have had the legal authority—even if it did not have the will—to punish those who discriminated against African Americans on the basis of their race. It would have possessed the power to eliminate the relics of slavery. The potential of such power is made evident by Justice Stewart's remark at the conclusion of his opinion: "when racial discrimination herds men into ghettos and makes their ability to buy property turn on the color of their skin, *then it too is a relic of slavery.*"[73] Judge Trieber never sought to challenge the system of racial segregation that existed in the South during his tenure on the bench. But from a legal standpoint, his interpretation of the laws and Constitution of the United States did exactly that when one considers the fact that it is recognized today that racial segregation, like residential discrimination, is a badge or relic of slavery.

Judge Trieber served on the federal bench for twenty-seven years. It was said of him that "he was a man of great integrity of purpose, unfailing industry and a vast knowledge of the law." The author of Trieber's obituary published by the Bar Association of Arkansas even asserted that Trieber "was probably more familiar with the Federal decisions and statutes than anyone else." When not tending to the business of the court directly, Trieber would spend his time reading and taking notes on all of the Federal decisions and statutes. Lawyers knew not to attempt to "waste his time in desultory conversation," as he had no patience for such things.[74]

His earnestness and work ethic gained him respect and led him to be frequently called upon to temporarily sit on other federal benches. In fact, U.S. Supreme Court Chief Justice (and former President) William Howard Taft asked Judge Trieber, in the summers of 1925 and 1926, to go to New York City to help the federal court there to clear its congested docket. When Chief Justice Taft requested that Trieber return to New York City again in 1927, the seventy-four-year-old Arkansas judge agreed despite his failing health. As it was described in his obituary, "the strain was too much, and he finally sank, a martyr to his sense of duty, and passed away at the home of his daughter, at Scarsdale, New York, on the 17th of September, 1927."[75] He left behind a wife, two children, and an extraordinary and historically significant interpretation of the Thirteenth Amendment.

Emory Speer, U.S. District Judge, Southern District of Georgia,
1885–1918, circa 1900.
Picture History.

- CHAPTER THREE -

Judge Emory Speer

ITH FEWER THAN two months remaining in his lame-duck presidency, Chester A. Arthur nominated Emory Speer (1848–1918) to be the federal judge for the Southern District of Georgia. Southern political leaders bitterly contested this move, hoping to delay any appointment to the position until the newly elected president, Grover Cleveland, a Democrat, took office. But on February 19, 1885, with only one vote to spare, the U.S. Senate confirmed Speer's nomination. The only Democrat to vote in favor of the appointment was Senator Joseph E. Brown of Georgia, who had governed that state during the Civil War. Speer, who was thirty-six years old at the time of his appointment, served on the bench for thirty-three years.[1]

Speer, who was born in 1846 in Culloden, Georgia, was a descendent of two fairly prominent southern families. His father and grandfather were both well-respected, educated Methodist ministers. In addition to being a pastor, Speer's paternal grandfather also served as secretary of state for South Carolina and made his mark politically by opposing the forces of nullification in that state during the tariff crisis of 1832–1833. Speer's maternal grandfather was also a pastor as well as the nephew of William Rufus King, who was elected vice president of the United States in 1853.[2]

As a fifteen-year-old boy, Speer ran away from home to join Brigadier General J. H. Lewis's "Orphan Brigade," which was attempting to halt General William Tecumseh Sherman's march through Georgia. Speer saw action at the Battle of Griswoldsville and remained with the brigade until the end of the war. Upon returning home, Speer enrolled at the University of Georgia, where his father was a professor of oratory. Speer excelled at the university, becoming the president of the debating club and co-editing the university magazine with Henry Grady, who later as editor of the *Atlanta Constitution* became the primary spokesman for the "New South" movement.[3]

After graduating from the university in 1869, Speer studied law under Benjamin H. Hill, a leading Democrat who represented Georgia in both the U.S. House of Representatives and Senate during the 1870s and 1880s. In 1870, Speer was admitted to the Georgia bar and began serving as editor of the *Southern Watchman,* an Athens-based newspaper through which Speer denounced Reconstruction and helped Georgia Democrats in their counter-revolutionary efforts. But when Georgia Democrats failed to help Speer in 1877, by denying him the party's nomination for congressman of the state's ninth congressional district, he bolted the party. The next year he ran as an independent candidate for the congressional seat and won, in large part because of the votes of black and white Republicans.[4]

As an Independent congressman, Speer quickly developed a friendly relationship with Republican Presidents James Garfield and Chester A. Arthur and demonstrated a willingness to vote with his Republican colleagues in Congress. It is not surprising then that when Speer ran for reelection in 1880 that the Georgia Republican Party did not field a candidate and instead urged its members to vote for Speer. Speer won in 1880, but his relationship with the Republican Party incensed Georgia Democrats, who resorted to election fraud and political violence to prevent Speer from winning a third term.[5]

Despite losing in 1882, Speer's votes in favor of Republican economic policies and his support of President Arthur's appointment of an African American as postmaster of Athens, Georgia, won him the president's support. Consequently, within days of Speer's election defeat President Arthur appointed him to the position of U.S. attorney for the Northern District of Georgia. Within weeks of taking the position Speer began a highly publicized and successful crusade to punish the white Georgia Democrats who had harassed African Americans for exercising their right to vote in the recent election.[6]

The events that led to Speer's successful prosecution of these Democrats began on July 25, 1883, when several white men, wearing black caps that partially concealed their faces, burst into the home of an African American family in Banks County, Georgia, around midnight. One of the intruders held Sallie Bryson down on her bed at gun point while his accomplices dragged her husband, Warren Bryson, outside to assault him.[7] After beating Bryson with a pistol and a whip, they told him that he had better have voted for the Democratic candidate in the recent election. They left his yard and proceeded to similarly harass other blacks in the area.

This group of whitecappers eventually made their way to the residence of Berry and Maria Sanders, who were sleeping with their infant in their

home for the first time in three days. Berry and his wife had begun periodi-
cally sleeping outside in a field after a mob came looking for him late in the
evening twelve nights earlier. He avoided an unpleasant encounter with the
mob that night, but was not so fortunate on the night of July 25. After the
gang threatened to burn down the Sanders's cabin if Berry did not come
out, he impulsively decided to flee. He burst through the front door and
across the yard. The armed whitecappers immediately opened fire, hitting
Berry three times. Although injured and bleeding, Berry did not stop running until he reached the home of the son of his former owner, a white
man named Minyard Sanders.[8]

Other than the minor wounds inflicted by the pistol shots, Berry Sanders
avoided the wrath of the mob. Cad Bush, also an African American, was not
as lucky. When the whitecappers pounded on his door they told him they
came in peace and only wished to search his premises. When he let them
inside they immediately grabbed him, dragged him outside, and stripped him
naked. The hostile intruders then proceeded to whip him with hickories,
counting out loud the 175 lashes that they inflicted upon him.[9] Matilda
David, a black female, also received a whipping at the hands of the whitecappers. She testified that nearly a dozen men had lashed her naked back
twenty-five times apiece.[10]

The U.S. marshals had little difficulty in learning the identity of those
who had caused what the *Atlanta Constitution* referred to as a "reign of terror in Banks County."[11] Some of the victims recognized the voices of their
tormentors and were able to provide the authorities with their names and
addresses. The guilt of the men named appeared to be confirmed when
authorities traced freshly made horse tracks from the victims' cabins to the
homes of the accused. The nine men arrested for beating and intimidating
the African Americans were described by the *New York Times* as being "men
of considerable property."[12] The gang was led by four members of the
Yarbrough family (Jasper, James, Dilmus, and Neal) and included five of their
neighbors. According to the *Atlanta Constitution,* the whitecappers were
motivated by a desire to oust those "negroes [who had] begun to accumu-
late some property."[13] It is apparent that the whitecappers were also motivated by a desire to punish the blacks for voting against the Democratic
Party, even though the Democratic candidate had defeated the incumbent,
Emory Speer. During the trial, the victims testified that members of the mob
made statements such as these: "We are going to whip every d—d Speer
negro they [*sic*] is" and "You see what your d—d Speer has done for you."[14]

Each of the nine members in the Yarbrough gang were charged with
violating section 5508 of the revised statutes and were tried in the U.S.

Circuit Court for the Northern District of Georgia during the fall of 1883.[15] The trial, in fact, began one day after the U.S. Supreme Court handed down its decision in the *Civil Rights Cases,* which invalidated an act passed by Congress mandating the integration of public facilities. It was in the midst of this racial climate that U.S. Attorney Speer directed the prosecution against the Yarbrough gang.

By October 26, 1883, the trial had reached its last phase and the lawyers for both sides began their closing arguments. Speer began his closing argument by explaining the motivation of the defendants. He asserted that they were not satisfied with their victory in the recent election, so they "proceeded to beat and maltreat all the colored men in their neighborhood who had exercised their right to vote as they pleased." He compared their actions to Indian squaws who tortured and killed captured opponents after a victorious battle. The actions of the whitecappers, he said, "should bring a blush of shame to every Georgian." Speer, knowing that the victims of the mob had voted for him, then commented that the blacks did not deserve to be harassed because "they exercised good judgement in voting for the gentleman for whom they did vote."[16]

After reciting much of the testimony given during the course of the trial, he portrayed the actions of the defendants as being harmful to the prosperity and success of the country. In urging the jury to find the defendants guilty he asked them "if crimes such as this diabolical, deliberate, premeditated, beating and murder, are to go unwhipt of justice, what baleful and portentous future is there overhanging our country?" The "grave problems" that American society faced regarding the races were serious, he admitted, but "they can never be solved by lawlessness and outrage." The "lash and the bullet" only succeeded in making things worse. Violence, he said, unsettled society, frightened capital, destroyed security, lowered property values, and inspired retaliatory bloodshed. The country was only as peaceful and productive as the whole of its parts. If one part of the region was in disarray, it would drag down the entire country.[17]

Speer then attempted to sway the jury by painting a picture of the South that differed greatly from that touted by white supremacists. The latter demanded that the results of the Civil War and emancipation be scaled back or negated entirely. They argued that if African Americans were treated as equal citizens then southern Anglo-Saxon civilization was in peril. In order to escape the specter of "negro domination," they insisted that African Americans be relegated to a status of second-class citizenship. Speer reminded the jurors that whites in the South had little to fear from blacks because the former firmly ruled the country and society at large. Rather than repressing the powerless and pitiful African Americans, he said, white southerners should treat them with compassion. By doing otherwise, specifically, by utilizing legal and extralegal means to subjugate blacks, the white south was legitimizing and setting an unwise precedent for discrimination and the use of violence. He reminded the jury, "The white people of this country control the Government, State and Federal. They enjoy every conceivable advantage. They have superiority in wealth, education, social influence, everything." "A magnanimous people," he continued, "a just people, they owe it to themselves, to be magnanimous and just to the colored people. The colored man is here, and he will remain here. He must be subject to the law; he must be protected by the law. He has his duties to perform, he must perform them. But just so sure as the lash and bullet of the midnight assassin is tolerated," Speer asserted, "there is an end to social order, and every interest of our people will be prostrated and destroyed."[18]

Speer accepted the results of emancipation. He recognized that it was impossible to return to the social arrangements that existed before the war without resorting to the use of ignoble methods. Such a course, he thought, would inevitably engender criticisms of the South. In addition, it would cause problems in the region itself. As respect for law and order decreased, the South would descend into barbarism. As a result, problems such as crime and corruption would increase, bringing disorder in their wake.

Not only did Speer wish to spare his home region the chaos and confusion caused by a concerted effort to repress a particular group of citizens, but he also wished to preserve the reputation of America. He gave voice to his patriotism and love for America in his closing argument. By widening his perspective to the national level, he was able see discrimination against blacks in the South not as a life-or-death battle for control of society, but rather as a blemish on America's character. Violence, intimidation, and bigotry were not qualities that civilized people admired in a society. But if a government could protect its citizens and treat them all alike and fairly, regardless of their race or income, then that country would see progress and be respected throughout the world. It was with this mindset, and with an intention to appeal to the patriotism of the jury, that Speer told them:

> For my part I love my country, I am proud of its traditions, I glory in the heroes and manhood of its people; I know they despise cruelty and barbarity to the helpless and the obscure. I know that its prosperity and happiness depends on the preservation of social order, and by

that love, that pride and that knowledge, I adjure you to do your whole duty in this important trial. Seldom indeed, in the annals of criminal trials has there been an opportunity for a jury so well to earn the gratitude of generations yet unborn, and wherever the intelligence of your verdict is flashed by the telegraph, the humane and the good, will take new courage in your firm resolution, and your sterling law-loving and law-obeying manhood. Seldom if ever has there been the opportunity to record so righteous a verdict for the punishment of crime, for the vindication of humanity, for the preservation of social order, for the perpetuation and advancement of those principals of eternal justice on which the social fabric has its essential foundation.[19]

Judge H. K. McCay, in his charge to the jury, suggested that Speer had not proven his case; but the jury, which consisted of seven white men and five African Americans, found the defendants guilty.[20] According to the *New York Times* it was "the first conviction of Kuklux [*sic*] in Georgia."[21] The newspaper also pointed out that "the charge of Judge McCay was so favorable to the defense that an acquittal was considered certain. When the verdict was read to-day convicting the entire gang several of them broke down and sobbed audibly."[22] They were sentenced to two years imprisonment, at hard labor.[23]

The members of the Yarbrough gang appealed to the U.S. Supreme Court, which heard their argument on January 23, 1884. Henry B. Tompkins, the lawyer for the petitioners, argued that their convictions were invalid because the federal court did not have proper jurisdiction. The U.S. Constitution, he argued, did not contain any provision empowering Congress to prosecute any private citizen who may have harmed another private citizen because of political animosity. He therefore asked the justices of the Supreme Court to overturn his clients' conviction. But on March 3, 1884, the Court announced that it was upholding the conviction of the petitioners. The verdict surprised many people, according to the *Atlanta Constitution,* because "the recent drift of [Supreme Court] decisions had been toward the assertion of state sovereignty to a degree unknown since the war."[24]

The Court's decision was, indeed, quite astonishing. First of all, it diverged greatly from the precedents that the Court had set in this area. In previous cases, primarily *Slaughterhouse* and *Cruikshank,* the Court rejected the notion that the federal government was empowered to protect citizens from private discrimination and violence. Secondly, the Court's strongly worded opinion sanctioning federal supervision of elections was unanimously adopted by the justices on the Court. And lastly, the opinion was written by Justice Samuel Miller, whose concurring vote in both *Cruikshank* and the *Civil Rights Cases* appeared to confirm his opposition to federal efforts to protect black civil rights.[25]

Justice Miller began the opinion of the Court by rebutting Tompkins's assertion that sections 5508 and 5520 of the revised U.S. statutes should be struck down because the Constitution does not explicitly empower Congress to protect voters from violence. This view of the Constitution, Justice Miller wrote, ignored the long-held doctrine that "what is implied is as much a part of the instrument as what is expressed." For instance, the Constitution does not provide express authority to Congress to punish those who steal from the U.S. Treasury. "Is there therefore," he asked, "no power in Congress to protect the treasury by punishing such theft and burglary?" Likewise, "Are the mails of the United States . . . to be left to the mercy of robbers . . . because the Constitution contains no express words of power in Congress to enact laws for the punishment of those offenses?" The answers to these questions, he said, are obvious. Congress has the power, as given in article I, section 8, of the Constitution, to pass laws that are "necessary and proper" for it to carry out its responsibilities. Just as the federal government is responsible for the U.S. mail, it is also obligated to make sure that congressional elections are free and fair. "If this government," Justice Miller wrote, "is anything more than a mere aggregation of delegated agents of other States and governments . . . it must have the power to protect the elections on which its existence depends from violence and corruption."[26]

Justice Miller concluded his opinion with unusually strong statements in support of black civil rights and the power of the federal government. For instance, Tompkins, in his brief to the Court, cited the Court's decision in *U.S. v. Reese* as evidence that the Fifteenth Amendment did not give African Americans the right to vote. Justice Miller refuted Tompkins's statement by arguing that the purpose of the amendment was "primarily to prevent discrimination against him [the African American] whenever the right to vote may be granted to others." The amendment, therefore, "was mainly designed for citizens of African descent." In this sense, then, the amendment "does *proprio vigore*, substantially confer on the negro the right to vote, and Congress has the power to protect and enforce that right."[27] The federal government, he said, has an obligation to make sure that those people who are elected to Congress are put there by the free votes of the electors. In light of the fraud and violence that marred elections in the South, including those for federal offices, Justice Miller concluded, "If the government of the United States has within its constitutional domain no authority to provide

against these evils, if the very source of power may be poisoned by corruption or controlled by violence and outrage, without legal restraint, then,
indeed, is the country in danger, and its best powers, its highest purposes,
the hopes which it inspires, and the love which enshrines it, are at the mercy
of the combinations of those who respect no right but brute force, on the
one hand, and unprincipled corruptionists on the other."[28]

Despite its strong, highly nationalistic rhetoric, the *Yarbrough* decision
proved to be a mere aberration in the pattern of the Court's decisions regarding federal protection of civil rights. The Court heard a similar case in 1903,
known as *James v. Bowman*.[29] In that case, the Court completely ignored its
Yarbrough decision and sanctioned a narrower yet generally accepted interpretation of the Fifteenth Amendment. In the *Bowman* decision, the Court
ruled that the amendment does not prohibit private individuals from disfranchising blacks, but only applies to state governments and government officials.[30] In surveying the Court's decisions regarding the amendment between
1898 and 1904, Alexander Bickel and Benno Schmidt declared that the Court
was guilty of providing "a judicial parallel to Congress' repeal in 1894 of the
statutes calling for federal oversight of elections and franchise practices." By
1905, they concluded, the Court had disarmed the Fifteenth Amendment.[31]

Although *Yarbrough* did not prove to be a watershed decision, Speer's
prosecution of the Georgia whitecappers was considered a stunning success
at the time. U.S. Attorney General Benjamin Brewster congratulated Speer
and asked him to serve as a special prosecutor in a crusade to suppress a
group, known as the "Red Shirts," that had used violence to maintain white
supremacy and Democratic hegemony in South Carolina.[32] Samuel Melton,
the U.S. attorney for South Carolina, had spearheaded an investigation of
the Red Shirts and had won indictments against "a group of influential
men" for stuffing ballot boxes.[33] An indicator of the forces and attitudes that
men such as Speer had to contend with when attempting to secure equal
justice for blacks is found in the fact that the South Carolina governor, a
Democrat, had instructed his attorney general to handle the defense of the
alleged Red Shirts. In addition, the South Carolina legislature appropriated
ten thousand dollars to pay for the expenses of the defendants. Battling
against such odds and fighting the perception that they represented federal
interference in a local matter, it is not surprising that Melton and Speer
failed to win any convictions against the defendants. Speer complained that
he had received death threats and Melton told Attorney General Brewster
that it was impossible to draw a South Carolina jury that would convict a
white man for violation of the election laws.[34]

Speer returned to Georgia after his stint in South Carolina and resumed his duties as U.S. attorney until narrowly confirmed for the federal bench in February 1885. As a U.S. attorney, he had conducted the first successful prosecution of Klan members in Georgia; as a federal judge, he would preside over the first conviction of whites who held blacks in a state of debt peonage in the state of Georgia. In the peonage case the sheriff of Ware County, Thomas McClellan, a white man, was charged with arresting blacks with the intent of selling them to others as debt peons. Sheriff McClellan's co-conspirator, William Crawley, a prominent white lawyer in the county, contacted white landowners in the area to arrange the transaction that would furnish them with peon laborers. In 1902, Sheriff McClellan arrested two black youths for stealing a watermelon. They were sentenced to one month in the Ware County jail. Crawley contacted Edward McRee, the owner of a plantation in Lowndes County, and arranged to have the youths transferred to his custody. McRee paid the jail fines of the two youths and then put them to work on his farm for seven months.[35]

McClellan, Crawley, and members of the McRee family were arrested and indicted for violating the federal anti-peonage law passed in 1867. The McRees admitted their guilt and paid a fine. McClellan and Crawley, though, decided to fight the charges, primarily by challenging the constitutionality of the anti-peonage statute. Their lawyers, in the demurrer to the indictment, asserted that the Thirteenth Amendment did not provide a sufficient basis for such a law. On March 15, 1904, Judge Speer overruled the defendants' demurrer in a case known as *United States v. Thomas McClellan and William Crawley*.[36] He began his opinion by stating that the power of Congress to enact the anti-peonage legislation was "unquestionable." The Thirteenth Amendment outlawed involuntary servitude in the United States. It was "an absolute declaration," he said, that slavery shall not exist in any part of America. Congress, therefore, was simply exercising its recognized authority under the Thirteenth Amendment when it passed the 1867 statute. The fact that debt peonage was a form of slavery or involuntary servitude, he stated, was conclusively demonstrated by Judge Thomas Goode Jones of the Middle District of Alabama in his recent charge to the grand jury in the *Peonage Cases*. For those who still doubted that peonage could be classified as such, he asked, "Is it not involuntary servitude to seize by force, to hurry the victim from his wife and children, to incarcerate him in a stockade, and work him in range of the deadly muzzle of the shotgun, or under the terror of the lash and continue this servitude as long as resentment may prompt, or greed demand?"[37]

Not content with demonstrating the constitutionality of the 1867 statute, Judge Speer concluded his opinion with a highly charged condemnation of the peonage system. Those who participated in such a practice, he said, were "lawless and violent men" who, "for their own selfish purposes," consigned "helpless and pathetic negroes" to "a life of involuntary servitude compared to which the slavery of *antebellum* days was a paradise." Such an ignoble and inhumane practice, he insisted, needed to be destroyed. If allowed to continue, he warned, it would prove detrimental to society as a whole. For instance, even though the peonage system appeared on the surface to victimize only blacks, it actually had a negative effect on whites in the community as well. Judge Speer, in making this point, asked, "How can the plain farmer or manufacturer of turpentine, or lumber who hired help, hope for fair play in the market when a huge saw mill in the vicinity or an unscrupulous planter with a stockade full of unpaid hands can underbid his prices? Why should one man through lawless methods be permitted to grow rich while his neighbors who piously respect the law, and the rights of their fellow man, however humble, shall forever toil on perhaps in poverty and want?" In addition, he asked how any progress could be made in the so-called race problem when such a practice continued to thrive in the South. What "hope can the respectable negro have, what incentive to better effort, or better life" could he strive for, Speer wondered, "if he, his wife, his daughters or his sons may in a moment be snatched from his humble home and sold into peonage?" Because this was happening mainly to African Americans and not whites, there had not been much of an outcry against the system. In response to this, Judge Speer urged his audience "to put ourselves in his place [the place of an African American] and imagine our furious indignation or hopeless despair if our loved ones or ourselves could be subjected to such a condition of involuntary servitude."[38]

Detecting in Judge Speer's comments a lack of sympathy for their plight, the defendants (McClellan and Crawley) hastily changed their plea to guilty. Before sentencing the men, Judge Speer lectured them and his audience about debt peonage and the race problem. In a prime example of turn-of-the-century paternalism, he stated that "there is a peculiar obligation upon our southern white people to do all we can for the betterment of this race which is among us, which was formerly servile, and yet which forms so important a part of our economy." He declared that "it is the Christian duty of every white man in the South to do all he can to give the Negro a fair chance."[39]

Judge Speer's rhetoric made it appear that he would impose a heavy sentence on the guilty men. After talking about the white man's duty to blacks, he declared that he was alarmed by the fact that peonage was so prevalent in the state of Georgia. "These conditions," he said, "make it imperative upon the Court to consider this as a very serious case." And although the defendants had made a strong appeal for clemency, Speer said that he "must consider the general interest and the effect of this sentence on other people who may be disposed to offend as these have done." He then declared that neither defendant would serve time in jail, but that they each had to pay a thousand-dollar fine. But then Speer suspended the fine, saying that it would "hang over them" for the duration of their good behavior and could be imposed at any time.[40]

Judge Speer can be criticized for failing to adequately punish McClellan and Crawley. But his denunciation of the practice and his upholding of the anti-peonage statute were significant and somewhat extraordinary for the time. It should be pointed out, for instance, that Judge William Newman, Speer's counterpart in the Northern District of Georgia, responded to these same events by publicly declaring the Anti-Peonage Law unconstitutional.[41] In addition, Judge Speer, in a letter to President Theodore Roosevelt, expressed his fear that the Supreme Court would overrule him on this issue. He warned Roosevelt of such a turn of events and told him that if the Court embraced Newman's view of the statute, then Congress's top priority should be to enact anti-peonage legislation that would be declared constitutional.[42] Judge Speer's actions, as disappointing as they were, earned him praise from some of the advocates of black civil rights. The *Voice of the Negro,* for instance, commended him for his fight against peonage and published portions of his charge to the jury.[43]

Years later, in 1911, Judge Speer again faced the issue of debt peonage. According to the *Crisis,* the official magazine of the National Association for the Advancement of Colored People (NAACP), which at the time was being edited by William Edward Burghardt DuBois, "four wealthy Georgians" were on trial in Speer's court for holding "hundreds of negroes" in peonage. During the course of the trial, DuBois pointed out, "Judge Speer reprimanded Attorney General Felder for continually using the word 'nigger.'" Judge Speer "remarked that he was tired of 'nigger, nigger, nigger,' and suggested that the lawyer choose a more pleasing form of address." Although Attorney General Felder protested the judge's suggestion, "Judge Speer was insistent and even hinted that he would not allow the lawyer to appear before him if he did not mend his manners." Attorney General Felder refrained from using the term from that point forward and completed his case. In his message to the jury, Judge Speer "charged that the Georgia contract labor [law] violate[d] the Constitution of the United States." Consequently, said DuBois, "the judge practically ordered a verdict of guilty." Much to Judge Speer's chagrin, the jury returned a verdict of not guilty after just five minutes of deliberation. According to DuBois, Judge Speer was "angered" by the verdict, particularly since he believed that the charged men had "by their own testimony . . . convicted themselves."[44]

Judge Speer was no stranger to the pages of both the *Crisis* and the *Voice of the Negro*. He was praised by the editors of the latter in 1905 for trying to destroy the chain gang system, which the editor called "a very great curse upon . . . every Southern state."[45] Convicted criminals in the South were frequently used as laborers, being chained together and forced to work on public lands and roads. Besides the humiliation that accompanied having to work in public on the chain gang, convicts also had to endure frequent whippings and harsh conditions. Macon, Georgia, like many other southern communities, had an ordinance that authorized a city official (in this case, the recorder of Macon) to sentence people to the local chain gang for violating minor municipal laws. This situation, according to the *Voice of the Negro,* led to "one-man power in the South." The men who wielded such power, the magazine said, were typically "bare-faced tyrants who rule supreme and who will send a Negro to the chain-gang if he dares try to defend himself before 'his highness.'"[46]

Judge Speer had long been an outspoken critic of the chain gang, but his effort to eradicate the practice did not occur until his wife prodded him into action.[47] On March 14, 1904, a sixty-year-old black man named Henry Jamison was sentenced by the recorder of Macon to serve seven months on the local chain gang for being drunk in public and for disorderly conduct. Because Jamison occasionally did odd jobs for Mrs. Speer, she urged her husband to keep him off of the chain gang. Judge Speer, in response, had the U.S. attorney file a petition for habeas corpus on Jamison's behalf, thus suspending the sentence and bringing before Speer's court the question of the constitutionality of the recorder's actions.

The habeas corpus proceedings in the Jamison case stretched from March 1904 to August of that same year. Judge Speer frequently intervened in the proceedings to defend the petition from the criticisms of Minter Wimberley, the lawyer for the city of Macon. Wimberley asserted that the federal court did not have proper jurisdiction for this case. Judge Speer retorted that the right of habeas corpus is designed to ensure that the law under which someone is being sentenced is constitutional. The purpose of the proceedings, he said, was to determine "if the Recorder's court has violated that clause of the Constitution of the United States which says that no state shall deprive any citizen of life, liberty, or property without due process of law."[48]

In his ruling on the petition, which he handed down on June 28, 1904, Judge Speer went to great lengths to justify his court's intervention in a local matter. He stated that his intention was to determine the legality of the chain gang, which he called "perhaps the most melancholy and distressing spectacle which afflicts the patriot and humanitarian." He sought, he said, to determine if "such a deplorable and degrading punishment . . . for minor municipal offenses" was "tolerable under the American system." As for the importance of his investigation, he said that "in no case previously decided by a state or national court has there been so fully and fairly made this inquiry, fraught as it is with the misery of thousands of humble men, women, and children, and fraught also with the hope of a possible return by local governments to more humane methods, with the resultant uplifting of millions of the people."[49]

The chain gang, according to Judge Speer, was a form of "involuntary servitude" and "infamous punishment."[50] To support this assertion, Judge Speer described the horrible conditions that characterized life on the chain gang. First of all, the convicts on the chain gang were forced to sleep in the same dirty clothes in which they worked throughout the day. Even if allowed to change clothes it would be nearly impossible for any of the convicts to get a proper amount of rest considering that they remained chained to one another and that their bedding consisted of pallets or straw on an otherwise bare floor. Upon waking they were forced to perform manual labor that was "as severe perhaps as any of which the human frame is capable."[51] Those who failed to maintain a torrid pace of work ran the risk of being whipped by one of the armed guards. He asserted that "the agony inflicted by this implement of torture" was "not surpassed by the Russian knout," which he called "the synonym the world around for merciless corporal punishment."[52]

One of the worst aspects of this system, he said, was how easy it was for someone to suddenly find themselves facing such conditions. Most of the people sentenced to the chain gang, he pointed out, were convicted of minor municipal offenses, such as "disorderly conduct, violations of the bicycle ordinances, walking or standing on the park grass, loitering in the depot or in the railroad yard, careless driving and the like." Numerous people were convicted of committing such petty crimes and were typically given excessive sentences. He calculated that in the month of March 1904 alone, 149 people were convicted by the recorder of Macon for violating municipal ordinances. These unfortunate persons were sentenced to a total of 6,751 days on the chain gang. This translated, he said, into a situation in which "one man is entrusted by the state with practically arbitrary power to impose cruel and infamous punishment for offenses of the most trivial" nature.[53] That such a situation exists in the South, he said, was both unfortunate and unprecedented. There was "no shred of authority," he asserted, in either American or British jurisprudence "where a sentence for petty offenses . . . to public chaingang, with the ignominious accessories of fetters, the stripes, lash, and of the degradation of convict life, has been sustained or even palliated."[54]

Besides being unable to find any authority upholding such a severe punishment for minor crimes, Judge Speer argued that the system, as it existed in Georgia, violated the Fourteenth Amendment, which stipulates that no state shall deprive any person of life, liberty, or property without due process of the law. The legal proceedings in the Recorders Court, he asserted, did not constitute due process. Those who are brought before that court are judged not by a jury of their peers, but simply by a sole individual. These proceedings typically occurred in a hurried, haphazard fashion in which little evidence was presented and the accused was not provided with proper legal representation and advice.[55]

As for the assertion that the federal district court did not have the jurisdiction to consider the petition for habeas corpus, Judge Speer responded by saying that such a "contention does not seem marked by any considerable merit." He cited several cases in which the U.S. Supreme Court upheld decisions by lower federal courts overturning a conviction at the state level which was based on an unconstitutional law. These convictions were reversed after the plaintiff filed a petition of habeas corpus in a federal court. "No case has been found," he said, "wherein there is a disapproval of the action of such courts . . . where it is fully averred and shown that the petitioner is held in custody in violation of the Constitution and laws of the United States."[56] He therefore ruled that since the recorder of Macon deprived people of their liberty without due process, Henry Jamison had the right to petition the court in order to have his constitutional rights protected by that court.

Judge Speer not only upheld Jamison's right to petition the federal court, he ruled in favor of it. He then declared the city ordinance under which Jamison was sentenced to be unconstitutional and void. The city of Macon, displeased with the verdict, appealed to the U.S. Supreme Court. In October of 1905 the Supreme Court rejected Judge Speer's arguments and ruled that the federal district court did not have appropriate jurisdiction in the matter.[57] Although the Supreme Court thwarted Speer's attempt to eradicate the chain-gang system in his home state, he received significant assistance from an unexpected source. Approximately six months after the U.S. Supreme Court handed down its decision, the Georgia State Supreme Court struck down the Macon ordinance that empowered the recorder to send people to the chain gang.[58]

Years earlier Judge Speer had intervened in a somewhat similar case, one in which federal intervention was questionable at best. In 1889 Judge Speer learned that a black prisoner had been chained to the grating in his cell by his neck so that only his toes touched the ground. Speer ordered the U.S. attorney to prosecute the jailer, Nat Birdsong, who explained that he only punished the prisoner after he became unruly and uncooperative. When brought before Judge Speer, Birdsong's attorney argued that Birdsong's actions did not fall under the federal court's jurisdiction because he was not a federal officer. Judge Speer ruled that since Birdsong was an officer in a jail sometimes used by the federal government, then a federal court did indeed have jurisdiction.[59] He initially found Birdsong guilty and assessed a fine, but then suspended the sentence on assurances that Birdsong would never repeat his cruel behavior.[60] According to Margo Schlanger, this is practically the only time, until the 1960s, that a federal judge intervened in a civil case in a matter regarding the treatment of prisoners.[61]

Just as Speer overstepped his bounds in the Jamison and Birdsong cases, he did so as well in the political realm when he attempted to force Republican delegates to the 1912 national convention to pledge their votes to Theodore Roosevelt rather than William Howard Taft. Taft's supporters in the Justice Department launched an investigation into Speer's conduct, which resulted in congressional hearings on the matter. Despite the fact that sixty-two individuals testified against Speer at the hearings, the members of the congressional committee voted against impeaching Speer. Judge Speer suffered a severe mental and physical breakdown in the midst of the affair and his health never fully recovered. On December 13, 1918, he died in a Macon, Georgia, hospital from complications that arose from a surgery for gall stones.[62]

Thomas Goode Jones, U.S. District Judge, Middle and
Northern Districts of Alabama, 1901–1914.

Alabama Department of Archives and History, Montgomery, Alabama.

- CHAPTER FOUR -

Judge Thomas Goode Jones

I N THE FALL of 1901, President Theodore Roosevelt appointed Thomas Goode Jones federal judge of the Northern and Middle Districts of Alabama. Roosevelt, a Republican, selected the Alabama Democrat on the recommendation of Booker T. Washington, the famous black leader of the early twentieth century who frequently advised the president on his political appointments in the South. Washington's relationship with Jones dated back to 1890, when he secretly urged blacks to vote for Jones in his successful race for the Alabama governorship. His support for Jones stemmed primarily from Jones's success, as head of the Alabama state militia, in saving an African American from a Birmingham lynch mob in 1883.[1]

Jones had become head of the Alabama state militia as a result of the military experience he garnered as a cadet at the Virginia Military Institute under the tutelage of Thomas J. "Stonewall" Jackson and then as aide-de-camp to General John B. Gordon during the Civil War.[2] Jones studied William Blackstone's commentaries on the laws of England while in winter quarters during the war and in 1866 began reading law in the office of John A. Elmore, "the acknowledged head of the Alabama bar" and a former law partner of secessionist leader, William Lowndes Yancey.[3] He then studied law under Abram J. Walker, who served as the chief justice of the Alabama State Supreme Court from 1859 until 1868, when he was forced out of the position as a result of congressional Reconstruction.[4] Judge Walker refused to administer the oath of office to his successor, Elijah Woley Peck, a prominent Republican, but Jones accepted an offer two years later from Peck to serve as the court's reporter, a position he retained for ten years. During that time, Jones also established a law practice with Samuel F. Rice, a former chief justice of the Alabama State Supreme Court (1856–1859), who enraged Democrats by switching allegiances to the Republican Party during Reconstruction. In the early 1880s, Jones became a lawyer for the

powerful Louisville and Nashville Railroad, and in 1887 he led the Alabama
Bar Association to adopt the nation's first code of legal ethics, which he
authored and which was adopted by the American Bar Association in 1908.[5]

Although Jones was obviously willing to work with Republicans, such
as his law partner Samuel Rice, his political allegiances clearly lay with the
Democratic Party. In fact, he actively participated in the Democratic Party's
counterrevolutionary campaign to "redeem" Alabama from Republican
rule. He was elected to both the Montgomery city council (1875–1884) and
the Alabama State Legislature (1884–1888) as a Democrat. In 1890, he won
the party's nomination for governor and easily defeated his Republican
opponent. His bid for re-election in 1892, although successful, was marred
by widespread election fraud as Alabama Democrats resorted to desperate
measures to rebuff the challenge of the insurgent Populist Party, which consisted primarily of poor whites and blacks seeking to overthrow the oli-
garchical Democrats.[6]

Although a prominent member of the party of white supremacy, Jones
was not a typical Gilded Age southern Democrat. His position on political
questions frequently diverged from the party line of economic retrenchment
and the repression of African Americans. It is significant to note that he won
the nomination for governor—and the position of party leader—not because
of his adherence to party doctrine, but because he was a compromise candidate. He had polled the fewest delegates out of the five men seeking the
nomination in 1890. But his delegates announced that their second choice
was Reuben Kolb, an agrarian who only needed a few more votes to secure
the nomination. Determined to forestall Kolb, who would later become
Alabama's leading Populist, the party leaders decided to throw their support
behind Jones.[7]

It did not take long for Governor Jones to demonstrate his willingness to
diverge from the party line. During his first inaugural address he shocked
many Alabamians by expressing his strong opposition to a popular bill pending in the general assembly that based the funding of black and white schools
upon the amount that each race paid in taxes. African Americans, he pointed
out, owned little taxable property. Consequently, their schools would be
grossly underfunded if the state adopted such a funding formula. In addition,
he dismissed talk of calling a constitutional convention so as to disfranchise
African Americans. Such a course of action, he said, would be unwise, unconstitutional, and unjust.[8] Newspaper editors throughout the state castigated
him for his heresy. The *Sumter Sun,* echoing comments from Democratic
newspapers across the state, declared that his position was "contrary to the
views of three-fourths of the white Democratic voters in Alabama."[9]

   His position on a number of other issues also proved to be controversial. During his two terms as governor he enacted reforms designed to bring the state's notorious convict-leasing system to an end. His advances in this area were reversed when his successor, a Democrat, with the blessing of a Democratic general assembly, reinstated the leasing system as the keystone of the state's penal system. The general assembly also rejected Jones's request to provide the chief executive with the authority to fire sheriffs who failed to protect (or attempt to protect) a prisoner from a lynch mob. A few prominent Alabama Democrats, such a J. Thomas Heflin, also criticized the governor's vocal opposition to the lynching of blacks.[10]

   Jones's leadership of the Alabama state Democratic Party represented a more moderate and temporary phase. By 1900, retrenchment and racial repression once again ruled. In the following year, Alabama Democrats sought to permanently enshrine their policies by writing them into a new state constitution. Jones, to his surprise, was elected as an at-large delegate to the 1901 constitutional convention. His actions there won him renewed support from Booker T. Washington and captured the attention of President Theodore Roosevelt. His primary contribution was his service as the leader of the small minority of delegates who were opposed to the disfranchisement of African Americans. He also gave passionate speeches against lynching and in support of educational opportunities for African Americans.[11] A few weeks after the convention ended, President Roosevelt, on the advice of Booker T. Washington, nominated Jones to the federal bench.[12]

   After being on the bench for less than two years, Judge Jones commenced a controversial crusade to rid Alabama of debt peonage. He described the practice to Attorney General Philander C. Knox, explaining that "a systematic scheme of depriving negroes of their civil liberty, and hiring them out, has been practiced for some time" in the state. "The plan," he wrote, "is to accuse the negro of some petty offense" so that he will seek to escape conviction by working for any white landowner who will pay his fine. The African American then becomes indebted to the landowner and "is made to believe he is a convict, and [is] treated as such."[13] Judge Jones asked the attorney general for assistance, arguing that any effort to eradicate peonage in Alabama would be fiercely resisted. He predicted that "a great effort will be made to suborn witnesses, to run others off and to manufacture testimony."[14] In fact, one black witness had been kidnapped after testifying to the grand jury. Although he was released soon thereafter, the event demonstrated the lengths to which some in the community would go in thwarting justice. An Alabama citizen writing to the attorney general to complain about peonage also warned about the difficulties that would be encountered

in a fight against peonage. He told the attorney general that "the enslavement of the colored people in Alabama" is "carried on by that class of men
who by reason of their party prominence in the community where they live
have so exercised influence over juries and public officials as to make the
local courts . . . powerless to enforce the law." Those men who held African
Americans in a state of peonage, he asserted, were "protected in their brutal
and inhuman conduct by that class of Democrats who believe that no law,
moral or otherwise, is violated in the enslavement of negroes." He added
that "the Federal officials here, surrounded by the Democratic influence as
they are, will not enforce the law."[15]

Judge Jones disproved this assertion when he commenced his attack on
peonage by assembling a grand jury in his district to indict those suspected
of placing African Americans in a state of peonage. With his charge to the
grand jury, Jones became the "first jurist in the United States to define
peonage" and "explain to Alabama citizens the foul makeup of the system."[16]
Jones's aggressive campaign against the system was detailed in the *Federal
Reporter* under the title of *The Peonage Cases.*[17] Jones began his charge by
tracing the migration of peonage from Spain to Mexico and into New
Mexico and the United States. He attributed the spread of peonage to "the
improvidence and the needs of laborers and servants, the greed of employers,
and the exercise, often corrupt, of almost irresponsible power of local mag-
istrates." Such factors, he asserted, "resulted in citizens becoming bound, in
constantly increasing numbers and length of service, to compulsory 'service
or labor' to coerce payment of debt or to compel the performance of real
or pretended obligations of personal service."[18] Because of the continued
existence of peonage in New Mexico—despite the ratification of the
Thirteenth Amendment in 1865—Congress passed an act banning peonage
in the United States.[19] Jones declared that the 1867 act of Congress outlawed both state and individual actions resulting in the holding or returning of a person to a system or condition of peonage. Therefore, Jones
contended, federal officials were authorized to prosecute individuals accused
of holding others in a state of peonage.[20]

Jones then explained the nature of peonage to the jurors, stating that it
consisted of a person consenting to a form of voluntary servitude that
becomes "involuntary the moment the person desires to withdraw, and then
is coerced to remain and perform service against his will." He explained that
the person who coerces another to serve involuntarily is not the only person guilty of putting that person in a state of peonage. Any judicial or law
officials who conspire together or with others to place a person in a system

of peonage are also guilty—as is anyone who falsely accuses another of a crime in a conspiratorial attempt to make the innocent person a peon.[21]

He concluded his charge by declaring the Alabama Labor Law of 1901 unconstitutional. This legislation had made it illegal for a laborer who was indebted to his employer to break his contract with that employer and sign a similar one with a different person, without the first employer's permission. Of the law, Jones asked, "What is this but declaring, if a man breaks his contract with his creditor without just excuse, he shall not work at his accustomed vocation for others without permission of the creditor?"[22] Echoing Judge Jacob Trieber's sentiments, as expressed in *U.S. v. Morris,* Jones argued that "one of the most valuable liberties of man" is the ability to choose his employer and to quit a job when he wishes. The Alabama law, in his opinion, was a "vicious species of class legislation" that discriminated against "persons in uninfluential and humble occupations." Because the law was "designed solely in the interest of the employer or landlord," he concluded that the labor law violated the U.S. Constitution by denying the poor and humble equal protection of the law.[23]

On June 15, 1903, U.S. Attorney William S. Reese Jr. submitted his report on the peonage cases to Attorney General Knox. After delineating the extent of the practice and describing the horrible conditions under which its victims lived, he updated Knox on the progress being made in the cases. The grand jury had, at that time, already handed down eighty indictments, some of them against local officials, such as sheriffs and justices of the peace.[24] In commenting on Judge Jones's charge, Reese called it "an actual and not a theoretical emancipation of the negro."[25]

The crusade against peonage appeared to be successful, and Jones received praise from the highest levels. Booker T. Washington, for instance, told Oswald Garrison Villard that "we owe to Judge Thomas G. Jones . . . a great debt of gratitude for what is being done in regard to exposing the peonage system in Alabama." He said that the judge was "as good a friend to the Negro as any white man in this country."[26] President Theodore Roosevelt also commented on the decision, telling Lyman Abbott, "You can hardly realize the immense service rendered by him [Jones] in his recent peonage decisions, or the great moral courage he showed in rendering them." Roosevelt then explained why he believed it took great courage for Jones to act as he did:

> Unfortunately there is in the south a very large element which because of the very fact that they have been let alone by the north as regards

dealing with the Negro have been resolute in their intention practically to reintroduce some form of serfage or slavery. This large white element in the south is not in the least concerned about those bugaboos, "social equality," "negro domination," and "miscegenation," all three of which are the merest phantoms. It hates and despises the Negro but is bent upon his continuing in the land. It is this element which in the black belt controls the towns and ran out the emigration agents who sought to get the Negroes to go to Oklahoma. This element strives to prevent the Negro's rising in any way and seeks to drive him from every trade in which he can be a rival to a white, and at the same time does not want to work. The absence of protest from the north has undoubtedly, whatever may have been its good effects in certain lines, had a bad effect in encouraging this white element; and the bold action of Judge Jones is therefore all the more valuable. Of course it is far better that such action should come from a Southerner, but the north ought in every way to uphold the hands of the southerner brave and wise enough to take it.[27]

A few weeks later Booker T. Washington addressed the National Afro-American Council and described Judge Jones's actions as a ray of hope for blacks in America. He told the delegates:

In the present season of anxiety, and almost of despair, which possesses an element of the race, there are two things which I will say as strongly as I may. First, let no man of the race become discouraged or hopeless. Though their voices may not be often or loudly lifted, there are in this country, North and South, men who mean to help see that justice is meted out to the race in all avenues of life. Such a man is Judge Thomas G. Jones, of Alabama, to whom more credit should be given for blotting out the infamous system of peonage than to any other. Judge Jones represents the very highest type of Southern manhood, and there are hosts of others like him. There is a class of brave, earnest men in the South, as well as in the North, who are more determined than ever before to see that the race is given an opportunity to elevate itself; and we owe it to these friends as well as to ourselves to see that no act of ours causes them embarrassment. The lesson for the other portion of the nation to learn is that, both in the making and the execution, the same laws should be made to apply to the Negro as to the white man. There should be meted out equal justice to the black man and the white man whether it relates to citizenship, the protection of property, the right of labor, or the protection of human life. Whenever the nation forgets, or is tempted to forget, this basic principle, the whole fabric of government for both the white and the black man is weakened and threatened with destruction.[28]

When the peonage investigations commenced, Jones had predicted that whites in Alabama would be hesitant to punish other whites for engaging in a generally accepted, widespread practice. White resistance had, indeed, been evident throughout the entire process, but did not significantly influence the federal government's efforts until the 1903 trial of Fletcher Turner, who was charged with holding African Americans in a state of debt peonage. After both sides presented their evidence in the trial, Judge Jones charged the jury to convict Turner of violating the peonage statutes. A few jurors, though, refused to find Turner guilty. Although Judge Jones explicitly told the jurors that they were obligated to convict the defendant and repeatedly extended their time of deliberation so they could reach a verdict, he eventually had to order a mistrial in the case. But, before discharging the jury, he chastised its members for basing their actions on public opinion rather than law and justice. "I say then, not only as a judge, but as an Alabamian, as a Southern man, and as an ex-Confederate soldier," that "I readily understand how disagreeable it may be, at times, for a man to discharge a duty that is unpleasant; to face hostile opinion, prejudice or passion, and to be misunderstood. These things come to everyone who courageously discharges his duty." "Nevertheless," he said, "I had hoped that this jury would be strong enough to do their duty and reach a conclusion, when the evidence was clear."[29]

Judge Jones then read into the record the efforts that he had made to steer the jury toward a proper verdict. He pointed out that he provided a "general charge [that] was so clear" that no one could fail to understand its intent. He did so, he said, to shift the responsibility for the verdict rendered [assuming Turner would be found guilty] from the jury to the court so as to protect the jurors from public reprisals. He added that, although the jury had no business considering the punishment, he alleviated their fears of a harsh punishment by telling them that Turner would not be sent to prison. In sum, he said, "I wished to relieve the jury, if it wished to do its duty, of any obstacle which [it] might feel made [its] path of duty hard."[30]

Judge Jones believed that the jury failed to convict Turner because of white public opinion. Indeed, a significant part of white public sentiment in Alabama appeared to be opposed to the peonage investigations or at least to the imprisonment of the offenders. Federal officials in the investigation complained of the hostile environment and believed that they were fighting against insurmountable odds. This attitude was evident in a letter written to the head of the Secret Service Division of the Treasury Department. The author, who was assisting an operative from the division in his investigation of peonage in Alabama, said, "Knowing public sentiment as I do, I fear, unless compromise verdicts can be secured [in the remaining cases], that no convictions will result." He continued, "The sentiment against the infliction of punishment to offenders finds its strongest exponent in Sec[retary] of State J. Thomas Heflin, an orator of no mean ability, and he is going about the state like a roaring lion. I merely write this to say, that whatever the result in the trial of the cases in this Court, the failure to convict and punish offenders, cannot be charged to our service."[31]

J. Thomas Heflin, who served as a U.S. senator from Alabama from 1920 to 1932, expressed approval of the mistrial and said that Jones's reprimand of the jury was "wholly uncalled for . . . and it tended in my judgment to intimidate rather than enlighten, to trespass on the domain of the jury, and to usurp its function."[32] Herbert D. Ward, who published an article on peonage in *Cosmopolitan,* disagreed with Heflin and stated that Jones's "scoring of the [Turner] jury was the cause not only of the rallying of the best element in the state to the banner of justice, but of freeing at least fifteen hundred negroes from an actual state of peonage."[33] How Jones's scoring of the jury accomplished this last feat, Ward does not say. In all probability the mistrial probably bolstered, rather than discouraged, the confidence of those who were holding blacks in a state of peonage.

After the mistrial, the assault on peonage in Alabama transformed into what Pete Daniel calls an "experiment in leniency."[34] After suffering a defeat in the Turner trial at the hands of those who were hostile to any effort to punish peon masters, Judge Jones encountered pressure—from African Americans, no less—to have those convicted of peonage pardoned. One newspaper printed a story that "influential colored men" from Coosa and Tallapoosa counties (where those convicted of peonage were from) were spearheading a movement to have George and Barancas Cosby pardoned.[35] Judge Jones had sentenced them to 365 days in the Atlanta Penitentiary for peonage. This rather strange turn of events is also mentioned by Jones in a letter to Booker T. Washington.[36] These African Americans organized several mass meetings and led a petition drive to convince the judge to pardon the Cosbys. The petition, which was signed by "several hundred negroes," stated that the peonage cases had "caused a bitter feeling between the two races." Since the system had been broken up, it stated, it would be beneficial to the relations between the races in the counties if the Cosbys were released from prison.[37]

Jones at first appeared to have rejected the notion that they should be pardoned. He told Washington that those urging such action based it partially on the fact that the Cosbys were poor and that their families were dependent upon them. But Jones rejected this line of reasoning, saying that such was usually the case whenever anyone was punished for committing a crime. But in the same letter, he revealed that he was giving the matter serious thought and that he was being swayed by the argument that pardons would improve race relations. He told Washington that the "object of all good men now is to lessen the friction between the races and put the blacks especially on as high a plane as possible." He then asked Washington, "Would or would it not confound those who are filled with low hates, if the representatives of the negro race, should publicly take the ground that it had no desire, now that the [peonage] system was broken up, for vengeance, or to subject the families of the men who are now in prison, to the suffering that they inflicted on others, and that believing it would redound to the public good, and promote friendship among good men of both races, they would be glad to see clemency extended to them? Would it not confound 'negro haters' and their friends to have your people take such a stand? Would or would it not lead to better things?"[38]

Jones's questions appeared to be an effort to convince Washington to call for the pardon of the Cosbys rather than being a simple request for assistance in finding answers to such questions. Nevertheless, he told Washington that he had "not maturely considered the question" and would appreciate it if Washington would give him his impression of the situation. Washington agreed with Jones and forwarded the letter to T. Thomas Fortune with a note saying, "I think his view of the matter is Statesman-like and that the action would go far to show other guilty ones that *it is* the peonage system and not the men guilty of it that it is desired to be destroyed."[39]

In September 1903, Jones took the necessary steps to have the Cosbys pardoned. In a letter to Booker T. Washington, he explained that he did this because African Americans in Coosa and Tallapoosa counties had urged him to and because he believed "it will smooth the pathway of the races" in the state. The compassion and generosity shown by blacks in advocating the pardon of the Cosbys, he said, "will put them in the strongest and most favorable contrast to those who think the legal rights of human beings ought to shrink or expand according their color."[40]

Jones, like Washington, believed that the highly publicized prosecutions against peon masters such as the Cosbys had effectively broken up the system and that their work had been done. This impression appears to have been widespread amongst those involved with the investigation. For example,

Stanley W. Frisch, an examiner for the federal government, told the attorney general, "The prosecutions . . . have attracted general attention, and accomplished extensive results in breaking up the peonage system in this district." This fact, he said, explained and justified Judge Jones's actions.[41]

The results of Jones's crusade against peonage in Alabama in 1903 were quite unimpressive. In 1905, Assistant Attorney General Charles W. Russell outlined the results of the *Peonage Cases,* saying that of the ninety-nine indictments, four persons served a total of five months in jail and those convicted of peonage paid a total of five hundred dollars in fines.[42] After the Turner mistrial and the pardon of the Cosbys, the prosecutions against accused peon masters ceased on the basis that the peonage system had been effectively destroyed. In addition, the Alabama legislature had responded to Jones's striking down of the 1901 Alabama Labor Law by passing a new contract-labor law in 1903. This law sought to maintain the practice of debt peonage by declaring that a laborer's failure to complete a contract, or repay his creditor, was prima facie evidence of the laborer's intent to defraud the employer.[43] Although this law seemingly undermined everything that Jones and other federal officials had sought to accomplish, it also provided Jones with a second chance to bring the authority of the federal government to bear upon the practice of peonage in Alabama.

In 1908, Alabama law enforcement officials arrested an African American laborer named Alonzo Bailey for violating the above-mentioned Alabama law by breaking his contract with his creditor/employer.[44] Jones and other opponents of peonage took the opportunity of Bailey's arrest to contest the state's labor law that facilitated the continued survival of the peonage system in Alabama. Jones, Booker T. Washington, and other Alabamians worked together behind the scenes to promote and prepare the Bailey case.[45] Throughout its long journey to the U.S. Supreme Court, Jones maintained correspondence with Roosevelt, requesting assistance in the case. On October 2, 1908, Jones wrote the president about the *Bailey* case, suggesting to him that it would be helpful if Roosevelt could get a representative of the government to file a brief in support of Bailey. He told Roosevelt that he had been assisting Bailey's attorneys and said, "If the case is won, I want these young lawyers to get all the credit, and therefore want to keep my letter to you off the files, and as far as possible to keep myself in the background."[46] Although Roosevelt neglected to provide Jones with his requested brief, the president supported his efforts.[47]

In 1910, Jones wrote an eighteen-page paper entitled "Suggestions in the Bailey Case," which he submitted to Bailey's attorneys and the Justice

Department. One of the attorneys, Fred Ball, submitted Jones's suggestions, with some revisions, as his brief to the U.S. Supreme Court.[48] In his paper, Jones argued, "If the state may punish a man for quitting a contract of personal service, because he abandons it without just cause, it may annihilate the 13th amendment, and reestablish involuntary servitude in the teeth of the Supreme Law." He contended that the purpose of the Alabama statute was not to punish fraud or protect public morals, as its supporters commonly asserted, but simply to compel workers to contract their labor without any ability to break the contract, regardless of conditions. By making breach of contract prima facie evidence of intent to defraud, he argued, the accused is guilty until proven innocent—a travesty of American justice. He also argued that the statute violated the Fourteenth Amendment by denying laborers equal protection of the laws.[49] In denouncing such discrimination, Jones said, "Justice is administered without respect of person or cause. A man's right in the court cannot be different from the like rights granted other men, either because of the manner in which he obtains advances, or the class to which he belongs, or whether he intended to defraud."[50]

On January 3, 1911, the U.S. Supreme Court ruled on behalf of Alonzo Bailey in *Bailey v. Alabama*.[51] The Court explained that the Alabama statute was unconstitutional because the state "may not compel one man to labor for another in payment of a debt, by punishing him as a criminal if he does not perform the service or pay the debt."[52] Justices Oliver Wendell Holmes and Horace H. Lurton dissented. Justice Holmes argued that the Alabama law simply provided an acceptable legal enticement to make laborers honor their promises to their employer. In his dissent, Holmes said, "Breach of legal contract without excuse is wrong conduct, even if the contract is for labor, and if a State adds to civil liability a criminal liability to fine, it simply intensifies the legal motive for doing right, it does not make the laborer a slave."[53]

Bailey proved to be one of the few Supreme Court decisions of the era that ruled on behalf of African Americans. Although it was a rare victory, it was, nevertheless, a significant one. By striking down as unconstitutional the contract-labor laws like the one passed in Alabama, the Supreme Court freed an increasing number of African Americans from involuntary servitude and thereby helped to make the first and second Great Migrations possible. Historians have long recognized that the migration of millions of African Americans to the North proved to be critical to the success of the civil rights movement. As African Americans crossed the Mason-Dixon line they improved their economic prospects and regained the right to vote. These economic and political gains enabled African Americans not only to directly aid the civil rights movement, but also to exercise greater influence over the nation's lawmakers.[54]

But many people disagreed with the decision. Jones had received threats and abuse throughout his battle against peonage, but the threats grew graver after the *Bailey* decision.[55] Jones complained to Roosevelt about the criticism, saying, "While I did nothing less than my duty in the peonage cases, I did it in a way to protect the good name of the people of Alabama and for that I should be thanked and not abused." After the *Bailey* verdict he told Roosevelt that he recently received anonymous letters threatening his assassination, "some of them saying such a fate ought to be meted out to a judge appointed by a 'nigger.'"[56] This, of course, referred to Booker T. Washington's role in Jones's appointment.

Despite such threats, Judge Jones continued to take steps to protect African Americans from hostile white southerners. In 1904 he handed down a decision, in a case known as *Ex parte Riggins,* that made him one of the first federal judges, if not *the* first, to declare that lynchers violated *federal* laws.[57] The case stemmed from an incident in Huntsville, Alabama, in which a mob set the jail on fire in an effort to flush out an African American prisoner named Horace Maples. By igniting the prison, the mob not only endangered the lives of federal prisoners who were being held in the jail, but also succeeded in getting the sheriff to force Maples to jump from a second-story window into the mob below. The crowd dragged Maples to the Huntsville town square and hanged him from a tree on the courthouse lawn.[58]

The lynching outraged Jones, and he sought advice from numerous sources regarding the federal government's ability to prosecute the members of the Huntsville mob. He asked Judge David D. Shelby of the U.S. Circuit Court of Appeals in the Fifth Circuit—which included Alabama—if it was ethical for them to correspond over such legal matters. Judge Shelby responded by saying, "I see no impropriety in our consulting about our respective judicial duties." He cautioned that "in these consultations our opinions of course would be tentative," but added that the exchange of ideas and opinions "might teach us more law."[59] He then told Jones that he agreed with his assertion that section 5508 of the Revised Statutes provided federal jurisdiction in a case of conspiracy to injure or kill federal prisoners by burning the jail in which they are confined. The incident, he said, was a serious one; he urged Jones to pursue the matter.[60]

On the same day that Judge Shelby wrote his initial response to Jones, the Alabama judge sent another letter to him, focusing on the question of whether or not the government possessed the authority to prosecute the mob for lynching Maples. Shelby replied by telling Jones, "Your letter and . . . a further examination of other authorities [has] convinced [me] that it is the duty of the U.S. Attorney to prosecute these cases." Writing from the Fifth Circuit courthouse in New Orleans, Judge Shelby stated that it "seems that the Federal court may have jurisdiction of the other branch of the case—the murder of the negro Maples." "There is evidence," he said, "that he was deprived of the right of trial on the account of *race*. Speeches by the mob show this to be a fact."[61] He told Jones to examine Judge Jacob Trieber's opinion in *U.S. v. Morris,* saying that it justified federal intervention when rights are deprived on the basis of race. It is possible that "the federal courts can stop the lynching of negroes," he wrote, "if juries will hold they are lynched because they are negroes."[62]

The federal government, of course, had done very little to stop the lynching of African Americans. The attitude that prevailed in the American legal community at the time was that the federal government did not possess the constitutional authority to intervene in such a matter as it was considered solely a state affair. Consequently, as state and local officials either acquiesced or participated in lynchings, there appeared to be no end in sight to this heinous practice—a practice disproportionately employed against black southerners. One court official in Huntsville, writing to Jones during the investigation, pointed to the chronic failure of the states to deal with lynching when he stated, "It will be difficult, if not impossible, to secure convictions in the state court." He said that they might "be able to get some of the guilty parties" if the federal Court was able to prosecute them.[63] Judge Shelby's suggestion that the federal government should intervene, it appears, provided the best hope for blacks seeking protection from the lynch mob.

Judge Jones and other federal authorities in Alabama decided to arrest members of the mob and charge them with violating federal laws. The case against the Huntsville mob was presented to the grand jury by U.S. Attorney Thomas Roulhac. Upon learning of the proceedings against the mob, Judge Shelby wrote Jones, urging him, "Write your instructions to the grand jury in such form that they might be reported as authority. In that way, your views would reach the other judges in the circuit, and to some extent mob murder might be checked."[64] These comments demonstrate that Judge Shelby was also a foe of lynching and accepted the idea that the federal government had the right to take steps against mob murder.

On October 11, 1904, Judge Jones delivered a two-hour-long charge to the grand jury in which he argued that the lynchers had violated federal

laws through their actions. In supporting this assertion he looked first to the
Thirteenth Amendment. The framers of the amendment, he argued, feared
that white southerners, who were accustomed to ruling African Americans,
would attempt to oppress and exploit them. Therefore, it was believed that
"unless the right of equality before the law were secured to the race, and its
members were freed in person and property against hostile acts and discrimination," the black race would essentially remain enslaved to the white race.
In order to avoid such a situation and to make the ex-slaves truly free, the
Thirteenth Amendment was created and adopted. By outlawing slavery, the
framers made the African American a freeman. "What constituted a freeman," he said, "was measured in the minds of [the] American people by the
civil rights which were accorded the dominant race." Anyone who did not
possess such rights, consequently, was a slave. In short, by outlawing slavery
the Thirteenth Amendment bestowed upon African Americans the same
civil rights enjoyed by white citizens, thus making them truly free. And by
empowering Congress to enforce this provision, it authorized the federal
government to take steps to ensure that these civil rights were accorded to
African Americans.[65] One of the civil rights enjoyed by whites, as Jones
mentioned, and hence given to blacks, was equality before the law. It was
this right, he asserted, that a mob denied to its victim when it lynched him
because of his race. In attempting to make this point Jones asked, "If the
master race, imbued with a sense of its superiority and the inferiority of the
former slave race, and for that reason not regarding it as entitled to the legal
equality which the law gave, were permitted, when disputes arose between
the races, or when one of the members of the master race were injured by
a member of the former slave race, to take the law into their own hands and
settle such controversies by violence, can anyone doubt that such things
would militate against the freedom, or enjoyment of civil equality, of the
race subjected to such treatment, and sooner or later reduce that race to the
condition of a subject race?"[66] The judge answered his own question by saying that "no candid man can deny" that the lynching of blacks was intended
"to prevent the enjoyment of equality before the law" and, therefore, "falls
within the power of Congress." In short, what Jones was asserting was that
whenever African Americans were treated differently from whites—because
of their race or previous condition of servitude—then that action was in
violation of the Thirteenth Amendment.[67]

　　In addition to providing a very broad interpretation of the Thirteenth
Amendment, Jones also asserted that lynching violated the Due Process
clause of the Fourteenth Amendment. He explained that the amendment
required state governments to afford due process of law and equal protec-

tion of the law to every person. The amendment "thereby creates an immunity or right . . . in favor of every person . . . to have such protection afforded by the State." The purpose of the amendment, therefore, was not simply to instruct the states to act in a certain manner, but rather to provide the people of the country with particular rights—in this case, the right to due process and equal protection. "The immunity of the citizen," he said, "is not merely to prevent the State from putting him to death 'without due process of law,' but to have the State see to it that he is not unlawfully deprived of his life when in its custody upon accusation of crime." It is the actual enjoyment of the right to one's day in court that the framers had in mind, not merely that the states follow particular guidelines. In making this argument he was seeking to discredit the universally accepted notion that the amendment only regulated the actions of states, not individuals. If individuals were capable of preventing the enjoyment of these rights to due process and equal protection, then Jones believed that the federal government possessed the authority to intervene and punish the guilty individuals. In discussing lynching in particular, he asked, "Do not such acts by preventing the protection which would follow from the enforcement of State laws, defeat the great object the amendment intended to secure to all persons; which was not merely that citizens should have a parchment acknowledgment of their rights and that officers should endeavor to do their duty, but that the duty should be so enforced that it would result in the enjoyment of the protection the amendment designed to secure?"[68] The amendment, he argued, obligated the states to take appropriate action to ensure that the rights enumerated in the amendment were enjoyed by all persons in the state, but the fact that the states had the primary responsibility for doing this did not preclude the federal government from intervening when necessary. This design, he asserted, was created in accordance with the prevalent doctrines of state-oriented federalism. The framers gave primacy to the state governments, but they also made it so that the federal government served as a watchdog, making sure that the states fulfilled their duties and that the rights enumerated were truly being accorded to the people. In the case of lynching in the South, it was obvious that the state governments in the region were not diligent in protecting the right of African Americans to due process of the law. In order to rectify this situation, he argued, the federal government possessed the authority to prosecute and punish the members of a lynch mob, particularly in light of state inaction.[69]

After having led the jurors through a long and tedious maze of legal arguments in order to convince them that lynching violated both the Thirteenth and Fourteenth Amendments, the judge ended his charge by

appealing explicitly to their patriotism and sense of justice. He warned the
jurors that the South's political leaders were steering the region in the
wrong direction. By "teaching that giving a negro his right under the law
would result in social equality," they were justifying and encouraging the
repression of African Americans. The jurors and the rest of the South needed
to realize, he said, that the "black man will remain here on the same soil
with us and with our children for countless generations." By mistreating and
oppressing the entire race the South was only creating future problems for
itself. If white southerners refuse to "lift the negro up," he warned, "the
negro . . . will drag us down."[70] Then, as Judge Trieber had done in the
Morris case, Judge Jones, before releasing the jury to reach a verdict, asked
them to remember the words of the founding fathers as expressed in the
Declaration of Independence: "that all men are endowed by the Creator
with certain unalienable rights; and that among these are life, liberty and the
pursuit of happiness."[71]

Local observers immediately recognized the novelty and significance of
Judge Jones's charge. The reporter who covered the court proceedings for
the *Montgomery Advertiser* called Jones's interpretation "unique" and added
that it was received with "a considerable measure of surprise." "Many of the
leading attorneys of Huntsville," the report[er] said, "believe that the
Thirteenth Amendment does not go so far as" Judge Jones contended. One
"prominent" member of the Huntsville bar warned the reporter that the
judge's interpretation would authorize the federal government "to interfere
in small cases as assault and battery between a white man and a negro, where
race prejudice was shown to exist," and in "contracts between colored servants and their employees, provided the negro was not paid the same wages
as a white person."[72]

A few days after Jones delivered his charge to the jury, they returned
indictments against the alleged mob members. The judge reassured the jury
that they had made the right decision by telling them, in contrast to the
view of the Huntsville bar, that they had "trod in no uncertain or doubtful
paths." He asserted, "The court, in advising you as to the range of your
duties, did not lay down any strange or hitherto unknown construction of
the constitution and laws of the United States, or the extent of the jurisdiction of its courts." Indeed, he asserted, "In the charge given you to the effect
that Congress had the power to deal with offenses by men of one race
against men of another race, when the object and intent of the offense was
to deprive the member of that race of civil equality before the law, and
induced by race prejudice, and not be mere ordinary felonious motive, the

court only was stating what has been the settled law of the United States since the great case of *Cruikschank v. United States.*"[73]

Jones sent copies of his charge to numerous people, including political leaders, professors, civic leaders, newspaper editors, and other federal judges. One of the first people to comment on the charge was Judge Trieber of Arkansas. He told the Alabamian that the U.S. Supreme Court would probably reject his interpretation, "although in my opinion it is right." But instead of discussing points of law, legal precedents, and the particulars of his interpretation of the Constitution, the Arkansas judge placed Jones's stance against lynching in the social and political context of the turn-of-the-century South. He told him:

> I see a rift in the clouds when men like yourself, Judge Speer of Georgia, and Judge [John Henry] Rogers[74] of this state, all natives of the South and ex-Confederates, lead in this patriotic movement to awaken the conscience of our people. If every man in the South who believes as we do would only have the moral courage exhibited by you and the others, I sincerely believe that this race question could be solved to the lasting benefit of our country and in conformity with the spirit of this civilized age.[75]

Judge Trieber believed that in order for the South to solve its race problem it was necessary for native southerners to take the lead in the call for justice for African Americans. He evidently believed that some of his colleagues on the federal bench constituted the core of such a movement.

Judge Trieber asserted that there were numerous white southerners who opposed racial oppression, but that they were too scared to speak their mind. In order "to influence a patriotic adjustment of this negro question," he said, all that is necessary is "to awaken their conscience and supply them with the moral courage necessary to give expression of their views on the subject." The Alabama judge, he said, "blazed the way for such an awakening." The reasoning in the charge, he said, "was not only convincing, but . . . is so calm and unprejudiced that every thinking man will appreciate it." This approach, he added, was more effective than that of Judge Emory Speer, who too often used vigorous language. "Although justified by the facts," Judge Speer's opinions were "too passionate" and consequently were often not well received by the public. In contrast, Jones's strategy, he concluded, would prove to be more beneficial; and, therefore, the day was not far off "when the people will realize what a debt of gratitude they owe" Jones for his efforts. He asked Jones to forgive him for expressing his views on the race problem so fully when all that had been requested was a legal analysis. His more expansive discussion rested, he said, on his perception that "judges cannot give publicity to our views on this subject, and it relieves me somewhat to be able to express them in confidence to a brother judge."[76]

Judge Eli Shelby Hammond of the Western District of Tennessee also expressed his appreciation to Jones for his charge to the Huntsville grand jury. Judge Hammond, without explicitly giving his opinion on the legal merits of the charge, did assert that Jones's interpretation, if accepted and acted upon, "will probably do more to restrain the crime [of lynching] than any remedy which has been suggested."[77] Judge Edmund Waddill Jr. of the Eastern District of Virginia likewise wrote to Jones and said, "The crime of lynching is one too horrible to think of, with its demoralizing effect upon the community and, unless the same can be in some manner stopped, will soon result in the substitution of force for law."[78] Inspired by Jones's actions, Judge Waddill said that he was considering taking action against the members of a mob that had recently lynched an African American in his district. He asked the Alabama judge to provide him with any information that would assist him in such a prosecution, particularly in justifying his court's involvement.[79]

Miriam Leakey, an assistant U.S. attorney for the Southern District of Georgia (Judge Speer's district) wrote Jones asking for more information in hopes of prosecuting the members of a lynch mob in his district. He said that the charge to the jury "opened up a mine of thought on the Thirteenth Amendment," and, consequently, "the idea has grown upon me that this act of the parties engaged in the mob was murder and in violation of the . . . Constitution."[80] Unfortunately, Leakey's plans to prosecute the Statesboro mob were squelched by the Justice Department, which forbade him from proceeding in the matter.[81]

In addition to federal officials, hundreds of ordinary citizens—white southerners among them—wrote to Jones, thanking him for his charge to the jury. A lawyer in Detroit, Michigan, wrote to say that he was impressed with the charge and that it "has been widely commented on all over the United States."[82] Another writer who identified himself only as "an ardent admirer (white)" said that after "having read your most able and manly charge . . . I can but exclaim in Kipling's words: 'Once in a time there is a man.'"[83] J. C. Styles of Americus, Georgia, commented on Jones's bravery in delivering such a charge, saying, "It requires courage and deep conviction for a man of your standing and position to speak out on such a matter." He reassured him that "when impartial history shall have a hearing, posterity, without regards to race or color, shall give you and your name the great and illustrious laurels which are justly due."[84] The African American president of the Alabama Penny Savings and Loan Company told Jones that his views "give encouragement to thinking, struggling, earnest men of my race," and "they go a long way toward the betterment of conditions."[85] Another African American thanked him profusely in an eight-page letter which ended with the author saying, "I know the heart of all good colored citizens beat with a memory of, and commends with silent applause, the action of your late court."[86] Booker T. Washington, in a letter to Jones, declared that "the whole country is your debtor . . . for your very able, wise, and courageous charge."[87] The charge, indeed, was courageous and necessary, according to H. J. Redd of Riverview, Alabama, because "numbers of men think no more of killing a negro than they would of killing a rattlesnake."[88] A. P. Agee, an Alabama lawyer, agreed that the court's actions were necessary, alleging that the state courts were virtually incapable of punishing criminals since there was widespread sympathy for the offense committed. "This impotency," he said, "is striking when it comes to suppressing mob law." He said that he regretted the intervention of a federal court, but reasoned that "law abiding and liberty loving citizens" have no choice but "to turn for protection to a Court that has not only the desire but the power to suppress this form of anarchy."[89]

U.S. Senator Augustus O. Bacon of Georgia disagreed with the idea that federal intervention was either necessary or desirable. If Jones's interpretation of the Constitution was accepted, he said, it would mean that "all offenses against the person, property or rights of negroes by two or more persons," in which the motivating factor was race, "would also be within the jurisdiction of the Federal Courts." Such a situation, the senator said, "would speedily make it impossible for the two races to live together in peace. . . . To vest the Federal Courts with jurisdiction practically in all cases affecting any injuries to negroes, or their rights or privileges, when under similar circumstances in troubles between whites the Federal Courts would have no such jurisdiction, would inevitably create disorders and scenes of violence of ten-fold more frequency than any which exists now."[90] Judge T. S. Maxey of the Western District of Texas also raised doubts about the jurisdiction of a federal court in the matter of lynching and told Jones, "Candor compels me to say that I am not fully satisfied as to the correctness of your views."[91]

Unfortunately, not everyone who disagreed with Jones's position was as cordial as Senator Bacon and Judge Maxey. Jones complained to President Theodore Roosevelt, "Quite a reaction has set in from the . . . adverse sentiment that politicians had created against the charge of the court.'"[92] He later told the president that the five wounds he received as a Confederate soldier had "not shielded [him] from some very mean and base insinuations, upon the part of the element which despises 'justice without respect of person.'"[93] That Jones had come under attack is evidenced by the encouragement he received from the state tax commissioner, who told him, "Dont [sic] be worried by the miserable skunks now attacking you." In time, he said, the "people will recognize and acknowledge that you and *you alone* broke up lynching in Alabama."[94]

Lynching in Alabama, of course, had not come to an end; and, in actuality, the process of punishing the Huntsville mob had just begun. The first hurdle that Judge Jones faced after the indictments had been handed down was a writ of habeas corpus filed by Thomas Riggins, one of the indicted members of the Huntsville mob. This petition questioned the constitutionality of the statutes under which the mob had been indicted. Jones's ruling on the petition for habeas corpus is known as *Ex parte Riggins.* In that opinion, he held that members of a lynch mob violate federal laws.[95]

Jones began his ruling on the petition for habeas corpus by arguing that the Thirteenth Amendment did not merely end slavery. Rather it was designed to ensure that the emancipated race would forever possess the same civil rights as white citizens of the United States. Whenever hostile white men, he said, sought to prevent an African American from the enjoyment of his civil equality, and did so on the basis of his race, then those whites were guilty of violating both the spirit and the letter of the Thirteenth Amendment. Jones therefore believed, as Judge Trieber asserted in *U.S. v. Morris,* that when an African American was harmed or injured *because of his race or color,* such action constituted one of the forms of repression that the authors of the Reconstruction amendments in general sought to abolish. Lynching, Jones believed, fit into this category. "Whatever may be said of any other murder of a negro by white men," Jones asserted, "it is undeniable, when a negro is taken by white men from the custody of the state authorities, when he is being held for trial on accusation of a crime against state laws, and put to death to prevent his having such trial, because of race hostility, that the manifest result, as well as intent, of such act, is to deprive him, because of his race, of the enjoyment of a civil right accorded by law to white freemen."[96] Therefore, like Judge Trieber, Jones believed that the federal government possessed a broad basis of authority for protecting African Americans. In particular, it had the power to intervene—as Senator Bacon feared—whenever a crime was committed against an African American *because* of his race, color, or previous condition of servitude.

Judge Jones, in establishing a specific basis for such federal power, argued that lynching violated the Fourteenth Amendment. He admitted that under the Equal Protection clause of the amendment, only state officials, through legislation, could breach the amendment. But, he contended, members of a lynch mob, through their actions, violate the Due Process clause. "From the very nature of the right [of due process], whenever the administration of due process involves the administration of judicial procedure," Jones said, "the state must not only pass fair laws, but through its officers must do, or cause to be done, certain physical and mental operations in individual cases, which operate directly upon a particular individual, the benefits of which he cannot enjoy unless the officers of the state are permitted to perform them or cause them to be performed, according to the established course of judicial procedure, when he is present and asserting his rights." "Undoubtedly, then," Jones concluded, "private persons may defeat enjoyment, in the constitutional sense, of the right, privilege, or immunity of the citizen to have the state afford him due process of law in many cases."[97] The duty of providing due process of law to citizens originally rested with the state, he said, but after the ratification of the Fourteenth Amendment by the states the performance of this duty became a matter of "national concern, and if need be, of national supervision." Federal involvement, he cautiously insisted, was limited to dealing with the evil of lynching and could not interfere with the state laws or the authority of its officers in executing them.[98]

He acknowledged that many legal experts considered it impossible for anyone but state officials to violate the Due Process clause. In rebutting this assertion, he argued that the members of a lynch mob, through their murderous actions, deprived their victims of their constitutional right to their day in court. Jones, in elaborating on this point, said, "The argument that Congress has no such power because the amendment is directed against denial of due process by the state, and that there is no denial by the state when neither its laws nor its officers are at fault, ignores the pregnant fact that the amendment creates a right, privilege, or immunity of a citizen of the United States to have enjoyment of the benefit of due process at the hands of the state." Likewise, it "ignores the further equally important fact that such lawless violence of private individuals, by preventing the state's giving the benefit of due process of law when it is endeavoring to do so, directly and inevitably defeats the enjoyment of his right or privilege, created by the Constitution of the United States, to have enjoyment of the benefit of due process at the hands of the state, and thus fatally impairs the enjoyment of the right, privilege or immunity."[99] The federal government, Jones concluded, had not only the right, but an obligation to prosecute individuals such as

Riggins who willingly and purposefully murdered African Americans so as to prevent their enjoyment of due process. Such action, in a broader sense, was simply an act of racism that constituted an important part of the general effort of some southern whites to repress blacks. After reaching this conclusion, Jones then declared that the writ of habeas corpus was denied and that Riggins would have to stand trial for violating federal laws through the lynching of Maples.

Before such a trial could begin, though, Riggins appealed the habeas corpus decision to the U.S. Supreme Court. The high court heard the Riggins case during the October 1905 term, the same session in which it considered the important Hodges case that came out Judge Trieber's court in Arkansas. The Court threw out the Riggins appeal on a technicality, thereby avoiding the constitutional issue that Judge Jones had raised through his novel interpretation of the Fourteenth Amendment.[100] But in the *Hodges* decision, the Court put forth a rather strict interpretation of both the Fourteenth and Fifteenth Amendments even though Judge Trieber's decision was based solely on the Thirteenth Amendment. In light of this, one of the members of the Huntsville mob, Robert Powell, applied to have the indictments quashed on the basis of the above-mentioned interpretation put forth by the Court in *Hodges*.

After hearing Powell's case in March of 1907, Judge Jones had to decide whether or not he would follow the Court's interpretation of the Fourteenth Amendment as expressed in *Hodges*. In a sense, he did both. On one hand, he acknowledged the Court's narrow reading of the amendment and ruled that the federal government did not possess the authority to prosecute private individuals who prevented another person from enjoying his or her right to due process of the law. But on the other hand, he devoted the entirety of the *Powell* opinion—with the exception of the last paragraph— to explicating a strong, impassioned argument *in support of* the idea that the members of a lynch mob did, indeed, violate the Fourteenth Amendment.

Jones began his unusual opinion in the case of *United States v. Powell* by maintaining that the Fourteenth Amendment should be interpreted broadly and on the basis of the spirit in which it was written. The Supreme Court, he alleged, focused too much on the negative, prohibitory language of the amendment ("No State shall deny . . ."; "No State shall deprive . . ."). In doing so, the Court concerned itself merely with state legislation dealing with equal protection of the law and due process of the law. In seeing only the prohibitions, he said, the Court missed the real purpose and meaning of the amendment. "In form, the prohibitions of the amendment," Jones argued, "were leveled at the means by which it was supposed those rights would most often be defeated, but it was the evil to be averted, and the rights thereby to be enjoyed, and not the particular form of the invasion, which were uppermost in the minds of the framers of the amendment. The true "intent and spirit" of the amendment, according to Jones, was that "the enjoyment of the rights, which the amendment declares shall not be denied by the state, shall be worked out for those to whom the right was secured by full performance of the duties the amendment put upon the state."[101] In other words, the framers of the amendment wished for all persons in America to possess the right to both the equal protection and due process of the law. Believing that the state governments were in the best position to deprive individuals of these rights, the framers directed the prohibitions against them. The Court, therefore, when attempting to determine the scope of the amendment, should not be distracted by a strict adherence to the prohibitions, but rather should be guided by the overall purpose of the amendment: the right to due process and equal protection for all people.

As for the Due Process clause in particular, the Court, he said, was likewise obligated to abide by its spirit and general intent. The strict interpretation of the clause employed by the Court during the previous decades simply held that a state had properly provided due process if it had enacted appropriate laws and had employed officials to dispense justice. This was true, as far as the Court was concerned, even if a person, such as Horace Maples, in reality, was not allowed to exercise, to the fullest extent, his due process rights. To Judge Jones, this signified nothing less than a willingness on the part of the Court to "surrender abjectly to the witchery of mere grammatical expression, and [to] utterly desert the spirit of the clause." "The dominant end and purpose" of the clause, he said, was "that the citizen shall have *actual, physical enjoyment* of the benefits of the right [of due process], as distinguished from fictitious enjoyment, in theory of law, of a right in the form of an enchanting declaration upon parchment."[102] The framers of the amendment did not mandate simply that the states have a system of dispensing justice. This, of course, was critical; but the overarching aim of the framers was to ensure that every person accused of a crime would actually have his or her day in court.

The states had a "positive duty" to provide all persons charged with a crime the full enjoyment of the established course of judicial procedure. One important aspect of this procedure, he said, included the obligation of the state to "safely keep and protect him [the alleged criminal] in prison until it can give him the opportunity, as well as the right, to appear before its tribunal" and address the charges brought against him.[103] If state authorities failed to follow the set procedure, then they, of course, were liable for denying the individual of his or her due process rights. Likewise, if private individuals somehow prevented the accused from enjoying access to every step of the judicial process, then they too were in violation of the Fourteenth Amendment. The purpose of the amendment, and particularly of its Due Process clause, was not simply to force states to abide by the accepted standards of judicial procedure until the process was interrupted by some person or persons. Rather, he said, "it is full performance which is exacted."[104] The amendment was designed to provide the *full* range of the judicial process to all alleged criminals and to ensure that the process would be fulfilled for every alleged criminal by bringing the power of the federal government to bear against anyone, including private individuals, who sought to prevent such an occurrence. "It is undeniable," Jones asserted, "that private individuals, in some phase of the duty, can prevent enjoyment, in the constitutional sense, of due process of law at the hands of the state." Those who created the amendment, he said, were cognizant of this fact. "The framers of the amendment," Jones asserted, "were not ignorant that the practice of mobs to take prisoners accused of crime from the custody of the state, and murder them, to prevent the state's administering its justice, was one great evil which prevented citizens or persons from having, at the hands of the state, the enjoyment of the benefit of the administration of the state's established course of judicial procedure, *which it was the purpose of the amendment the prisoner should enjoy,* and from the enjoyment of which he is forever cut off, when the mob works its will upon him."[105] In sum, Jones believed that the framers fully expected private persons to be prosecuted whenever they denied someone of his due process rights.

Jones believed that it was undeniable that Congress had the authority to punish individuals. To support his position he pointed to a number of Supreme Court decisions, including *Ex parte Yarbrough,* which Emory Speer had argued as a U.S. attorney. In that decision the Supreme Court upheld the right of the federal government to punish individuals who deprived others of a constitutional right, which, in this case, was the right to vote in a federal election. As the right to due process was also a constitutional right, he argued, the federal government had the authority to prosecute those who interfered with it. But this was not accepted doctrine, he said. In particular, the U.S. Supreme Court refused to acknowledge that the government possessed such power. In a biting question seemingly directly at the Supreme Court and its view in this matter, Jones asked, "What right have we . . . to impute to the framers of the amendment, when it gave Congress the power 'to enforce' the command, any intention to withdraw from the power, by the very same words which conferred it, all strength to protect the means by which alone the right can be enjoyed, against attacks of lawless private persons upon the state's efforts to do things the Constitution commands it to do, simply because the state has vainly attempted to obey the constitutional command?"[106]

After establishing—in his mind at least—that Congress possessed the authority to punish individuals, he addressed the popular idea that congressional authority of this sort infringed upon the rights of the state. In doing so, Jones—a proud Confederate veteran—took the position that the Civil War had altered the nature of both the Constitution and the American federal system. He acknowledged that the idea of the federal government being able to punish lynchers constituted "a far-reaching departure from the traditions and time-honored maxims of our government."[107] With emancipation and the North's victory, it became obvious that "race and sectional feeling, state action, and private lawlessness . . . might hamper or prevent the enjoyment of these rights ['to life, liberty, or property'] and it was not deemed wise to leave their safeguarding wholly to the states, as in the past, though they were still primarily to depend upon the execution of their laws." Jones said, "Congress was therefore given power to see that the states accomplished their task."[108] The framers of the Reconstruction-era amendments and the people who adopted them "were not building upon the old system" of states' rights, he asserted, "but laying on new foundations a different system for the enjoyment" of fundamental human rights. Although the states essentially retained all of their power and authority, the new amendments had given the federal government the responsibility to ensure that the country benefited from a uniform, constantly enforced standard of basic human rights. The Fourteenth Amendment played a crucial role in bringing about this situation. The amendment's "dominant idea," he argued, is that the United States has a rightful concern in the actual enjoyment by citizens of a state, who are also citizens of the United States, of due process within the state, and ought therefore to have a part in seeing that the administration of due process in state tribunals accomplishes the enjoyment of those rights which it was the purpose of the Fourteenth Amendment to afford.[109] The amendment, he contended, clearly "repudiat[ed] the old thought and practice." It "conferred a new power for a benevolent purpose." Therefore, he concluded, "We ought not to shrivel the power by treating it as a mere penal enactment against faithless state officers."[110]

As for those who raised the cry that the Thirteenth, Fourteenth, and Fifteenth Amendments had destroyed the federal system, Jones pointed out that things had essentially remained the same. The amendments, he said, put "no new duty upon the state or its citizens, and [did] not change, in any way, the relations of the state to the federal government." "The authority of the state to give the law which regulates and controls its own domestic and political affairs" had remained undisturbed.[111] Those who opposed his view of the amendments were merely deceiving themselves by believing that there was anything to fear in such an interpretation. "The only moral or legal consequences which can result" from the federal government punishing individuals who deny others their due process "is that the power of the United States is arrayed behind the power of the state to accomplish obedience to its own laws." In short, the net result of his interpretation, he said, would be to "double the guard about the state's altars of justice which enforce the duties which man owes to man around the fireside and home."[112]

After completing his argument in support of a broad view of the Reconstruction-era amendments, he shifted his attention to the ruling he was about to make in the case. First, he took a shot at the Supreme Court by complaining "of its uniform habit not to pass upon constitutional questions when a ruling upon them can fairly be avoided." He was referring to the case of *Ex parte Riggins,* which the Court dismissed on a technicality. In light of this dismissal, he had little to base his decision on except the remarks about the Fourteenth Amendment made by the Court in the *Hodges* decision. In that case, the Court stated that the amendment did not apply to private individuals, but reached state officials only. Jones said, "It would be hazardous for this court, in view of the circumstances, to hold that these remarks were made without consideration of their effect upon other cases of the kind. If they were not inadvertently made, and the court intended to bind itself on this point, it is the duty of this court to follow unhesitatingly. While there may be doubt as to what it intended, the Supreme Court is the only court which can properly solve that doubt."[113] Judge Jones then reluctantly concluded that he "must therefore take the *Hodges* case as a binding authority" even though it eviscerated the Due Process clause. Although submitting to the Supreme Court, Jones made sure to point out in his last sentence that the Court's view of the amendment meant "that no immunity whatever is secured under the Constitution or laws, in a case like this, against the lawlessness of private individuals *which frustrates the state's efforts to perform its constitutional duty, although thereby all enjoyment of the benefits of due process be prevented.*"[114]

So, after devoting sixteen pages to explaining why he believed that the federal government possessed the authority to prosecute lynchers, Judge Jones, in the last paragraph of his ruling, announced that he must release an alleged member of a lynch mob because his view conflicted with that of the Supreme Court. He explained that if he had mistakenly misapplied the Court's statements to the case at hand, then the Court was in a position to rectify the situation. But in 1909, after reviewing Jones's decision in *United States v. Powell,* the Supreme Court upheld the decision without comment.[115]

With its decision in the *Hodges* case then, the Supreme Court rejected outright the arguments of Thomas Goode Jones and Jacob Trieber that the federal government had the right, indeed the obligation, to punish individuals who, respectively, lynched African Americans or used violence to intimidate them. In doing so, the Court helped to facilitate the southern counterrevolution that left southern blacks at the mercy of the leaders of the "Solid South," who saw to it that African Americans were relegated to a position of second-class citizenship. As for Judge Jones, the *Bailey* case constituted his last legal encounter with the civil rights of African Americans. He died three years later.

CHAPTER 5

Conclusion

T HE PREVIOUS CHAPTERS demonstrate that Judges Jacob Trieber,
Emory Speer, and Thomas G. Jones embraced a broad interpretation of
the Reconstruction-era amendments when such a view was being rejected
by the U.S. Supreme Court. A complex admixture of cultural, political, legal,
and personal ideas and ideals all coalesced to shape their more dissident—
and unpopular—judicial perspective. Fundamentally, Trieber, Speer, and
Jones acted in accordance with the prevailing legal philosophy of the day,
classical legal thought (or legal formalism). They struggled to ground their
decisions on precedent-based interpretations of legal sources, namely, the
Constitution and relevant statutes.[1] An examination of their opinions reveals
a general adherence to this concept. These judges reached the conclusions
that they did largely through their deferential adherence to proclamations
made by justices of the Supreme Court. This deference to the high court
was not without irony, for although the justices made statements that occasionally appeared to sanction a broad interpretation of the Reconstruction
amendments, the Court essentially emasculated these same amendments
during the Gilded Age.

It is significant and, again, probably ironic that, in his opinion in *U.S. v.
Morris*, Judge Trieber utilized ten separate and in some cases quite lengthy
quotes from previous Supreme Court rulings to make the case that the
Thirteenth Amendment empowered Congress to protect blacks from racial
discrimination.[2] Likewise, Judge Speer quoted Justices Wood, Bradley, and
Miller in his *U.S. v. McClellan* opinion on peonage. In his *Riggins* decision,
Judge Jones quoted from several Supreme Court decisions in an effort to
show that the Thirteenth and Fourteenth Amendments obligated the federal government to prosecute individuals who sought to deny African
Americans their constitutional rights:

In the *Civil Rights Cases,* 109 U.S. 20, the Supreme Court said that the thirteenth amendment "is undoubtedly self-executing, and by its own unaided force and effect abolished slavery and established universal freedom." It was further said that "it authorized legislation for the protection of the freedom it intended to secure, which might be direct and primary in its nature, operating upon the acts of individuals, whether sanctioned by legislation or not." In *Ex parte Virginia,* 100 U.S. 339, speaking of the thirteenth amendment, as well as of the fourteenth and fifteenth amendments, the court said: "One great purpose of these amendments was to raise the colored race from that condition of inferiority and servitude, in which most of them had previously stood, into perfect equality of civil rights with all other persons within the jurisdiction of the state." It is further said of the thirteenth amendment, as well as the others, in the *Slaughterhouse Cases,* 16 Wall. 36: "One pervading purpose found in them all, and lying at the foundation of each, and without which none of them would have been even suggested, was the freedom of the slave race, and the security and firm establishment of that freedom, and protection of the rights of the newly made freeman and citizen from the oppression of those who had previously exercised unlimited dominion over them."[3]

Despite using the justices' own words against them, the U.S. Supreme Court nevertheless rejected Jones's arguments.

In addition to citing the pronouncements of Supreme Court justices, the southern judges also went to great lengths to demonstrate that their assertions were in harmony with the original intent of the framers of the Reconstruction-era amendments. In seeking to determine the extent and meaning of the Reconstruction-era amendments to the Constitution, they sometimes quoted from the congressional debates over those amendments. Jones's charge to jury in the Riggins lynching case, for instance, consisted primarily of an explanation of the intentions of those who wrote the Thirteenth Amendment. Speer and Trieber, likewise, expressed the importance of determining and following the original intentions of the framers of the Reconstruction-era amendments.[4] They referred to the original intent of the framers in their major decisions regarding race relations.[5]

It is not entirely surprising that their investigations into the intent of the framers led them to a broad reading of the amendments. Even though many scholars dispute whether or not the original intent of the Constitution or any of its amendments can truly be ascertained, it is generally accepted that the Congress that wrote and passed the Reconstruction-era amendments intended and expected them to be interpreted more broadly than the Supreme Court did during the first decades of the twentieth century.[6] In fact, the justices of the Supreme Court admitted as much in the *Jones v. Alfred H. Mayer Co.* decision, in which they cited the work of Jacobus TenBroek, who argued in his book, *Equal under Law,* that the framers of the Thirteenth Amendment clearly intended for it to outlaw slavery *and* its incidents and badges.[7] Several recent studies have expanded upon TenBroek's work and likewise argue that, relatively speaking, the original intention of the amendments can be discerned and that Trieber, Speer, and Jones were essentially correct in their assertions regarding the authority and responsibility that they gave to Congress to protect African American civil rights.[8]

Even though it would have been entirely possible for Trieber, Jones, and Speer to interpret the amendments as they did on the basis of Supreme Court precedents and their reading of the historical record, it appears that these things alone did not form the basis of their judicial decisions. In their written opinions and their personal correspondence, the judges indicate that their rulings were influenced, to some degree, by their personal values and other cultural and political factors. How else can one explain Judge Trieber's statement to Jones that he saw "a rift in the clouds" of southern racism in the actions of Jones and others? He was evaluating Jones's actions not on the basis of how closely they adhered to legal precedent or original intent, but on how they affected contemporary society.

Legal realists insist that one cannot evaluate or understand judicial interpretation without considering the judge's social context, values, and beliefs. It appears that this holds true for Trieber, Speer, and Jones. Examining the decisions of these judges reveals opinions replete with moral and political arguments—as well as legal reasoning and constitutional interpretation. Judge Speer, for instance, began his opinion in *Jamison v. Wimbish* not with a constitutional justification for federal intervention in a state chain-gang case, but rather by denouncing the system as "the most melancholy and distressing spectacle which afflicts the patriot and humanitarian."[9] Likewise, in a case concerning the cruel and unusual punishment of a state prisoner, Judge Speer began his opinion by expressing his astonishment that such "a repugnant act" could take place "in this day of Christian civilization."[10] Through such utterances, Speer, Trieber, and Jones seem to indicate that they did not limit themselves to merely "finding the law" when formulating their opinions, but actually gave voice to some of their most closely held ideals of civilized decency. And, clearly, they hoped their decisions would encourage what they perceived as Christian or civilized conduct in the larger southern society.

Consequently, in order to better determine why these judges acted as they did, it is necessary to look beyond their legal citations and arguments. An examination of their public utterances and personal correspondence reveals that all three of the judges were greatly influenced by the Civil War and its aftermath, especially the white southern response to Reconstruction.[11] It is apparent from their public utterances and personal correspondence that, unlike many other white southerners, Trieber, Speer, and Jones ultimately accepted the results of the Civil War; and they believed it unwise and undesirable to try to reestablish the social conditions that existed in the region before the war. As a result of this they came to believe that slavery had hindered the development of the South and that the inhabitants of the region should look to the future and to the victors in the war for guidance in creating a modern, diversified, industrialized "New South."

Trieber, Speer, and Jones were patriotic southerners who were devoted to their region. Speer and Jones, in fact, had shed blood for the South fighting as young men for the Confederacy during the Civil War. But they, along with Trieber, did not respond to defeat and the problems caused by the war with resentment toward the North or hostility toward the freedmen. Rather, they treated defeat as a lesson learned and sought to get southerners to look to the future rather than longing for the past. All three accepted emancipation and the fact that African Americans had been made citizens of the United States. They readily admitted that the conditions were far from ideal. But they viewed the situation as being irreversible. And rather than repeating the mistake of slavery—the repression of one race by another—they called for the white South to deal with African Americans fairly. The progress and development of the South, they believed, was dependent upon the advancement of its people—including African Americans. They concluded, therefore, that it would be better for the South and the country if whites helped blacks instead of exploiting and repressing them. Jones expressed as much in a statement he made at the 1901 Alabama constitutional convention. In seeking to defeat an attack on African American education in the guise of basing educational expenditures on the taxes each race paid, he said:

> I remember seeing it related somewhere of Robert E. Lee, when he was asked why he took so much interest in a worthless soldier, and why he seemed to have solicitude for his welfare, that that grand old man answered, "Because he is under me." The negro race is under us. He is in our power. We are his custodians . . . [and] we should extend

to him, as far as possible, all the civil rights that will fit him to be a decent and self-respecting, law-abiding and intelligent citizen of this State. We are not dealing merely with conditions which are to affect our children, and our children's children. This race is here. It cannot be transplanted. It cannot be deported. He is part of our economic system. We come in contact with him everywhere. If we do not lift them up, they will drag us down. . . . You cannot in a constitutional government like ours, where these people [African Americans] are citizens and entitled to equal civil rights, use the taxing power, the police power, or any other power of government, so as to diffuse the blessings or ills of government according to races. You cannot make distinctions of that sort. To attempt to do so, is not only wrong in itself, but in violation of the Supreme law, and will only entail complication and trouble in the administration of our school laws.[12]

It is apparent from this statement that Jones's main concern was the advancement of the South. His call for treating African Americans fairly and uplifting them was merely a by-product of this concern. If the ex-slaves were not lifted up, he argued, then they would drag the South down. This is what he hoped to avoid and explains why he embraced such a paternalistic attitude toward African Americans.

Speer and Trieber were likewise motivated by the same spirit. For instance, U.S. Attorney Speer, while prosecuting the Yarbrough whitecappers, called upon the federal government to punish individuals who attacked and intimidated blacks because such violence stunted the South's progress, economic and otherwise, and resulted in increasing social disorder.[13] He, like Jones, realized that African Americans were a permanent part of southern society and that the advancement of the South was in part based upon their progress. He urged his fellow white southerners to acknowledge this basic but frequently overlooked fact. "The colored man is here," he explained, "and he will remain here." Therefore, white southerners should "be magnanimous and just to the colored people." "There is a peculiar obligation upon our southern white people," he asserted, "to do all we can for the betterment of this race, which is among us, which was formerly servile, and yet which forms so important a part of our economy. Most of them are ignorant; many of them are degraded, but it is the Christian duty of every white man in the south to do all he can to give the negro a fair chance." Speer concluded, "We must proceed under the Providence of God to give the negro justice and enforce obedience to the law by him, and let the slow process of time work out the solution of the problem for us. This is the condition which confronts us."[14]

Judge Trieber likewise believed that the South would not advance until it began to provide equal justice for its African American inhabitants. Moreover, as a devoted Republican, his concern embraced a new political vision, which he defined as the development of a true two-party system in the region. The Democrats dominated the region so thoroughly that it became known as the "Solid South." Trieber, who desperately wished to change this situation, realized that the Democrats had established their dominance, in part, by depriving African Americans (who were generally pro-Republican) of their political rights. He believed that without the state election laws which disfranchised black voters, the Republican Party would be victorious in Arkansas.[15] He told the editor of the *St. Louis Globe-Democrat* that "if a fair election could be had throughout the State, we have no doubt but [t]hat Col. H. L. Remmel [the Republican candidate for governor in 1900] could carry the State by about 15,000 majority, but we have no right to expect that, as our election laws make it impossible to have a fair election."[16] Although the repeal of the discriminatory election laws would greatly increase the chances of a Republican election victory in the state, Trieber realized that the racist rhetoric of the Democrats would still prevent most Arkansas whites from voting Republican. He frequently complained to Powell Clayton, the leader of the Arkansas Republican Party, that the Democrats were poisoning the political climate in the state by never ceasing to engage in race-baiting.[17] The worst practitioners of this art, he said, were the faction known as "the swamp Democrat[s], whose sole platform is 'D— the Nigger.'" "I am sorry we have so much of the latter in Arkansas," he said, "but I honestly believe, it is the most popular platform for a Democrat, and carries more of them into office, than any other, silver [the unlimited coinage of silver] not excepted."[18] He added, "Too many [whites] are prone to vote the Democratic ticket regardless of who were its nominees because of that party's anti-black policies."[19] It appears, therefore, that Trieber opposed the racism of the white South in large measure because of its negative consequences for the Republican Party. As the South grew more racist in its attitude and political discourse, the Republican Party, the party of Lincoln, fell deeper into political oblivion while the Democratic Party, the party of white supremacy, further consolidated its already overwhelming power.

It is not surprising then that Trieber believed that the solution to the race problem was to treat African Americans fairly. In discussing this issue at length with President Theodore Roosevelt, he briefly summarized his answer to the South's woes: "Justice, common justice on the one hand, and a little patience on the other, will solve the [race] problem, not immediately, but in the course of time."[20] He wished for white southerners to discuss the problems of the region rationally, without scapegoating African Americans or appealing to the basest passions of the masses. In order to create a society in the South where blacks and whites could live with one another peacefully and civilly, the inhabitants of the region would have to be patient and sensible. It would take a long time, he believed, for both races to adapt to the changed conditions brought about by the Civil War. In short, he said that those who sought to solve the South's race problem needed to ignore proposed short-term answers and view the matter from a long-term perspective. In a letter written while he was serving on the bench, Trieber asserted that "the prejudice which is still to be found among many people is not easily overcome, and in my opinion, instead of attempting to overcome it by force or abuse, it is the better part of wisdom to act along conservative lines and remove the prejudice by acts of wisdom. Of course, it takes a longer time to accomplish a great deal along that line; at the same time, we are more sure of success." He concluded by saying, "Free discussion without bitterness of feeling, appealing to the justice of the people instead of trying to arouse their prejudices and passions, are bound to succeed in the end, and my efforts shall always be along that line."[21]

Jones and Speer also evidenced a long-term perspective when considering the racial tensions and problems that plagued the South around the turn of the century. Each seemed to believe that peaceful co-existence would not be realized during their lifetime, but that they owed it to their descendants to set the region on such a course for the future. This is especially evident in statements made by Jones, who appeared to be concerned with how the policies of his day would affect future generations. As for the disfranchisement of African Americans, he argued that "the withdrawal from freemen, who have once exercised the right of suffrage, of all political power, in a popular government, which shapes their destinies and makes their laws, is sure to create a servile class." "If the number is large," he said, "the change nurses a cancer on the life of the State. Their resentments and their constant struggle to regain lost rights, which are sure to be aided by some who have political power, will inevitably breed continued and ever increasing discontent and agitation, the magnitude of which, in the end, will bring greater evils to the State than any which the disfranchisement was intended to cure."[22] From today's perspective, his statement appears prophetic. Southern Democrats did disfranchise African Americans, and, as he predicted, over the next half-century blacks and their white allies fought strenuously to regain what had been stolen from them—and the struggle did bring in its wake much agitation and discontent. In order to avoid such friction between the races Jones had called upon his contemporaries to treat African Americans fairly. The clearest expression of this sentiment came during a debate in the 1901 Alabama constitutional convention in which he said:

> I hope for better things in the time to come in the relation between these two races. . . . Let us make him feel that while we intend to rule this land, that at the same time we intend to be just to him, to be his friend, and that he ought to rely on us. Let us take hold of him in his schools and elsewhere, and teach him what he ought to learn, that while he can not rule us, that his interests, his prosperity, and his happiness are things for which we care. Let us make him feel that we are too great to legislate on the lines of race hatred, or unworthy race passions. When he is convinced of this, a condition of things will come about which will make a contented race which will be glad to be with us. But let him once be convinced that the white man hates him and intends as far as possible to oppress him, and let the idea glow with him for generations that the power of the white man is to be exerted not merely to govern the land but to cast the negro down as far as possible, and bar him of opportunity to improve, and deny him rights as a human being, and his condition will grow worse and worse. Where he can, he will leave. Such a policy on our part will bequeath a legacy to our children of perpetual discord, race hatred, and it may be, here and there, race conflict. Why not hope and plan for better things?[23]

This classic statement of paternalism reveals part of the motivation for the judges' actions regarding African American civil rights.[24] Trieber, Speer, and Jones wished for a peaceful, stable, and orderly South that was controlled by intelligent, conservative whites. Such conditions were necessary if the region was ever going to develop economically and attract northern and foreign capital. They greatly desired for the South to develop a diverse, industrialized economy.[25] Trieber's biographer, for instance, called him "an unabashed supporter of economic development in Arkansas" who thought "that Arkansas should encourage railroads and manufacturers to come to the state through tax breaks and promises of profitability.[26] Likewise, Speer's biographer also emphasized Speer's concern for the South's economy and said that he "favored a high protective tariff" to "help Southern industry to develop."[27] Historian Paul Gaston has studied those white southerners who embraced this philosophy and called them "New South advocates." Trieber,

Speer, and Jones, although not mentioned by Gaston, are worthy of the label.[28]

With the emergence in the 1890s of a more radical, violent form of racism in the South, the judges began to believe that the South was moving away from the New South blueprint. Instead of directing the South toward a peaceful and prosperous future, the leaders of this movement, they feared, were pushing the region backwards. These demagogues, who were willing to sacrifice the future of the South for their own political careers, had won the support of the people by scapegoating the African Americans. Trieber complained of this in a letter to Jones, saying, "I do not know what conditions exist in your state, but in our state the rabble seems to have obtained absolute control of the politics of the state, and what is worse than anything else is the fact that their supremacy has been obtained solely by appealing to the prejudices existing in the mind of many against the negro."[29] Jones evidently agreed with Trieber. In a 1903 letter to Theodore Roosevelt, in which he defended the president from accusations that his racial policy had increased tensions, he recalled the racial climate in the South during the 1890s and asserted that white southern leaders in that decade "were proclaiming the statesmanship of 'I hate the nigger,' and consistently appealing to the basest and lowest passions of the ignorant and lawless class of whites. . . . On the stump, in the press, everywhere, the people were constantly told of negro vices and the peril he was to civilization. The cry was often raised to drown out the influence of the more conservative southern leaders."[30] Believing that peace between the races was essential to the social stability and prosperity of the South, it is not surprising that they were willing to publicly oppose certain aspects of the southern counterrevolution, such as lynching, whitecapping, and debt peonage. This was especially true when one considers that their position as federal judges, appointed for life, protected them to a great extent from the political consequences of their actions.

Although their rulings from the bench, particularly in regards to the civil rights of African Americans, were quite unpopular and controversial, their racial beliefs were deeply marked by antebellum paternalistic racial attitudes. Trieber, Speer, and Jones believed that whites should control the South and that the races should not intimately intermingle. The judges generally regarded African Americans as a benighted, semi-civilized people requiring paternal solicitude—and governance. But as paternalists, Trieber, Speer, and Jones, in marked contrast to the more radical racists, believed it unnecessary, unwise, and even morally wrong to "grind the Negro down," as Jones put it.[31] Some white southerners and leaders of the radical racism movement, in contrast, did not seem to be satisfied until the African American was crushed and pushed to the brink of extinction. Trieber, Speer, and Jones appeared to believe that as the African Americans were pushed down, the South would be dragged down with them. Instead, what needed to be done was to uplift African Americans, thus encouraging the white South to grow and advance along with the ex-slaves.

On one hand, what Trieber, Speer, and Jones advocated was nothing extraordinary. They merely wished to see the South become more civilized, peaceful, and prosperous. They did not call for integration or for providing African Americans with unchecked political power. Rather, they called upon the federal government to fulfill its duty, as expressed in the Reconstruction-era amendments and the laws based upon them, to protect African Americans from those who wished to oppress them. But, as it turned out, the conditions that surrounded their actions made those actions extraordinary. Their call for simple justice came at a time when many political leaders in the South openly advocated the brutal repression of African Americans. At the same time, the U.S. Supreme Court was in the process of establishing a narrow interpretation of the Reconstruction amendments. While the white South sought to negate the revolutionary changes brought about by the Civil War, the Supreme Court, through its decisions, aided and abetted the southern counterrevolution. This situation provided the context in which moderates such as Judges Jacob Trieber, Emory Speer, and Thomas Goode Jones could provide a rare ray of light for African Americans at a time when the skies surrounding them were filled with dark clouds.

Revised Statutes, U.S. Compiled Statutes 1901

Section 1978

That all persons born in the United States and not subject to any foreign power, excluding Indians not taxed, are hereby declared to be citizens of the United States, and such citizens of every race and color, without regard to any previous condition of slavery or involuntary servitude, except as punishment for crime whereof the party shall have been duly convicted, shall have the same right, in every state or territory of the United States, to make and enforce contracts to sue, be parties and give evidence, to inherit, purchase, lease, sell, hold and convey real and personal property, and to full and equal benefit of all laws and proceedings for the security of persons and property, as is enjoyed by white citizens and shall be subject to like punishments, pains and penalties, and to none other, any law, statute, ordinance, regulation or custom to the contrary notwithstanding.

Section 5508

If two or more persons conspire to injure, oppress, threaten, or intimidate any citizen in the free exercise or enjoyment of any right or privilege secured to him by the Constitution or laws of the United States, or because of his having so exercised the same; or if two or more persons go in disguise on the highway, or on the premises of another, with intent to prevent or hinder his free exercise or enjoyment of any right or privilege so secured, they shall be fined not more than five thousand dollars and imprisoned not more than ten years; and moreover, be thereafter ineligible to any office, or place of honor, profit, or trust created by the Constitution or laws of the United States.

Section 5510

Every person, who, under color of any law, statute, ordinance, regulation, or custom, subjects, or causes to be subjected, any inhabitant of any state or territory to the deprivation of any rights, privileges, or immunities, secured or protected by the Constitution and laws of the United States . . . on account of such inhabitant being an alien, or by reason of his color or race . . . shall be punished by a fine of not more than one thousand dollars, or by imprisonment not more than one year, or by both.

Judge Jacob Trieber's Charge to the Jury, Helena, Arkansas, October 6, 1903

My attention has been called by the district attorney to some matters to be laid before you for your investigation and action thereon which are somewhat extraordinary and of great importance.

Under the laws of the United States, section 5508, Rev. St., it is a serious offense "for two or more persons to conspire to injure, oppress, threaten or intimidate any citizen in the free exercise or enjoyment of any right or privilege secured to him by the constitution or laws of the United States or because of his having exercised the same." Since the adoption of the thirteenth amendment to the constitution of the United States slavery has ceased to exist in this country and every citizen thereof is entitled to enjoy those rights which are inherent in every free man. Without enumerating what all of these rights are, it is sufficient to say that among them are, in the language of the Declaration of Independence, the corner-stone of our republican form of government, the following: "That all men are created equal; that they are endowed by their Creator with certain unalienable rights, that among these are life, liberty, and the pursuit of happiness." The framers of the present constitution of this state are no less emphatic on this subject, for in the bill of rights they say: "All men are created equally free and independent, and have certain inherent and inalienable rights; among which are those of enjoying and defending life and liberty, of acquiring, possessing and protecting property and reputation; and of pursuing their own happiness. To secure these rights governments are instituted, deriving their just power from the consent of the governed."

The right to own, hold, dispose, lease and rent property, either real or personal, and to perform honest work for the support of himself and his family are natural rights belonging to every free man without any statute or written law. Deprive a man of these rights and he ceases to be a freeman.

Congress, in order to leave no doubt on that subject, has enacted a statute declaring:

"That all persons born in the United States and not subject to any foreign power, excluding Indians not taxed, are hereby declared to be citizens of the United States and such citizens of every race and color, without regard to any previous condition of slavery or involuntary servitude, except as punishment for crime whereof the party shall have been duly convicted, shall have the same right, in every state or territory of the United States, to make and enforce contracts to sue, be parties, and give evidence to inherit, purchase, lease, sell, hold and convey real and personal property, and to full and equal benefit of all laws and proceedings for the security of persons and property, as is enjoyed by white citizens and shall be subject to like punishments, pains and penalties, and to none other, any law, statute, ordinance, regulation or custom to the contrary notwithstanding." Chapter 31, Act of Congress, April 9, 1866, 14 St. at L. 27.

Under these acts the court charges you, gentlemen of the grand jury, that it is unlawful for two or more persons to conspire for the purpose of preventing by force, threats or intimidation any citizen of the United States from renting lands and cultivating the same, or performing any honest labor, when hired to do so, on account his being a negro or a citizen of African descent. If the evidence which will be laid before you is of such a nature as to satisfy you that two or more persons have in the district, within the last three years, conspired to deprive persons from renting lands, or from cultivating them after they have rented them, or from performing honest work, when employed to do so, and that this conspiracy was on account of the fact that the persons who had thus rented lands, or were hired to perform labor, were negroes, then it is your duty, under the law, to find a true bill against these persons. If the acts of these conspirators were simply against those men as neighbors, not on account of their race or color, then this court would be without jurisdiction, although the parties are amenable to the laws of the state of Arkansas in its courts. But so far as this court is concerned, the cause of these lawless acts must have been the fact that the parties against whom they were directed were colored persons or Negroes. The owner of the lands and tenements has the right to lease or convey them to whomsoever he pleases or to employ any person he desires. If he sees proper to rent lands to negroes, or employ negroes as laborers, and the negroes are willing to enter into such agreements, they have a perfect right to do so and no persons can, under the constitution and laws of the United States, prevent by force, threats or intimidation the exercise of these privileges because they happen to be negroes. If a person should be injured in his property or person by any wrongdoer for the mere felonious or wrongful purpose of malice, revenge, hatred or gain, without any design to interfere with his rights of citizenship or equality before the laws, on account of the person being of a different race and color from the white race, it would be an ordinary crime punishable by the state laws only, but the rule is otherwise if the tort is committed against persons for no other reason than that they are negroes. Therefore, to constitute an offense within the jurisdiction of this court, the design of these parties must have been to injure these persons or deprive them of their equal right of enjoying the protection of the laws on account of their color or previous condition.

You will carefully investigate these matters and act upon the evidence in the same manner as you would in any other case. These are the first instances of offense of this nature which have been committed in this state, so far as the court has any knowledge, and it behooves the courts, of which the grand jury is a very essential part, to see to it that those who are guilty of these acts should be punished, if the law and evidence justify it. Nothing tends more to bring the courts into disrepute and lead to mob rule than a failure of the courts and juries to enforce the laws of the country. The people at large have a right to look to the courts for protection and it has always been the pleasure of this court to be able to say that grand jurors as well as petit jurors, selected in this district have never been found unwilling to discharge the parts of the duty honestly and in strict accordance with their oath of office.

(Reprinted from the *Arkansas Gazette,* October 7, 1903, 1.)

Judge Jacob Trieber's "A Rift in the Clouds" Letter to Judge Thomas Goode Jones, October 14, 1904

I thank you very much for your kind letter of the 9th instant and copy of your charge to the jury in the lynching case. I have read it very carefully, and I have no doubt that if an appeal is taken to the Supreme Court of the United States, that part of it which declares an attempt to burn the jail where federal prisoners were kept at the time an offense against the United States will be unanimously affirmed. As to the other portion, in relation to the lynching of the negro, the court, I fear, will be divided, although in my opinion it is right.

In any event, it is such action on the part of Federal Judges, especially by one like yourself, who is a native of the South, has served in the Confederate Army, and whose former political views cannot be questioned by the people of the South, which will arouse public opinion to the enormity of the crime. While I am not a native of the South, I have lived here ever since childhood, having resided in the state of Arkansas thirty-six years. I have no doubt my environments have somewhat influenced my views; still a charge from me would not have the effect that yours has. The responsibility for this unfortunate condition we have in this section is in part due, I think, to the spirit of some of the gentlemen connected with the press of the South. They seem to think that any criticism of any of the acts of irresponsible mobs is a stab at the South, when in fact it is for the benefit of the good people of the South.

I do not know the conditions existing in your state, but in our state the rabble seems to have obtained absolute control of the politics of the state, and what is worse than anything else is the fact that their supremacy has been obtained solely by appealing to the prejudices existing in the minds of many against the negro. The true representatives of our section, that is, those who are intelligent, have most at stake, and the greatest interest in the welfare of our section, are practically barred from participation in the administration of the affairs of the state.

Another misfortune is that many good people of the Northern states think that their advice to the people of the South in this matter can be of assistance to us, in the solution of this difficult problem, and while no doubt they mean well, our people resent their acts as unwarranted interferences, and thus their well meant acts add fuel to the flames and aid the worst elements among us. But I see a rift in the clouds when men like yourself, Judge Speers [sic] of Georgia, and Judge Rogers of this state, all natives of the South and ex-Confederates, lead in this patriotic movement to awaken the conscience of our people. If every man in the South who believes as we do would only have the moral courage exhibited by you and the others, I sincerely believe that this race question could be solved to the lasting benefit of our country and in conformity with the spirit of this civilized age, provided those well meaning people of the North could be induced to keep quiet and trust the good people of the South with the solution to this problem. When I tried the whitecapping cases here the jury which convicted the parties was composed exclusively of natives of the South; yet there was no trouble to secure a righteous verdict. This shows that the rabid expressions found in many of our leading newspapers, and so freely indulged in by petty politicians, do not express the sentiment of the better class of people. To awaken their conscience and supply them with the moral courage necessary to give expression of their views on the subject is all that, in my opinion, is necessary to influence a patriotic adjustment of this negro question. You have blazed the way for such an awakening, and I have no doubt that the day is not far off when the people will realize what a debt of gratitude they owe you for it.

I am glad that you had your charge printed, so that it can be given wide circulation. The reasoning of it is not only convincing, but it is so calm and unprejudiced that every thinking man will appreciate it. The only objection I have ever been able to make to Judge Speer's views in these cases is that the vigorous language he uses, although justified by the facts, seem to some as being too passionate, and for that reason will fail, to some extent, to have that beneficial effect your calmer tone will exercise.

Pardon me for expressing my views on this subject so fully, when all that your charge called for was an expression of the soundness thereof, from a legal standpoint; but you know we judges cannot give publicity to our views on this subject, and it relieves me somewhat to be able to express them in confidence to a brother judge.

I am sorry that we are not in the same circuit so that we could exchange occasionally, but I sincerely hope that some day I may have an opportunity of meeting you in person; in the meantime permit me to assure you of my admiration of you as a judge and a man, for I know what it means for one with our environments to act as you do. Thank God we still have men who have the courage of their convictions.

(Thomas Goode Jones Papers, Alabama Department of Archives and History, Montgomery, Alabama, box 3, file 29.)

Judge Jacob Trieber to President Theodore Roosevelt, February 27, 1905

I have read with a great deal of interest your remarks at the Philadelphia banquet on Washington's birthday touching the race question. Having lived practically all my life in this state, and for 29 years in that part of it, known as 'the black belt' and having given the subject careful consideration, based not only on information but actual observation, I feel that I am somewhat familiar with this grave issue confronting the Nation, and more especially this section. Your remarks are the first I remember reading, which indicate a thorough comprehension of this serious problem on the part of one who has never resided in the South.

It is not my intention to worry you with an essay on this subject, but merely to say a few words to assure you that in my opinion you have approached the subject in a way which will greatly aid in the solution thereof. It is a great mistake to suppose that all the people of the South, or even a large majority of them are so prejudiced against the negro, as to oppose his elevation, and in favor of depriving him of all his political rights. On the contrary the better element, and more especially the former slave owners, and their descendants entertain the kindliest feelings for him. It is the ignorant, lower element, and that class of politicians, whose entire stock of trade consists of appeals to the prejudices of the ignorant masses who cause the mischief. It is that element which opposes the education of the Negro, and insists on the segregation of school taxes, and thereby prevent the progress of the black race. In this state these efforts, although favored by the Governor, have twice been defeated in the Legislature, at the sessions of 1903 and 1905, in obedience to the wishes of the better elements of the state. The great trouble is that the better element of the state, the men who are building it up, who develop its resources, and sincerely believe in what you have so aptly called, "opening the door of hope to every citizen" have not the moral courage to assert themselves, and insist upon having meted out to every citizen that justice, which of right belongs to him, and more especiall [sic] to what they call, "the inferior race." The inconsiderate suggestions, if not interference of those well meaning philanthropists of the North, with suggestions mostly impracticable owing to the conditions prevailing, is often the excuse of these people, overlooking as they do that nothing would prevent such "interference" more readily than the assertion of these people, and carrying out their good intentions, based upon personal knowledge of the prevailing conditions. Your remarks at Philadelphia have touched the right chord, and and [sic] they begin to realize the grave duties devolving upon them, and will result in restoring to them that "backbone" which of late they have, it seems, lost entirely. Justice, common justice on the one hand, and a little patience on the other, will solve the problem, not immediately, but in the course of time. Your words are an encouragement to these people, and a continuance of that course, will in my opinion accomplish a great deal of good.

The advance of the Negro race in this country has within the last few years been much greater than is realized by those, who fail to give this matter careful attention. That crime is still very prevalent among them is unfortunately true, but a comparison with a like number of people of other races, if selected according to the same percentage of illiteracy, and like environments will show that it is not out of proportion. The morals of the Negro are much improved, and while at first this advance has been rather slow, it is now much more perceptible. A large number of Negroes is found in every community, whose citizenship is exceptionally good. In the courts of my district, the Commissioners charged with the selection of the juries, are instructed by me to make no discrimination on account of race or color, with the result that on every jury, grand or petit some negroes serve. An experience of 8 years, three and one half, as U.S. Attorney, and the rest as U.S. District Judge has shown, that those selected, who of course are the best representatives of their race, make good jurors, honest and intelligent, as well as determined to aid in the honest enforcement of the laws, without fear or favor. The same experience I have always had with white jurors. They are carefully selected from the best citizens, and I am proud to say that I do not remember a single instance, in which white or colored jurors were influenced in the determination of a cause by racial influences. It may interest you to hear of one cause especially. In one section of my state, some white men, ignorant and vicious had determined not to permit colored people to work in saw mills, or rent lands, threatening them with violence, if they did not leave that vicinity. My attention having been called to that fact I charged the Grand Jury to indict all such persons, as violators of the Act of Congress, making it an offence for two or more persons to conspire for the purpose of depriving any citizen of the United States of any right guaranteed to him by the constitution or laws of the United States. The Grand Jury composed of 17 whites and three colored men promptly returned indictments against the parties, and the trial jury composed of white men exclusively unhesitatingly convicted those proved to be guilty. The majority of both juries I was informed was composed of natives of the South, and a number of them ex-confederate soldiers. The good citizens of the neighborhood, where it occurred, as well as the county officials aided the federal officers in procuring evidence, and arresting the parties. I mention these matters merely to show that the unreasonable prejudice against the Negroes, and which results in violence in many instances is due more to a lack of moral courage on the part of the better element, than a general feeling of hatred against the race. In my opinion the large majority of the people of the South want to see justice done to the Negro, but when the cry of "Negro domination" and "social equality" is raised by the political demagogue for selfish purposes, there is want of firmness, which prevents carrying out the real feelings of the people. Your speech will supply some "backbone" to many of these people, and to those of the North a little patience. If they have that effect, the race question will be solved in the near future.

(Theodore Roosevelt Papers, Library of Congress, microfilm, series 1, reel 53.)

Opinion of Judge Emory Speer in the Case of *United States v. Thomas McClellan and William F. Crawley,* March 15, 1904

The indictment in this case charges that the prisoner, one of whom was the Sheriff of Ware County and another an attorney at law practicing in the courts, with forcibly seizing certain citizens, known under the law of Georgia as "persons of color" and selling them to other persons to be held by force, and compelled by force to labor in a state of involuntary servitude, which is termed "peonage." A demurrer to the indictment was interposed. There are a number of such cases and it is agreed *in judicio* by the Assistant District Attorney [Alexander Akerman] who represents the Government and by the counsel for the prisoners, that the arguments made in this case shall suffice for all.

The indictment is as follows:

The Grand Jurors of the United States, selected, chosen and sworn in and for the Eastern Division of the southern District of Georgia, upon their oaths present: That heretofore, to wit, on the eleventh day of August, in the year of our Lord one thousand nine hundred and two, on Thomas J. McClellan, late of said Division and District, within said Division and District and within the jurisdiction of this court, did then and there knowingly and unlawfully cause one John Wesley Boney to be held to a condition of peonage; for that the said Thomas J. McClellan in the county of Ware, in the State of Georgia, did forcibly seize the body of the said John Wesley Boney, without his consent and without authority of law, and did then and there sell the body of the said John Wesley Boney, without his consent and without authority of law, to Edward J. McRee, William McRee and Frank I. McRee and did then and there forcibly and against the will of him the said John Wesley Boney, and without authority of law, deliver him, the said John Wesley Boney, into the custody of the said Edward J. McRee, William McRee and Frank I. McRee, then and there causing him, the said

John Wesley Boney, to be held by the said Edward J. McRee, William McRee and Frank I. McRee to a condition of peonage; for that the said Edward J. McRee, William McRee and Frank I. McRee than and there so having obtained the custody of the body of the said John Wesley Boney, did then and there by force and against the will of him, the said John Wesley Boney, and without authority of law, transport the body of the said John Wesley Boney to the county of Lowndes in said State, and did then and there hold the said John Wesley Boney, against his will, to labor for them, to work out a debt which they, the said Edward J. McRee, William McRee and Frank I. McRee, claimed to be due them by the said John Wesley Boney, and to labor under the terms of the alleged contract, between them, the said Edward J. McRee, William McRee and Frank I. McRee, and said John Wesley; he, the said Thomas J. McClellan then and there well knowing that the said John Wesley Boney would be so held as aforesaid by the said Edward J. McRee, William McRee, and Frank I. McRee, whereby, in the manner aforesaid, the said Thomas J. McClellan did cause the said John Wesley Boney to be held to a condition of peonage; contrary to the form of the statute in such case made and provided, and against the peace and dignity of the said United States.

The law upon this subject is found in the Act of Congress approved March 2, 1867, entitled "An Act to abolish and forever prohibit the system of peonage in the Territory of New Mexico and other parts of the United States." This Act, by the codifiers of the Revised Statutes, has been distributed in several sections, 1990, 1991, 5526 and 5527. It is, however, serviceable to the correct understanding of the law, that the Act should be considered in the precise form in which it was enacted. The material section is the first. It provides:

That the holding of any person to service or labor under the system known as peonage, is hereby declared to be unlawful, and the same is hereby abolished and forever prohibited in the Territory of New Mexico, or in any other Territory or State of the United States; and all acts, laws, resolutions, orders, regulations, or usages of the Territory of New Mexico, or of any other Territory or State of the United States, which have heretofore established, maintained or enforced, or by virtue of which any attempt shall hereafter be made to establish, maintain or enforce, directly or indirectly, the voluntary or involuntary service or labor of any persons as peons, as liquidation of any debt or obligation, or otherwise, be, and the same are hereby declared null and void; and any person or persons who shall hold, arrest, or return, or cause to be held, arrested, or returned, or in any manner aid in the arrest or return of any person or persons to a condition of peonage, shall, upon conviction, be punished by fine not less than one thousand nor more than five thousand dollars, or by imprisonment not less than one nor more than five years, or both, at the discretion of the court.

This act is denounced by the demurrers, first, for the alleged reason that is was beyond the constitutional power of Congress, and secondly, because it does not apply to the illegal sale, holding in imprisonment and labor of the citizen.

It is perhaps not inappropriate that the court should express its appreciation of the erudite arguments based upon careful research made by the learned counsel for the prisoners and for the Government. Nor is it unmindful of the voluntary aid afforded by statesmen and others trained in the same school of constitutional construction with the prisoners counsel that a chairman of a penitentiary committee of the Georgia Senate appeared for the prisoners, that a Member of the House Judiciary Committee in Congress from the District of the prisoners, contributed a brief in their behalf, that a solicitor General of the State court in their State judicial district, charged with the prosecution of such offenses under the State law, sat with the prisoners and their counsel during the hearing, taken altogether is somewhat persuasive of the conclusion that if there is no system of peonage *dejure,* to which the statute applies, there is yet a de facto system of some equivalent sort which has evoked the liveliest apprehensions of those who participate in its operations and emoluments, and of others whose sentiments toward it are not wholly antipathetic.

Notwithstanding the comprehensiveness of the arguments, the inquiry presented by the demurrers may somewhat succinctly [be] presented. Did Congress have the power to enact this legislation; does the legislation itself apply to the illegal arrest and sale of a citizen into involuntary servitude as set out in the indictment, and is the indictment technically sufficient.

It does not seem difficult to find authority in the Constitution for this legislation. The Thirteenth Amendment provides:

SECTION 1: Neither slavery nor involuntary servitude, except as a punishment for crime whereof the party shall have been duly convicted, shall exist within the United States, or any place subject to their jurisdiction.
SECTION 2: Congress shall have power to enforce this Article by appropriate legislation.

This Amendment went into effect on the 18th day of December, 1865. This long antedated the Reconstruction period. The white people of the Southern States reorganized their State government with unreserved acquiescence in the abolition of slavery. Here then is the constitutional power of Congress to enact this legislation. The power is as unquestionable, as that to regulate interstate and foreign commerce, to establish post offices and post roads, or to provide a uniform system of bankruptcy. Then Congress by appropriate legislation can prevent involuntary servitude. It is wholly fallacious to contend that this legislation must be directed as State action. There is no such limitation in the Thirteenth Amendment. That this is true of the Fourteenth Amendment as argued at length may be conceded without impairing the grant of power in the Thirteenth Amendment which Congress exercised. No recourse then need be had to the Fourteenth Amendment, and why embark into a discussion of the powers of Congress therein granted? . . .

The case of *United States vs. Harris,* 106 U.S. 629, on which the prisoners counsel rely, related to another and wholly different section of the Revised Statutes. This was an attempt to secure citizens against conspiracies to deprive them of the protection afforded by State laws. It impinged upon state authority, and the court declared it unconstitutional, but even there, Mr. Justice Wood for the Court, observes:

> It is clear that this Amendment (the Thirteenth), besides abolishing slavery and involuntary servitude within the United States, gives power to Congress to protect all persons within the jurisdiction of the United States from being in any way subjected to slavery or involuntary servitude, except as punishment for crime, and in the enjoyment of that freedom which it was the object of the amendment to secure.

Again in the *Civil Rights Cases,* 109 U.S. 3, where the Supreme Court of the United States, in pursuance of the uniform policy of the national judiciary to conserve the just rights of the States, denied the power of Congress to enact measures of incalculable consequence to the peace and happiness of the Southern States, Mr. Justice Bradley discussing the Thirteenth Amendment said:

> By its own unaided force and effect, it abolished slavery and established universal freedom. Still, legislation may be necessary and proper to meet all the various cases and circumstances to be affected by it, and to prescribe proper modes of redress for its violation in letter or

spirit. And such legislation may be primary and direct in it character; for the Amendment is not *a mere prohibition of State laws* establishing or upholding slavery, but an *absolute declaration* that slavery or involuntary servitude shall not exist in any part of the United States.

And said Mr. Justice Miller in the *Slaughter House Cases,* 16 Wallace 36:

Undoubtedly while negro slavery alone was in the mind of the Congress which passed the 13th Article it forbids any other kind of slavery, now or hereafter.

Indeed the denunciation of involuntary servitude by the first clause of the Thirteenth Amendment would be an ample grant of power to enact this law if the second clause of the Amendment had been wholly omitted. To hold otherwise, is in the language of Justice Miller in *ex parte Yarborough,* 110 U.S. 651, to "destroy at one blow, in construing the Constitution of the United States, the doctrine universally applied to all instruments of writing, that what is implied is as much a part of the instrument as what is expressed." The denial of this power can only be supported by what the same learned Justice in the same case terms, "the old argument, often heard, often repeated, and in this court never assented to, that when a question of the power of Congress arises the advocate of the power must be able to place his finger on words which expressly grant it."

Our whole postal system is based upon the terse power of Congress "to establish post offices and post roads." There is no provision in the instrument authorizing an enactment to punish burglary of a post office, or the forgery of a postal note, or the theft of a letter, and yet there are a multitude of statutes defining and punishing such offenses the validity of which are unquestioned. Why? Because the government of the United States not only possesses and exercises all the powers which the Constitution expressly grants but all other powers which are necessary to the effective operation of those thus granted. Indeed Congress by clause 18 of section 8, Article I, of the Constitution is expressly empowered "To make all laws which shall be necessary and proper for carrying into execution the foregoing powers, and all others powers vested by this constitution in the government of the United States, or in any Department or officer thereof."

As in a multitude of cases which from time to time have been argued since the organization of the government, great use is sought to be made of the Tenth Amendment which reserves to the States "the powers not delegated to the United States by the Constitution, nor prohibited by it to the

States." But, as we have seen, all powers are delegated which are necessary to the effectiveness of those powers which are expressly delegated.

If the interesting but somewhat archaic argument which has been so often presented before, and which is pressed now, should prevail, the Constitution of the United States must *ex necessitate* have been practically as voluminous as the Constitution and statutes combined.

We concluded then the denunciation of slavery or involuntary servitude in the Constitution is the grant of power to Congress to prevent it in every foot of that territory under the aegis of the Stars and Stripes.

It is however urged that the term a "condition of peonage" imports a system of peonage. This however does not follow. A general condition of peonage might be synonymous with a general system of peonage, but a citizen held and worked by lawless methods against his will for the purpose of compelling him in this manner to discharge a real or alleged obligation, is in contemplation of law held in a condition of peonage. The words a condition of peonage as used in this sense should be broadly construed in favor of the liberty of citizen. There can be no more salutary rule of statutory construction. This is the view of Judge Jones of the Middle District of Alabama, as expressed in his charge to a Grand Jury reported in *The Peonage Cases,* 123 Fed. 679.

> The phrase "condition of peonage" means the actual status, physical and moral, with the inevitable incidents to which the employee, servant, or debtor was reduced under that system, when held to involuntary performance or liquidation of his obligation.

It is moreover urged that even if Congress was granted power to make laws which impose penalties on those who hold the citizen in involuntary servitude, it did not intend to do so by this legislation. The familiar expedient of reference to the debates in Congress is resorted to, to support this contention. This recourse is superfluous, for, when the words of the statute are plain and unambiguous, they are taken to import what they plainly mean. What can be plainer than this language of the Act, all of which has been hereinbefore set out, "and any person or persons who shall hold, arrest, or return, or cause to be held, arrested or returned, or in any manner aid in the arrest or return to any person or persons to a condition of peonage, shall upon conviction be punished etc."

It is however urged that the debate in the Senate shows Congress started out merely to abolish the system of peonage which existed in New

Mexico. This is probably true. But Congress may start out to do one thing and do much more. Congress may set out to appropriate money for the support of the War Department, and may attach a measure giving the Secretary of War primary jurisdiction over the Philippine Islands. Innumerable indeed are the provisions of positive law which have been enacted upon appropriation bills. It is quite possible that when the Senate of the United States began to frame this stature, it had chiefly in mind the hapless condition of the New Mexican peons, but reflection, the wisdom of which subsequent history has unhappily made manifest, may have convinced them that there might be peonage in every material sense, elsewhere in this land of the free. But whether this be true or not here is the unequivocal denunciation of the crime and the court and the country need not look beyond it, to ascertain what was in the breast of the legislators.

It does not seem to me that this is a question upon which the courts of the country should be astute to discover reasons to nullify an Act of Congress made in *favorem libertatis*. The substantial inquiry is, did the accused consign or hold the citizen in a condition of involuntary servitude for the purpose of compelling him to work out a real or alleged obligation. This if done created a condition of peonage. A peon is defined as "a debtor held by his creditor in a qualified servitude to work out the debt." Black's Law Dictionary. The involuntary servitude, and this "consists in the subjection of one person to another; if it consists in the right of property which a person exercises over another; it is slavery. When the subjection of one person to another is not slavery it consists simply in the right of requiring of another what he is bound to do or not to do; this right arises from all kinds of contracts or quasi contract." 2 Bouvier p. 986. It follows then that an unwilling servitude enforced by the stronger to collect a debt is to reduce the victim to the condition of a peon, and logically to a condition of peonage.

It is however insisted that while the conduct described in the indictment may be within the letter of the stature, it is not within the statute, because not within the spirit of the law, and this quotation from Lord Coke is cited, "Acts of Parliament are to be so construed as no man that is innocent or free from injury or wrong be, by a literal construction punished or undamaged." But how can it be contended that the conduct of the prisoners as described in this indictment, is innocent or free from injury or wrong. Is it not inimical to the Amendment of the Constitution which defines involuntary servitude? Is it not involuntary servitude to seize by force, to hurry the victim from wife and children, to incarcerate him in a stockade, and work him in range of the deadly muzzle of the shotgun, or under the terror of the lash and continue this servitude as long as resentment may prompt, or greed demands? It is true that a literal construction will not be favored, if the object be to punish those who are innocent, or free from injury or wrong. This was the decision of the Supreme Court in the case of the *Trustees of Holy Trinity Church,* 143 U.S. p.457 on which counsel for the accused rely. There it was held that although the Act of Congress prohibited a contract with an alien for labor and services of any kind in the United States, yet it did not apply to the rector of a church although his pastoral duty implied both services and labor. There, the statute was construed in favor of liberty. But what parallel is there between the holy ministrations of the man of God, though serviceable and laborious, and the conduct of lawless and violent men who would seize helpless and pathetic negroes, and for their own selfish purposes consign them to a life of involuntary servitude compared to which the slavery of *antebellum* days was a paradise. And it otherwise appears that the construction of this Act which seems to us proper, is in salutary accord not only with the spirit of Congress in adopting it, but with other statutes for the same general purpose which portray unmistakable the consistent purpose to stamp out on American soil any & every form of involuntary servitude. We refer to the Act of May 21, 1866, Sec. 5525 E.S., which provides:

> Every person who kidnaps or carries away any other person, with the intent that such other person be sold into involuntary servitude, or held as a slave; or who entices, persuades, or induces any other person to go on board any vessel or to any other place with the intent that he may be made or held as a slave, or sent out of the country to be so made or held; or who in any way knowingly aids in causing any other person to be held, sold, or carried away to be held or sold as a slave, shall be punished by a fine of not less than five hundred nor more than five thousand dollars, or by imprisonment not more than five years, or both.

This legislation was also enacted before the proclamation of the Fourteenth Amendment, and its author was the honorable Charles Sumner, Senator from Massachusetts. Primarily designed, as appears from the preceding Section, 5524, and the debate in Congress, to prevent kidnapping and sale of Southern negroes to Cuba, and other slaveholding countries, it was so framed as to make penal the act of any person "who kidnaps or carries away any other person, with the intent that such other person be sold into involuntary servitude." This is another instance of the exercise of Congress of the power granted by the Thirteenth Amendment to prevent involuntary servitude by a penal statute acting directly on the individual offender. The Act of June 23, 1874, c.464, (18 Stat. L. 251), is another pertinent illustration of this constant purpose. Again the bill was introduced by the Honorable Charles Sumner, but he died before its passage. It appears that subsequently it was reported by Mr. Cessna from the House Judiciary Committee, was adopted by the House, and as amended by the Senate became the law on the date mentioned. In advocacy of the bill, Mr. Sumner stated that there were about five thousand Italian children in the United States who had been kidnapped or inveigled, brought to this country and held in a condition of involuntary servitude. It provides:

> That whoever shall knowingly and willfully bring into the United States, or the Territories thereof, any person inveigled or forcibly kidnapped in any other country, with intent to hold such person so inveigled or kidnapped in confinement or to any involuntary service, and whoever shall knowingly and willfully sell or cause to be sold, into any condition of involuntary servitude, any other person for the term willfully hold to involuntary service any person so sold or bought, shall be deemed guilty of a felony, and, on conviction thereof be imprisoned for a term not exceeding five years and pay a fine not exceeding five thousand dollars.

Its special purpose was manifest not only by this title but by its phraseology, but in its broader scope, before it was completed, appears this vivid and vital language, "and whoever shall knowingly and willfully sell or cause to be sold into any condition of involuntary servitude any person for any term whatever, shall be deemed guilty, etc." It is not necessary in the opinion of the court to hold that the count of the indictment hereinbefore set out will find additional support in one or both of these statutes, although this might be argued on strong grounds of reason and authority. They are mainly cited to show a constant purpose on the part of the national legislature to protect all persons within our boundaries from involuntary servitude of whatever sort, and further to demonstrate the reiterated exercise by congress of the salutary constitutional power now challenged. Of the illustrious author of these statues to preserve human liberty we may all now adopt the language which was spoken of him many years ago by the not less illustrious son of Georgia, and Representative of Mississippi, the late L.Q.C. Lamar: "Charles Sumner was born with an instinctive love of freedom, and was educated from his earliest infancy to the belief that freedom is the natural and indefeasible right of every intelligent being having the outward form of man. In him, in fact, this creed seems to have been something more than a doctrine imbibed from teachers, or a result of education. To him it was a grand intuitive truth, inscribed in blaxing letters upon the tablet of his inner consciousness, to deny which would have been for him to deny that he himself existed."

In view of the political complexion of this question to which somewhat veiled reference has been made, the court deems it appropriate to refer to the degrading and un-American effect of involuntary servitude upon every concern of a self-respecting people. Already protests are heard from organized labor, and from manufacturers as well, against the baleful competition of convict made goods. How much worse will be that competition, with the labor, or products of the peon? The first are manufactured under the control of law, the other under the will of taskmaster, merciless perhaps as the Egyptian who drove the energies of the ancient people of God. How can the plain farmer or manufacturer of turpentine, or lumber who labors for himself, with the assistance of his sons, or hired help, hope for fair play in the market when a huge saw mill in the vicinity or an unscrupulous planter with a stockade full of unpaid hands can underbid his prices. Why should one man through lawless methods be permitted to grow rich while his neighbors who piously respect the law, and the rights of their fellow man, however humble, shall forever toil on perhaps in poverty and want. The demoralization of the spectacle to the plastic mind of youth, the incalculable harm flowing from the triumphant defiance of law, the reproach to the fair fame of our beloved state, all are involved in this supreme question. And besides what hope can the respectable negro have, what incentive to better effort, or better life if he, his wife, his daughters or his sons may in a moment be snatched from his humble home and sold into peonage. Let us for a moment put ourselves in his place and imagine our furious indignation or hopeless despair if our loved ones or ourselves could be subjected to such a condition of involuntary servitude. Nor if conditions like these described in the indictment shall continue, will the negro remain the sole victim of peonage. Crime is ever progressive. Very many poor and ignorant white people are scarcely less hapless than negroes, and cases are already reported where white men have been made in this way the victims of powerful and unscrupulous neighbors.

But it is urged that the courts of the State have jurisdiction of this crime under the name of kidnapping and false imprisonment. So they have, and no word we say ought to discourage their officers in the performance of their duty to prosecute and convict. So they have jurisdiction of the burglary of a post office but that does not nullify the jurisdiction of the national courts to try the same crime. The jurisdiction of both courts is here concurrent, and no man would be quicker than the presiding Judge of this court to applaud righteous convictions for these crimes, in the courts of the State. There are innumerable illustrations of the concurrent jurisdiction of the State and the national courts. They afford no reason however why either court with a case properly before it should refuse to proceed in the exercise of such jurisdiction. And after all what just cause of compliant is there? These prisoners if tried will be tried by Georgians; a Georgian Judge, a Georgian prosecuting attorney, a Georgia marshal appear and no one but Georgians are eligible as jurors. Away then with the pretence that the rights of Georgians are here imperilled or threatened. If here the guilty are not permitted to escape, here the innocent are never punished.

From these considerations it is concluded that the Act of March 2, 1867, denouncing peonage and involuntary servitude in any form, is a valid exercise of a power granted to Congress by the Thirteenth Amendment to the Constitution of the United States, and that the court has jurisdiction.

We are further of the opinion that a condition of peonage comprehended by that Act is described in these indictments. It is the illegal holding of any person to involuntary servitude to work out a debt or contract claimed to be due by the person so held to the person so holding.

Little stress was made in the argument on the insufficiency of the indictment and it seems to the court in all respects sufficient.

The demurrers will be ordered overruled and the prisoners put to plead.

(Record Group 21, National Archives, Southeast Region, East Point, Georgia, District Court, Northern District of Georgia, Case 10165 and 10166.)

Judge Thomas Goode Jones's
"Suggestions in the Bailey Case"

After the many decisions of the Supreme Court upon the subject, it is unnecessary to cite the authorities as to due process of law, the equal protection of the laws and involuntary servitude.

The Fourteenth Amendment in forbidding the states to deny—thereby commanding them to afford—"due process" and "equal protection of the laws" in the administration of their government, created no new right in these respects, save to place their enjoyment under the final arbitrament of the Federal authority. What the Fourteenth Amendment commands the state to afford, when it prosecutes a person for violation of its law, is the enjoyment of "its established course of judicial procedure" and the benefit of "the law of the land," as established by the constitution, statutes and decisions of that state.

In *Hurtado v. California,* 110 U.S. 516, the court says, "the commands of the Fourteenth Amendment are not too vague and indefinite to operate as a practical restraint," and that it "forbids any course of procedure, unless it hears before it condemns and proceeds upon fixed principles, and not arbitrarily, and renders judgment only after trial."

With these limitations, the state is free from any restraint in the constitution of the United States, to establish and enforce such rules as it thinks proper to constitute "due process." So also, whether it denies "the equal protection of the laws" is to be determined by the natural and ordinary operation of the statutes. The constitution, statutes and decisions of the state are adopted by the Fourteenth Amendment as the standard by which to determine whether under the operation of a particular statute, due process is afforded, or the equal protection of the laws is denied to any person.

The decisions of the state Supreme Court that the act under which Bailey was convicted was not in violation of the state constitution foreclosed further inquiry on that point, and is conclusive on all other courts. The only question the Supreme Court of the United States can consider is whether the statute as administered in this case, violates any right of Bailey under the constitution and laws of the United States.

Viewing this statute in the light of the constitution of the United States, it is apparent that it offends several of its provisions. To constitute the offense the statute denounces, the defendant must entertain the fraudulent intent on three different occasions: First, when he enters into the contract of personal service; Second, when he obtains the money or advances from his employer; and, Third, when he fails to refund the money. But the fraudulent intent and acts at these different periods, antecedent to the quitting of the contract, does not constitute any offense whatever under this statute. Standing alone, these bad acts, under this statute, are grievances only under the civil law. The situation which brings the defendant under criminal condemnation, and puts life in the statute, which up to that time is inert, is not that the defendant did these things fraudulently, but that after doing of them, he failed or refused to perform the contract of personal service, "without just cause." In no jurisprudence that we are aware of, has it ever been held that the abandoning of any contract with just cause, whatever its nature, can subject the party to any liability whatsoever, either civil or criminal. So that the punishment for which this statute provides is rested on, and can be justified only, because there has been an unjust abandonment of the contract—"without just cause." It cannot be based upon anything else, because none of the antecedent frauds mentioned in the statute, or all of them combined, are criminal offenses. The dominating, controlling and sole fact which puts this statute in motion is the failure without just cause to perform the contract of personal service. The 13th amendment and the statutes passed in pursuance thereof, secure to every person the absolute right to abandon the performance of a contract for personal service, whether with or without just cause, and to exercise it at his pleasure, and forbids his being subjected to any pains or penalties because he so acts, except the ordinary civil liabilities for the breach of contract. This is necessarily so, because otherwise the State can by compulsory, criminal, means compel performance of labor or service against the will of the servitor, and thus destroy a right which it is the end and design of the constitution and statutes to protect and safeguard. In its last analysis, therefore, this statute punishes an American citizen because he exercises the fundamental right of quitting, without just cause, the performance of a contract of personal service, the enjoyment of which right is secured to him by the constitution and laws. What stronger assault can be made upon the enjoyment of a right the constitution secures than to punish the person to whom the right is secured because he exercises it? If the state may punish a man for quitting a contract of personal service, because he abandons it without just cause, it may annihilate the 13th amendment, and reestablish involuntary servitude in the teeth of the Supreme law. The right thus given to quit performance of a contract is absolute and unconditional. It cannot be taken away or undermined directly or indirectly under the guise or the device of regulating the right. *Railroad Company v. Morris,* 65 Ala. 199; *Joseph v. Randolph,* 71 Ala. 499. The state has no power to declare that person shall not exercise this absolute right, because prior to its exercise, he may have offended against some law of the state. That would be to outlaw a man, and destroy a right he has under the Federal constitution, because he had offended in some other respect against the laws of the state. If the legislature may constitutionally declare that a man shall not exercise a right secured to him by the constitution, because he has fraudulently obtained advances, it may likewise so declare if he commits any other crime, or is guilty even of a civil breach of the rights of another. The legislature has no constitutional power to declare that a certain line of conduct shall, or shall not be an offense, accordingly as the person exercise or refrains from exercising an absolute right which he has under the constitution of the United States. To uphold such a doctrine, we must add a new cannon to our jurisprudence,—that a man may be punished criminally because he exercises a constitutional right.

The ordinary, natural and inevitable result of the statute here if allowed effect, being the compulsory performance of labor against the will of the employee, the statute is void, no matter what the language it employs, or however it clouds the issue by cunning words and phrases to disguise the real object and purpose of the framers of the statute.

But this aside, the words and framework of the statute conclusively demonstrate that its purpose is not to punish fraud, or to protect public morals, but merely to compel performance of a contract for personal service. The obtaining of money or property by a fraudulent promise to render personal service in the future, not meant to be kept, in whatever form accomplished, can undoubtedly be made a crime by the state, whether or not the thing fraudulently obtained is restored, and whether or not the contract under which it was obtained was breached, with or without just cause. The statute purposely and studiously refrains from making the fraud that is mentioned in it the crime, with which the statute deals. The fraud is treated only as an incident, and not worthy of the notice of the legislature, said to be bent on protecting public morals, but the real grievance is, that there is failure to perform a contract of personal service without just cause. The

quitting of the service without just cause is the thing the statute is designed
to prevent. The purpose is to compel performance by stress of criminal
penalties. The fraud is brought into the statute only incidentally, and solely
to cloak the design to punish non-performance of the contract, and to bol-
ster up the pretense, that under this statute the offender is not punished
because he quit the contract without just excuse, but for the fraud perpe-
trated in getting advances before he quit without just excuse. The legislature
as we have seen has the undoubted power to punish the fraudulent obtaining of advances by criminal enactment, whether the advances are afterwards
returned or not, but it cannot use this power so as to hamper and under-
mine a positive right secured by the constitution. Under the constitution a
man cannot be punished criminally, directly or indirectly, or in any manner,
shape or form, or by any device, because he exercises his constitutional right
to abandon a contract without just cause. Such conduct on his part, cannot
be made an element of the fraud. The 13th amendment excepts from the
power of the state in dealing with fraud all authority to make such quitting
of a contract for personal service as an element of any fraud, which it may
otherwise punish. Having imported into the statute, as one of the elements
of fraud for which an offender is to be punished, the ingredient that the
offender exercised a right under the constitution, and the provision of the
law in this respect being inseparable, the design to promote one end, the
compulsory performance of a contract of personal service, the whole act is
void.

This statute also violates the 14th Amendment. The state constitution
ordains that the right of trial by jury shall remain inviolate. The right to
enjoy it as it is afforded to all other person in like circumstances is a part of
the due process the 14th Amendment commands the state to afford, when
it prosecutes persons for crime. There can be no difference in the state court
in the measure of rights which the defendant shall there enjoy, because he
belongs to a particular class, or occupation, or in the nature of the presumption which the law indulges as to his innocence because of the means by
which the offense was committed. The enjoyment of the right cannot be
burdened in the case of particular persons or particular offenses by exactions
or burdens which are not put upon all others. Under the general law of the
land the defendant goes before the jury with the presumption of innocence,
and that remains with him during the whole trial, until, upon the whole
case all the facts establish his guilt as a matter of fact, beyond a reasonable
doubt. *Ogletree v. The State,* 28 Ala. 693. *Coffin v. The United States,* 156 U.S.
432.

Here, the charge is that the advances were obtained by fraud. The party quit the service without just cause, without repaying them. The statute upon these facts raises the presumption as matter of law that the defendant is guilty. It takes away [from] him the right to decide as a matter of fact whether, under all circumstances, the quitting, etc., proves guilt. It says as a matter of law, if these facts are shown, the law presumes the defendant guilty, unless he proves himself innocent. This burden is placed upon no other person who is indicted for fraud. In all other cases the presumptions of guilt are presumptions of fact which the jury, under the direction of the court, must draw from the circumstances of the whole case. Not only [have] defendants in this class of cases to meet a presumption of law rigidly fixed in the statute, which is not authorized under the law of the land in similar cases, but the statute arbitrarily, and without any justification in reason or morals, requires the jury, in this class of cases only, to repudiate the great general and essential principle of justice that where an act equally denotes one of two intentions, one of which points to innocence and the other to guilt, that the jury must adopt that construction and draw those inferences which lean to innocence rather than those which lean to guilt. Under this statute, if it be conceded to be valid otherwise, the jury, in order to convict, must find, beyond reasonable doubt, that he had the fraudulent intent at the three different periods of time, first, when he made the contract; second, when he obtained the advances; third, when he quit without repaying them. If the defendant did not have the fraudulent intent at the time he made the contract, or at the time he obtained the advances, he cannot be guilty under this statute, although he had the fraudulent intent of cheating his employer when he quit the service. How can the *law* say that the mere fact of quitting proves that the fraudulent intent was formed prior to the quitting rather than at the time of quitting? That is not the experience of mankind. Ordinarily men who make contracts and get advances under them do not intend at the time to defraud, but rather expect to repay the advances, and the formation of the criminal intent generally arises subsequently, in consequence of poverty, disappointment in the results of the contract, or of the pressure of other vicissitudes to which men are subjected in the struggle for subsistence and the pursuit of happiness. There is no presumption that men intend to defraud one another, and there is no presumption of law, where there is an intent to defraud, that it was formed at one time rather than another, when the facts relied on point equally to any period of time anterior to the quitting, as well as the time of the quitting of the contract. To make a rule and presumption of law, merely because the party quit without just cause, that the fraudulent

intent was formed at one time rather than another, is to destroy the right of
the defendant to be tried by jury, and his right to have the jury determine
the significance of the facts as to the time when the fraudulent intent was
formed, as matter of fact, in view of the whole case. This right is given by
the law of the land in all other cases.

Chief Justice Brickell, a great jurist, in *Gassenheimer v. The State,* 52 Ala.
319, emphatically condemned as a violation of the legal rights of defendant,
any rule which required or authorized the jury to draw inference of guilt,
when the facts admitted of inference in favor of innocence. Speaking of the
fact relied on there to justify an inference unfavorable to the defendant, he
said (on page 320), "Why that inference? It is the most uncharitable which
can be drawn, and must juries, despite the charity of the law which does not
permit crime or fraud to be presumed when the facts are consistent with
innocence, be invited to indulge such inference? We are of opinion that the
evidence was improperly admitted." This statute compels the jury to draw
the inference of guilt, merely from the unlawful quitting, that the fraudulent
intent existed before the quitting—a fact which must be proved to uphold
a conviction under this statute—when the inference may as well, if not better, be indulged from the quitting that the intent was formed then and not
at any earlier period. That decision shows, as do numerous others, the established course of judicial procedure. The application of the statutory presumption here, therefore, amounts to a denial of the equal protection of the
laws. It not only strikes down the great general and essential principle which
inheres in all our jurisprudence, that the defendant shall not be convicted
until guilt is proved beyond a reasonable doubt, but puts upon him arbitrarily the burden of overcoming a statutory presumption of guilt, arising from
one fact—the quitting of the service—which does not, and cannot, prevail
in any other case. See *Birmingham Water Works Co. v. the State,* 159 Ala. 120,
wherein the Supreme Court of the state reaffirms *Railroad Co. v. Morris,* 65
Ala. 193, and *Smith v. Railroad,* 75 Ala. 449, and holds in the case then under
consideration that there was arbitrary distinction, which under like circumstances, in principle, it held in the Bailey case was not arbitrary. See Cooley
Constitutional Limitations, Sec. 391–3.

These cases, which are in line with like decisions everywhere in the
United States, declare that "unequal, partial and discriminatory legislation,
which secures rights to some favored class or classes, and denies them to
others similarly circumstanced, who are thus excluded from the equal protection of the law, designed to be secured by the general law of the land, is
in clear and manifest opposition to the letter and spirit of these provisions."

The provisions of the Alabama constitution there alluded to are found in the bill of rights.

This statute also amounts to a denial by the state of due process of law, because of the vague and uncertain terms in which the rule of action which the statute intends to enforce is expressed. Section 7 of the constitution of 1901, which the 14th amendment requires to be observed, when the state prosecutes for violation of its laws, provides that "no person shall be accused or arrested or detained, except in cases ascertained by law and according to the forms it has prescribed, and no person shall be punished but by virtue of law established and promulgated prior to the offense and legally applied."

What constitutes "just cause" for breach of a contract for personal service? The statute does not undertake to furnish any guide. Its language furnishes no clue to the causes which the legislature intended to treat as just or unjust. No person who refuses to perform a contract, no matter how honestly he believes he has cause for quitting it, can tell when the court and jury will convict or acquit him, or what they will deem to be just or unjust cause in any particular case. The statute here is not a law, because the statute itself does not "ascertain" the case, but it leaves it to the judge and jury to ascertain the cause and declare the law in view of the facts of the particular case. When the judge and jury undertake these functions, they exercise usurped authority, and the legislature illegally delegates to them under this statute power which the constitution of the states says the law making power alone shall exercise. The "law of the land," which the 14th amendment requires to be applied, requires that the rule of action, for non-conformity to which the citizen may be punished criminally, shall be defined with such certainty that a person of ordinary intelligence, on reading the statute, may know what he may do and what he may not do.

But, if this obstacle were out of the way, we are confronted with the further obstacle that the law must be "promulgated" before the offense. There is no promulgation of the law covering the particular offense until the verdict of guilt or innocence. The only way a defendant can know of the promulgation of the law, is after his act is performed, when he is brought in the prisoners dock, and the jury promulgate the law by their verdict, based upon such instruction as the judge may give. See *Tony against the State,* 141 Ala. 120, which adopts the conclusion in this respect, in *The Peonage Cases,* 123 Fed. Rep. 671. The statute might as well have attempted to declare in general terms that, if a man does any wrong to his neighbor about the performance of a contract, or fails to do equity regarding it, he shall be guilty of a criminal offense. The statute prescribes no rule of conduct whatever.

No one on reading it can tell what abandonment of the contract the legislature intended to be within, and what without, the influence of the statute. A person punished for violation of such a statute is not punished by due process of law. *U.S. v. Reese,* 92 U.S. 214. In the words of the Supreme Court of Louisiana in the *State vs. Castor,* 41 La. Annual, S.C. Sou. Rep. 739: "Language of such wide an indefinite import as to leave absolutely uncertain what acts are within, and what acts are without, the statutory provision, cannot operate as a valid criminal statute." See also Bishop on Statutory Crimes, Sec. 41, *Ex parte Bell,* 22 Tex. Criminal Reports, 31. *Carney v. Andrews,* 5 Stockton Chancery Reports, N. J.

We are far from contending that the legislature may not lawfully create a criminal offense by using terms which have a well defined and settled meaning at the common law, the known meaning of which, includes all the constituent elements of the offense thus defined. In that case the very words employed inform the defendant of what he is forbidden to do. Hence, the legislature may lawfully provided for the punishment of arson, burglary, larceny and like, without defining them more particularly, or prohibit certain games of chance by referring to them only their popular and well known names such as the keeping of a gaming table, betting at faro, and the like. In these and like instances, the terms used have a well defined, settled and certain meaning, and everybody, knows when the statute uses them what it means to forbid and what conduct it prescribes. But the word "just cause" in this connection has no popular or settled legal meaning, and the very statute shows on its face that the justice of the cause is to be ascertained by the judge and jury in view of the facts of the particular case. They have no constitutional history or meaning as has the term "just compensation" as used in the 15th amendment; nor have they any well defined, settled meaning at the common law. To uphold this statute is to repudiate Section 7 of the Alabama Bill of Rights.

The defendant in error cannot derive any comfort from the decision in *Freeman v. United States,* 217 U.S. 539. The defendant was convicted for embezzling money. No element of performance of a contract was involved. The local statute imposed punishment for violation of the law for certain term of imprisonment, to uphold the offended dignity of the local sovereign there. It further provided for "subsidiary" punishment according to the value of the property embezzled, etc. The latter it imposed to compel restoration to the wronged party. If the embezzled money be refunded, the subsidiary punishment may be avoided. If it is not, the offender must submit to the punishment, first, for violating the laws of the island, and, secondly, to further punishment to compel restoration to the wronged individual. Of course an embezzler by undergoing punishment for the crime against the state, is not thereby absolved from civil liability for the conversion. There was no violation of any constitutional right or of the Acts of Congress, which stands in lieu of the constitution in the Philippine Islands. That case involved no question of due process of the law, or the denial of equal protection of the laws, or unjust discrimination in the terms upon which a jury trial can be had, or arbitrary presumption of guilt. It involves only a question whether or not there was imprisonment for debt.

The argument in support of the statute confounds throughout different things and proceeds on the supposition that, as the legislature can, under certain circumstances, make certain rules for the government of persons in particular occupations and the liabilities that may result therein, and sometimes justly discriminate between them by imposing different burdens and liabilities, that this same power of classification obtains as to the rights that these persons may enjoy in the courts of justice. But, such persons are not engaged in their calling or occupation when they seek their rights or defend their liberty in a court of justice. Justice is administered without respect of persons or causes. A man's right in the court cannot be different from the like rights granted other men, either because of the manner in which he obtains advances, or the class to which he belongs, or whether he intended to defraud. Justice is not subject to classification, and this statute attempts to make an arbitrary distinction between defendants in these cases and other defendants, as to the extent of the privileges they shall enjoy when proceeded against in the courts of the country for like crime. What is said in *Peonage Cases* 123 Fed. 671, as to the validity of the original statute, 4730 of the Code of '76, before it was amended by the Act of '85, is pure dictum. It was not enquired about in the questions propounded by the grand jury. The Judge's attention was called to the different acts which he declared unconstitutional. In answering questions put by a grand jury, the judge does not have the benefit of argument of counsel, and it is quite apparent from the reasoning of the court as to the case before it, that had the statute have been before it, and the judge's attention been directed to it, and the objections now urged against it, the court would have declared it unconstitutional. The statute then before that court, did not contain the arbitrary legal presumption, embodied in the present statute. However, this may be, in a case which presents such momentous issues, this court will rely upon its own judgment, not attach influence to a mere dictum of an inferior court, in dealing with a different statute.

The fact that Bailey did not offer to testify to his intention does not avoid the effect of the decisions that such evidence cannot be received. It is not deferential to courts to offer evidence which counsel well know the highest court has repeatedly decided is illegal. It is true Bailey had the right to testify in his own behalf, but the statutes of this state prescribe that no presumption shall be drawn against him if he does not testify in his own behalf, and therefore no presumption can be drawn in this case that Bailey had any intention to defraud, because he did not essay the vain task of testifying to his mental status or intent.

The strange contention is made, although the amendment to the statute making the quitting, etc., prima facie evidence of intent to defraud, be stricken out of the statute, yet that a conviction in a court which held that legal presumption warranted and upon which the case was submitted to the jury, should nevertheless be affirmed. If the presumption could not be drawn as a matter of law, and the defendant was convicted by reason of it, the conviction would be illegal, although the remaining parts of the statute were severable from the other feature and capable of carrying out the legislative intent standing alone. See on the general proposition Cooley's Con. Lim. Sec. 178 page 196 and note, where he says, speaking of the presumption in favor of an act as a whole and where parts of it have been declared invalid: "In one case the act should be sustained, unless its invalidity is clear; in the other the whole should fall, unless it is manifest the portion not opposed to the constitution can stand by itself, and that in the legislative intent it was not modified or controlled in its construction and effect by the part which was void."

Again he says, in another place: "We do not know that the legislature would have been willing that a part of the act should be sustained if the remainder were void, and there is generally a presumption, more or less strong, to the contrary." Cooley Con. Lim. note page 197.

(The Peonage Papers, reel 4, frames 722–740, Library of Congress, Washington, D.C.)

Notes

Chapter One: Dark Clouds

1. Michael J. Klarman, *From Jim Crow to Civil Rights: The Supreme Court and the Struggle for Racial Equality* (New York: Oxford University Press, 2004); Frank J. Scaturro, *The Supreme Court's Retreat from Reconstruction: A Distortion of Constitutional Jurisprudence* (Westport, CT: Greenwood Press, 2000); Donald E. Lively, *The Constitution and Race* (New York: Praeger, 1992); Rayford W. Logan, *The Betrayal of the Negro: From Rutherford B. Hayes to Woodrow Wilson* (New York: Collier Books, 1965); Rayford W. Logan, *The Negro in American Life and Thought: The Nadir, 1877–1901* (New York: Dial Press, 1954); Owen M. Fiss, *Troubled Beginnings of the Modern State, 1888–1910,* vol. 8 of The Oliver Wendell Holmes Devise: *History of the Supreme Court of the United States* (New York: Macmillan, 1993), chapter 12; Alexander M. Bickel and Benno C. Schmidt, *The Judiciary and Responsible Government, 1910–1921,* vol. 9 in The Oliver Wendell Holmes Devise: *History of the Supreme Court of the United States* (New York: Macmillan, 1993), chapter 8; John R. Howard, *The Shifting Wind: The Supreme Court and Civil Rights from Reconstruction to Brown* (Albany: State University of New York Press, 1999); and Harold M. Hyman and William W. Wiecek, *Equal Justice under Law: Constitutional Development, 1835–1875* (New York: Harper and Row, 1982).

2. Although Chief Justice Melville W. Fuller (1888–1910), Justice Edward D. White (1894–1910), and Justice Rufus W. Peckham were Democrats appointed to the bench by President Grover Cleveland, Justices Oliver Wendell Holmes (1902–1932), Henry B. Brown (1890–1906), William H. Moody (1906–1910), George Shiras Jr (1892–1903), William R. Day (1903–1922), David J. Brewer (1889–1910), and Joseph McKenna (1898–1925) were Republicans and residents of the North. Justice John Marshall Harlan (1877–1911) was also a Republican but a resident of Kentucky.

3. For more information on the reestablishment of Democratic control over the South after Reconstruction, see C. Vann Woodward, *Origins of the New South, 1877–1913* (Baton Rouge: Louisiana State University Press, 1951). For an overview of race relations in the South after the reestablishment of Democratic control, see Leon F. Litwack, *"Trouble in Mind": Black Southerners in the Age of Jim Crow* (New York: Knopf, 1988).

4. See David M. Oshinsky, *"Worse than Slavery": Parchman Farm and the Ordeal of Jim Crow Justice* (New York: Free Press, 1996), and Matthew J. Mancini, *One Dies, Get Another: Convict Leasing in the American South, 1866–1928* (Columbia: University of South Carolina Press, 1996).

5. See William Cohen, *At Freedom's Edge: Black Mobility and the Southern White Quest for Racial Control, 1861–1915* (Baton Rouge: Louisiana State University Press, 1991). For the exploitative (and racist) nature of the South's labor laws at this time, see Jennifer Roback, "Southern Labor Law in the Jim Crow Era: Exploitative or Competitive?" University of Chicago Law Review 51 (fall 1984): 1161–1192.

6. See, Pete Daniel, *The Shadow of Slavery: Peonage in the South, 1901–1969* (Urbana: University of Illinois Press, 1972); Daniel A. Novak, *The Wheel of Servitude: Black Forced Labor after Slavery* (Lexington: University Press of Kentucky, 1978); Harold D. Woodman, *New South—New Law: The Legal Foundations of Credit and Labor Relations in the Postbellum Agricultural South* (Baton Rouge: Louisiana State University Press, 1995); and Cohen, *At Freedom's Edge*, 228–247.

7. Herbert Shapiro, *White Violence and Black Response: From Reconstruction to Montgomery* (Amherst: University of Massachusetts Press, 1988), 5.

8. Quoted in Daniel, *The Shadow of Slavery*, 28.

9. Ibid., 30.

10. Ibid., 32.

11. Novak, *The Wheel of Servitude*, 84.

12. Joel Williamson, *The Crucible of Race: Black-White Relations in the American South since Emancipation* (New York: Oxford University Press, 1984), 114. On whitecapping, see Jeannie M. Whayne, *A New Plantation South: Land, Labor, and Federal Favor in Twentieth-Century Arkansas* (Charlottesville: University Press of Virginia, 1996), 47–55; Christopher Waldrep, *Nightriders: Defending Community in the Black Patch, 1890–1915* (Durham, NC: Duke University Press, 1993); Richard Maxwell Brown, "The American Vigilante Tradition," in *Violence in America: Historical and Comparative Perspectives*, ed. Hugh Davis Graham and Ted Robert Gurr (Beverly Hills: Sage Publications, 1979); and the following articles by William F. Holmes: "Whitecapping: Agrarian Violence in Mississippi, 1902–1906," *Journal of Southern History* 35 (May 1969): 165–185; "Labor Agents and the Georgia Exodus, 1899–1900," *South Atlantic Quarterly* 79 (1980): 436–48; "Moonshiners and Whitecaps in Alabama, 1893," *Alabama Review* 34 (Jan. 1981): 31–49.

13. Whayne, *A New Plantation South*, 48.

14. Logan, *The Negro in American Life and Thought*, and W. Fitzhugh Brundage, "The Darien 'Insurrection' of 1899: Black Protest during the

Nadir of Race Relations," *Georgia Historical Quarterly* 74 (1990): 234–253. On the radical phase of racism in the South, see Joel Williamson, *Black-White Relations in the American South since Emancipation* (New York: Oxford University Press, 1984), 111–323.

15. Woodward, *Origins of the New South,* 321.

16. See Michael Perman, *Struggle for Mastery: Disfranchisement in the South, 1888–1908* (Chapel Hill: University of North Carolina Press, 2001); Glenn Feldman, *The Disfranchisement Myth: Poor Whites and Suffrage Restriction in Alabama* (Athens: University of Georgia Press, 2004); Kent Redding, *Making Race, Making Power: North Carolina's Road to Disfranchisement* (Urbana: University of Illinois Press, 2003); and J. Morgan Kousser, *The Shaping of Southern Politics: Suffrage Restriction and the Establishment of the One-Party South, 1880–1910* (New Haven, CT: Yale University Press, 1974).

17. Williamson, *The Crucible of Race,* 184.

18. On lynching, see Christopher Waldrep, *The Many Faces of Judge Lynch: Extralegal Violence and Punishment in America* (New York: Palgrave Macmillan, 2002); W. Fitzhugh Brundage, *Lynching in the New South: Georgia and Virginia, 1800–1930* (Urbana: University of Illinois Press, 1993); Philip Dray, *At the Hands of Persons Unknown: The Lynching of Black America* (New York: Random House, 2002); Margaret Vandiver, *Lethal Punishment: Lynching and Legal Executions in the South* (New Brunswick, NJ: Rutgers University Press, 2006); and Michael J. Pfeifer, *Rough Justice: Lynching and American Society, 1874–1947* (Urbana: University of Illinois Press, 2004).

19. Brundage, *Lynching in the New South,* 199.

20. Williamson, *The Crucible of Race,* 263.

21. Charles W. Wynes, ed., *Forgotten Voices: Dissenting Southerners in an Age of Conformity* (Baton Rouge: Louisiana State University Press, 1967), 5.

22. Ibid., 3.

23. Timothy S. Huebner, "The Southern Tradition: Southern Appellate Judges and American Legal Culture in the Nineteenth Century" (PhD diss., University of Florida, 1993), 14. See also, Timothy S. Huebner, *The Southern Judicial Tradition: State Judges and Sectional Distinctiveness, 1790–1890* (Athens: University of Georgia Press, 1999), 190–191.

24. *Slaughter-House Cases,* 83 U.S. (16 Wallace) 36 (1873). Quote taken from Hyman and Wiecek, *Equal Justice under Law,* 478.

25. For more on this decision, see Ronald M. Labbe and Jonathan Lurie, *The Slaughterhouse Cases: Regulation, Reconstruction, and the Fourteenth Amendment* (Lawrence: University Press of Kansas, 2003); Michael A. Ross, *Justice of Shattered Dreams: Samuel Freeman Miller and the Supreme Court during the Civil War Era* (Baton Rouge: Louisiana State University Press, 2003);

Michael Les Benedict, "Slaughter House Cases," in *The Oxford Companion to the Supreme Court of the United States,* ed. Kermit L. Hall, 789–791 (New York: Oxford University Press, 1992); and Donald G. Nieman, "The Fourteenth Amendment Receives Its First Judicial Construction," in *Historic U.S. Court Cases, 1690–1990: An Encyclopedia,* ed. John W. Johnson, 252–260 (New York: Garland Publishing, 1992).

267. John A. Campbell had served as an associate justice of the U.S. Supreme Court from 1853 to 1861 and had concurred with the Court's infamous Dred Scott decision. Campbell reluctantly left the Court when his native Alabama seceded from the Union. See Robert Saunders Jr., *John Archibald Campbell, Southern Moderate, 1811–1889* (Tuscaloosa: University of Alabama Press, 1997).

27. Campbell's argument appears in *Slaughter-House Cases,* 45–57.

28. Both quotes are found in *Slaughter-House Cases,* 69.

29. Quote by Benjamin Butler, quoted in Jonathan Lurie, "Civil Rights or Last Rites," in *Historic U.S. Court Cases,* ed. Johnson, 368. Original quote found in Congressional Record, 43 Cong., 1st sess. (Dec. 19, 1973), 341.

30. *Slaughter-House Cases,* 82.

31. Donald E. Lively, *The Constitution and Race* (New York: Praeger, 1992), 68.

32. Ibid., 68.

33. *U.S. v. Harris,* 106 U.S. 629 (1883).

34. *Civil Rights Cases,* 109 U.S. 3 (1883).

35. Ibid., 20, 23; *Plessy v. Ferguson,* 163 U.S. 537 (1896).

36. Garner failed to pay a "capitation tax" to vote. He accused the election officials of allowing whites to pay the tax at the polls, but of denying this privilege to those blacks who, like himself, had failed to pay earlier but were willing to do so at the polls as well.

37. *U.S. v. Reese,* 92 U.S. 214 (1876).

38. Explanations of *U.S. v. Reese* can be found in Robert M. Goldman, *Reconstruction and Black Suffrage: Losing the Vote in Reese and Cruikshank* (Lawrence: University Press of Kansas, 2001); Charles Fairman, *Reconstruction and Reunion, 1864–88* (New York: Macmillan, 1987), part 2, 225–261; and Robert M. Goldman, "No 'Right' to Vote: The Reconstruction Election Cases," in *Historic U.S. Court Cases,* ed. Johnson, 363–366.

39. For a discussion of *U.S. v. Cruikshank,* see: Goldman, *Reconstruction and Black Suffrage,* Fairman, *Reconstruction and Reunion,* part 2, 239–374, and Goldman, "No 'Right' to Vote," 363–366.

40. "The Supreme Court and the Negro," *Voice of the Negro* 1 (June 1904): 217.

41. Logan, *The Betrayal of the Negro,* 105.

42. Linda Przybyszewski, *The Republic According to John Marshall Harlan* (Chapel Hill: University of North Carolina Press, 1999), 1–13.

43. Benjamin N. Cardozo, *The Nature of the Judicial Process* (New Haven: Yale University Press, 1921), 12.

44. Jacob Trieber to Thomas Goode Jones, Oct. 14, 1904, Jones Papers, Alabama Department of Archives and History, Montgomery, AL, hereafter cited as ADAH.

45. Michael J. Klarman, *From Jim Crow to Civil Rights: The Supreme Court and the Struggle for Racial Equality* (New York: Oxford University Press, 2004).

46. Ibid., 5–6.

47. Ibid., 5–6, 447–450.

48. Ibid., 6, 447; *Brown v. Board of Education,* 347 U.S. 483 (1954).

49. Ibid., 263, 266, 273, 294, and 459.

50. Ibid., 446–447.

51. Ibid., 450.

52. Ibid.

53. In his article "Race Relations Law and the Tradition of Celebration: The Case of Professor Schmidt," *Columbia Law Review* 86 (1986): 1622–1661, Randall Kennedy makes a similar point, showing that Supreme Court justices during the nadir could not but be aware of the arguments of those championing racial equality.

54. Paul M. Gaston, *The New South Creed: A Study in Southern Mythmaking* (New York: Alfred A. Knopf, 1970).

55. On paternalism, see George M. Frederickson, *The Black Image in the White Mind: The Debate on Afro-American Character and Destiny, 1817–1914* (New York: Harper, Row, 1971), 198–227.

Chapter Two: Judge Jacob Trieber

1. Gerald Heaney, "Jacob Trieber: Lawyer, Politician, Judge," *University of Arkansas at Little Rock Law Journal* 8 (1985–86): 422–424. See also, Jacob Trieber Collection, Arkansas History Commission, Little Rock, AR, which contains the material Heaney collected for his article on Trieber.

2. Heaney, "Jacob Trieber," 425–428. Trieber founded and served as the president of the First National Bank of Helena. In addition he served fifteen years on the Helena City Council (1882–1897) and five years as the treasurer of Phillips County (1892–1897).

3. Heaney, "Jacob Trieber," 425–428.

4. *Proceedings of the Thirty-First Annual Session of the Bar Association of Arkansas* (Hot Springs, AR: n.p., 1928), 132.

5. The African American, Benjamin Moreland, "acted as the agent of the other defendants in their dealings with the negroes [held in a state of peonage]." *Arkansas Gazette,* April 8, 1905, 1.

6. Charge to Grand Jury, *Peonage Cases,* 136 Fed. 707 (District Court, E.D. Arkansas, W.D., April 8, 1905).

7. Ibid., 708. This quote also appears in Heaney, "Jacob Trieber," 452.

8. Ibid., 709–710.

9. *Arkansas Gazette,* April 8, 1905, 1.

10. Ibid., April 9, 1905, 2.

11. Ibid., April 18, 1905, 6.

12. Ibid., April 19, 1905, 5. The peonage cases are discussed in Heaney, "Jacob Trieber," 451–452.

13. Quoted in Richard C. Cortner, *A Mob Intent on Death: The NAACP and the Arkansas Riot Cases* (Middletown, CT: Wesleyan University Press, 1988), 29. Quote taken from Walter White's article in the *Chicago Daily News,* Oct. 18, 1919. White served as executive secretary of the NAACP from 1931 to 1955.

14. Cortner, *A Mob Intent on Death,* 29–30; Heaney, "Jacob Trieber," 453; Arthur Waskow, *From Race Riot to Sit-In, 1919 and the 1960s,* (Garden City, NY: Doubleday & Co., 1966), 120–174. On the race riot, see Grif Stockley, *Blood in Their Eyes: The Elaine Race Massacres of 1919* (Fayetteville: University of Arkansas Press, 2001); and Jeannie Whayne, "Low Villains and Wickedness in High Places: Race and Class in the Elaine Race Riots," *Arkansas Historical Quarterly* 58 (autumn 1999): 285–313.

15. Stockley asserts that as many as 856 blacks may have been killed in the riot, many of them by National Guardsmen sent in to quell the violence. This figure is disputed by Jeannie Whayne. See, Grif Stockley and Jeannie Whayne, "Federal Troops and the Elaine Massacres: A Colloquy," *Arkansas Historical Quarterly* 61 (autumn 2002): 272–283. On Trieber's involvement in the affair, see Stockley, *Blood in Their Eyes,* 203–210; Cortner, *A Mob Intent on Death,* 78–81, 114–117, and 131.

16. The whitecapping cases are discussed in Heaney, "Jacob Trieber," 442–449.

17. *Arkansas Gazette,* March 17, 1904, 1.

18. Section 1978, Revised Statutes, U.S. Comp. Stat. 1901, 1259. See Appendix A for full text of section 1978.

19. Section 5508, Revised Statutes, U.S. Comp. Stat. 1901, 3712. A history of section 5508 is contained in *United States v. Williams,* 341 U.S. 84 (1951). See Appendix A for the full text of these statutes.

20. Judge Trieber's charge to the grand jury was published in the *Arkansas Gazette,* Oct. 7, 1903, 1–2. The full text of this charge is reprinted in Appendix B.

21. *Arkansas Gazette,* Oct. 7, 1903, 1.

22. Ibid., 1.

23. Ibid., 2.

24. Ibid., Oct. 10, 1903, 1.

25. *United States v. Morris, et al.,* 125 Fed. 322 (District Court, E.D. Arkansas, Oct. 9, 1903).

26. *U.S. v. Morris,* 322–323

27. *Civil Rights Cases,* 109 U.S. 23.

28. *U.S. v. Morris,* 323.

29. Ibid., 327.

30. Ibid., 328.

31. Ibid.

32. Ibid.,

33. Ibid.

34. *Prigg v. Pennsylvania,* 16 Pet. 539.

35. *U.S. v. Morris,* 330.

36. Ibid., 330.

37. Judge David D. Shelby to Judge Thomas Goode Jones, Sept. 14, 1904, Thomas Goode Jones Papers, Alabama Department of Archives and History, Montgomery, Alabama, box 3, file 29; hereafter cited as ADAH. The underlining of the term "race" appears in the original.

38. Thomas Roulhac to Judge Jones, Oct. 5, 1904, Jones Papers, ADAH, box 3, file 29.

39. Richard L. Niswonger, "James Paul Clarke," in *The Governors of Arkansas: Essays in Political Biography,* ed. Timothy P. Donovan and Willard B. Gatewood Jr., (Fayetteville: University of Arkansas Press, 1981) 97–102.

40. *Arkansas Gazette,* Oct. 14, 1903, 4.

41. Ibid.

42. Ibid.

43. Ibid., Oct. 18, 1903, 4.

44. *Pine Bluff Daily Graphic,* March 18, 1904, 1; *Arkansas Gazette,* March 18, 1904, 1; Heaney, "Jacob Trieber," 445.

45. Ibid.

46. *Arkansas Gazette,* March 20, 1901, 1; Heaney, "Jacob Trieber," 445.

47. Ibid.

48. Ibid.

49. *Arkansas Gazette,* March 20, 1904, 1; Heaney, "Jacob Trieber," 446.

50. Judge Jacob Trieber to Judge Thomas Goode Jones, Oct. 14, 1904, Jones Papers, ADAH, box 3, file 29.

51. Trieber to Jones, Sept. 23, 1904, Jones Papers, ADAH, box 3, file 29.

52. *Hodges v. United States,* 203 U.S. 1.

53. Ibid., 16–17.

54. Ibid., 18.

55. Ibid., 27.

56. Ibid., 31.

57. *Clyatt v. United States,* 197 U.S. 207, 25 Sup. Ct. Rep. 429.

58. *Hodges v. United States,* 34.

59. Ibid., 37.

60. Statement of Federal Grand Jury, Case No. 2650, Case Files, U.S. District Court, Eastern District of Arkansas, Little Rock Division Criminal Records, Record Group 21, National Archives, Regional Branch, Southwest Region, Fort Worth, TX.

61. *Arkansas Gazette,* May 30, 1906, 6.

62. Term Docket Book, Vol. 3, Texarkana Criminal Records, U.S. District Court, Eastern District of Texas, Case numbers 798, 894, 895, 896, 921, and 922, Record Group 21, National Archives, Southwest Region, Fort Worth, TX.

63. Gerald W. Heaney, "Busing, Timetables, Goals, and Ratios: Touchstones of Equal Opportunity," *Minnesota Law Review* 69 (April 1985): 760–761.

64. Harold M. Hyman and William M. Wiecek, *Equal Justice under Law: Constitutional Development, 1835–1875* (New York: Harper and Row, 1982), 501.

65. Mary Frances Berry, *Black Resistance, White Law: A History of Constitutional Racism in America* (New York: Appleton-Century-Crofts, 1971), 128, n.88. Heaney, "Jacob Trieber," 449.

66. Whayne, *A New Plantation South,* 52–53.

67. *Jones v. Alfred H. Mayer Co.,* 392 U.S. 409 (1968).

68. Ibid., 419. Section 1978 is now known as 42 U.S.C. 1982 and is referred to as such in the *Jones* opinion.

69. Ibid., 442–443, n.78.

70. Ibid., 439.

71. Ibid., 421–22.

72. Ibid., 422.

73. Ibid., 443, emphasis added by author.

74. All quotes and information taken from *Proceedings of the Thirty-First Annual Session of the Bar Association of Arkansas* (Hot Springs, AR: n.p., 1928), 132–133.

75. Ibid. Judge Trieber also heard more than 350 cases while sitting on the U.S. Court of Appeals for the Eighth Circuit in St. Louis, Missouri. See Heaney, "Jacob Trieber," 437.

Chapter Three: Judge Emory Speer

1. Mary Ann Hawkins, "'He Drew the Lightning': Emory Speer, Federal Judge in Georgia, 1885–1918" (MA thesis, Georgia State University, 1984), 55. This work provides a good overview of Speer's career but devotes special attention to the attempt made in Congress to impeach him and other judges in the early twentieth century.

2. Hawkins, "'He Drew the Lightning,'" 19–21, and Timothy S. Huebner, "The Southern Judicial Tradition: Southern Appellate Judges and American Legal Culture in the Nineteenth Century" (PhD dissertation, University of Florida, 1993), 294. An adaptation of his dissertation, Timothy S. Huebner's *The Southern Judicial Tradition: State Judges and Sectional Distinctiveness, 1790–1890* (Athens: University of Georgia Press, 1999) does not retain his chapter on Emory Speer. Speer never served as a state judge.

3. Hawkins, "'He Drew the Lightning,'" 21–23; Huebner, "The Southern Judicial Tradition," 294–296.

4. Hawkins, "'He Drew the Lightning,'" 24–27; Huebner, "The Southern Judicial Tradition," 296–298.

5. Hawkins, "'He Drew the Lightning,'" 28–47l; Huebner, "The Southern Judicial Tradition," 298–300.

6. Hawkins, "'He Drew the Lightning,'" 21–25, 48–49; Huebner, "The Southern Judicial Tradition," 296–301.

7. Taken from the official testimony of Sallie Bryson. Quoted in Emory Speer, *Argument of Emory Speer, United States Attorney, in the Case of the United States versus Jasper Yarbrough* (Atlanta: W. H. Scott, 1883), 10–11, located in Special Collections Department, Robert W. Woodruff Library, Emory University, Atlanta, GA.

8. Ibid., 24–26. Based on the testimony of Berry and Maria Sanders.

9. Ibid., 31–33. Based on the testimony of Cad Bush.

10. *Atlanta Constitution,* Oct. 14, 1883, 11.

11. Ibid.

12. *New York Times,* Oct. 28, 1883, 1.

13. *Atlanta Constitution,* Oct. 14, 1883, 11.

14. Ibid., Oct. 24, 1883, 7.

15. See Appendix A for the full text of Statute 5508.

16. Speer, *Argument of Emory Speer,* 9.

17. Ibid., 57–58. Speer mentions the "murder" of blacks, but the Yarbrough gang was not accused of such a crime. The alleged nightriding activities of the Yarbrough gang were but one part of the racial violence that Banks, Jackson, and Cobb counties experienced during July and August of 1883. This racial violence did include a few blacks being murdered by white-cappers, but the Yarbroughs were not tried for murder. See *Atlanta Constitution,* Aug. 2, 1883, 4; Aug. 12, 1883, 3; and Oct. 5, 1883, 7.

18. Speer, *Argument of Emory Speer,* 59.

19. Ibid., 60.

20. For Judge McCay's charge, see *Atlanta Constitution,* Oct. 27, 1883, 7, and Oct. 28, 1883, 5. The makeup of the jury is given in the *Atlanta Constitution,* Oct. 23, 1883, 7.

21. *New York Times,* Oct. 28, 1883, 1.

22. Ibid.

23. Stated in Justice Miller's opinion for the Supreme Court in *Ex Parte Yarbrough,* 110 U.S. 653.

24. *Atlanta Constitution,* March 4, 1884, 1.

25. Robert J. Cottrol, "Miller, Samuel Freeman," in *The Oxford Companion to the Supreme Court of the United States,* ed. Kermit Hall, 548 (New York: Oxford University Press, 1992).

26. *Ex Parte Yarbrough,* 657–658.

27. Ibid., 665.

28. Ibid., 667.

29. *James v. Bowman,* 190 U.S. 127 (1903).

30. Ward Y. E. Elliott, "Yarbrough, Ex parte," in Hall, *The Oxford Companion to the Supreme Court of the United States,* 946–947.

31. Alexander M. Bickel and Benno C. Schmidt Jr., *The Judiciary and Responsible Government, 1910–1921* (New York: Macmillan Publishing Co., 1984), 923.

32. Hawkins, "'He Drew the Lightning,'" 50.

33. Ibid., 50. See also George B. Tindall, *South Carolina Negroes, 1877–1900* (Columbia: University of South Carolina Press, 1952), 71–72.

34. Hawkins, "'He Drew the Lightning,'" 51.

35. Background information on this case is based on Huebner, "The Southern Judicial Tradition," 322; Hawkins, "'He Drew the Lightning,'" 66;

and John Dittmer, *Black Georgia in the Progressive Era, 1900–1920* (Urbana: University of Illinois Press, 1977), 72–75. For a glimpse into the life of a black Georgia peon, see "The Life Story of a Negro Peon," *The Life Stories of Undistinguished Americans as Told by Themselves,* ed. Hamilton Holt (New York: J. Pott and Company, 1806), 183–199.

36. "Opinion of Judge Emory Speer," *United States v. Thomas McClellan and William Crawley,* March 15, 1904, District Court, Southern District of Georgia, Eastern Division, Case No. 10165 and 10166, in Record Group 21, National Archives, Southeast Region, East Point, GA. The full text of Speer's charge is in Appendix E.

37. Ibid.

38. Ibid.

39. "Sentence by Judge Speer," *United States v. Thomas McClellan and William Crawley,* March 15, 1904, District Court, Southern District of Georgia, Eastern Division, Case No. 10165 and 10166, in Record Group 21, National Archives, Southeast Region, East Point, GA.

40. Ibid.

41. Hawkins, "'He Drew the Lightning, '" 68; *Savannah Press,* March 22, 1905, 1.

42. Emory Speer to Theodore Roosevelt, April 9, 1904, Theodore Roosevelt Papers, Library of Congress, Washington, DC, microfilm, series 1, reel 43.

43. "Judge Speer on Even-Handed Justice," *Voice of the Negro* (Jan. 1905): 683–684; Hawkins, "'He Drew the Lightning, '" 68.

44. *Crisis* 2 (July 1911): 96.

45. "Judge Speer and the Chain Gang," *Voice of the Negro* 1 (Aug. 1904): 300–301.

46. Ibid., 300.

47. Hawkins, "'He Drew the Lightning, '" 80.

48. Court Transcript, Henry Jamison testimony, Habeas Corpus Proceedings, March 23, 1904, 4, in box 1, file 13, Habeas Corpus cases, Southern District of Georgia, Western (Macon) Division, RG 21, National Archives, Southeast Region.

49. Opinion, *Wimbish v. Jamison,* 1, in box 1, file 37, Habeas Corpus Cases, Southern District of Georgia, RG 21, National Archives, Southeast Region.

50. Ibid., 6.

51. Ibid., 2.

52. Ibid., 6–7.

53. Ibid., 10.

54. Ibid., 12.

55. Ibid., 10–11, 14–15.

56. Ibid., 14.

57. *Wimbish v. Jamison,* 199 U.S. 599.

58. Hawkins, "'He Drew the Lightning, '" 80.

59. *In re Birdsong,* 39 Fed. Rep. 599 (1889).

60. See Huebner, "The Southern Judicial Tradition," 320.

61. Margo Schlanger, "Beyond the Hero Judge: Institutional Reform Litigation as Litigation," *Michigan Law Review* 97 (May 1999): 2000.

62. For the impeachment attempt against Speer, and his death, see Hawkins, "'He Drew the Lightning, '" 84–122.

Chapter Four: Judge Thomas Goode Jones

1. Louis Harlan, *Booker T. Washington: The Making of a Black Leader, 1865–1901* (New York: Oxford University Press, 1972), 255–256.

2. For biographical information on Jones, see Paul M. Pruitt Jr., "Thomas Goode Jones," in *Alabama Governors: A Political History of the State,* ed. Samuel L. Webb and Margaret E. Armbrester (Tuscaloosa: University of Alabama Press, 2001); John A. Eidsmoe, *Warrior, Statesman, Jurist for the South: The Life, Legacy, and Law of Thomas Goode Jones* (Harrisonburg, VA: Sprinkle Publications, 2003); and John Witherspoon DuBose, "A Historian's Tribute to Thomas Goode Jones," *Alabama Lawyer* 14 (Jan. 1953): 1–13.

3. Paul Pruitt, "Thomas Goode Jones, 1844–1914: Personal Code of a Public Man," in *Gilded Age Legal Ethics: Essays on Thomas Goode Jones' 1887 Code and the Regulation of the Profession,* ed. Carol Rice Andrews, Paul M. Pruitt Jr., and David I. Durham, 67–72 (Tuscaloosa: Occasional Publication of the Bounds Law Library, 2003). Quote taken from John Witherspoon DuBose, "A Historian's Tribute to Thomas Goode Jones," *Alabama Lawyer* 14 (Jan. 1953): 11. It should be noted that Blackstone emphasized the importance of rule of law and of precedent, both of which help to explain Jones's rulings on civil rights (see Conclusion, this chapter).

4. Thomas McAdory Owen, *History of Alabama and Dictionary of Alabama Biography* (Chicago, IL: The S. J. Clarke Publishing Company, 1921), 1714.

5. Andrews, Pruitt, and Durham, *Gilded Age Legal Ethics;* Benjamin P. Crum, "The Alabama Code of Legal Ethics," *Alabama Lawyer* 2 (July 1941): 245–246; Walter B. Jones, "Canons of the Professional Ethics, Their Genesis and History," *Alabama Lawyer* 2 (July 1941): 247–258, reprinted from the

Notre Dame Lawyer 7 (May 1932): 483–494; Joe D. Phelps, "Bust of Governor Jones Presented Law School," *Alabama Lawyer* 17 (Jan. 1956): 5–17; Walter B. Jones, "History of the Alabama Lawyers' Code of Ethics," *Alabama Lawyer* 17 (Jan. 1956): 18–24; and John J. Sparkman, "Thomas Goode Jones, Author, First Lawyers' Code of Ethics," *Congressional Record: Proceedings and Debates of the 85th Congress, Second Session,* 1–4.

6. Karl Rodabaugh, "The Alliance in Politics: The Alabama Gubernatorial Election of 1890," *Alabama Historical Quarterly* 34 (spring 1974): 54–80; Karl Rodabaugh, "'Kolbites' Versus Bourbons: The Alabama Gubernatorial Election of 1892," *Alabama Historical Quarterly* 38 (winter 1975): 275–321; Charles Summersell, "The Alabama Governor's Race in 1892," *Alabama Review* 8 (Jan. 1955): 5–35.

7. Rodabaugh, "The Alliance in Politics," 54–80.

8. Governor Jones's inaugural address can be found in the *Montgomery Advertiser,* Dec. 2, 1890, 1.

9. A number of newspaper excerpts, including this one from the *Sumter Sun,* were quoted in *Montgomery Advertiser,* Dec. 2, 1890, 7.

10. For an overview of Jones's political career, see Brent J. Aucoin, "Thomas Goode Jones and African American Civil Rights in the New South," *Historian* 60 (winter 1998): 257–271.

11. *Official Proceedings of the Constitutional Convention of the State of Alabama, May 21st, 1901 to September 3rd, 1901* (Wetumpka, AL: Wetumpka Printing Co., 1901), 4:4303, 3:4085–4088, and 3:2887–2889.

12. For Washington's role in getting President Roosevelt to nominate Jones for the bench, see Louis R. Harlan, *Booker T. Washington: The Making of a Black Leader, 1856–1901* (New York: Oxford University Press, 1972), 308–311.

13. Thomas Goode Jones to P. C. Knox, Attorney General, March 21, 1903, National Archives (hereafter cited as NA), Department of Justice files (DOJ), file folder (ff) 5280–5203, Record Group (RG) 60.

14. Ibid.

15. B. W. Walker to P. C. Knox, Attorney General, May 14, 1903, NA, DOJ files, ff 5280–5203, RG 60.

16. Sara Elizabeth Oswald Stoddard, "An Experiment in Progressivism: Alabama's Crusade against Peonage, 1900–1915" (MA thesis, Auburn University, 1979), 16, 114.

17. *The Peonage Cases,* 123 F. 671 (M.D. Ala. 1903).

18. Ibid., 674.

19. Sections 1990 and 5526 of the Revised Statutes of the United States (U.S. Comp. St. 1901, 1266, 3715); *The Peonage Cases,* 675.

20. Jones utilized the same argument to battle lynching. The Supreme Court rejected the idea that Congress had power to prosecute individuals accused of lynching, but upheld it in the case of peonage; *The Peonage Cases,* 676.

21. *The Peonage Cases,* 680, 682.

22. Ibid., 685.

23. Ibid., 688, 690.

24. W. S. Reese Jr. to P. C. Knox, Attorney General, June 15, 1903, "Report on Peonage Cases in the Middle District of Alabama," NA, DOJ files, ff 5280–5203, RG 60.

25. Ibid.

26. Booker T. Washington to Oswald Garrison Villard, June 16, 1903, and Booker T. Washington to Charles Waddell Chestnutt, July 7, 1903, both in *The Papers of Booker T. Washington,* ed. Louis Harlan and Raymond Smock, 7:178–179 and 7:197, respectively (Urbana: University of Illinois Press, 1972).

27. Theodore Roosevelt to Lyman Abbott, June 22, 1903, in *The Letters of Theodore Roosevelt,* ed. Elting E. Morrison, 3:500–502 (Cambridge, MA: Harvard University Press, 1954).

28. Booker T. Washington's address before the National Afro-American Council, Louisville, Kentucky, July 2, 1903, in *The Papers of Booker T. Washington,* ed. Harlan and Smock, 7:187–190.

29. *Montgomery Weekly Advertiser,* July 17, 1903, 9.

30. Ibid.

31. E. P. Maudaure to John E. Wilkie, Aug. 28, 1903, NA, DOJ files, ff 5280–5203, RG 60.

32. *Montgomery Daily Advertiser,* July 24, 1903, 8.

33. Herbert D. Ward, "Peonage in America," *Cosmopolitan Magazine* 39 (Aug. 1905): 426.

34. Pete Daniel, *The Shadow of Slavery: Peonage in the South, 1901–1969* (Urbana: University of Illinois Press, 1972), 67.

35. The unidentified newspaper clipping was enclosed with E. P. Madaure's letter to John E. Wilkie, Aug. 28, 1903, NA, DOJ files, ff 5280–5203, RG 60.

36. Thomas Goode Jones to Booker T. Washington, Aug. 17, 1903, in *The Papers of Booker T. Washington,* ed. Harlan and Smock, 7:268–369.

37. E. P. Maudaure to John E. Wilkie, Aug. 28, 1903, NA, DOJ files, ff 5280–5203, RG 60.

38. Thomas Goode Jones to Booker T. Washington, Aug. 17, 1903, in *The Papers of Booker T. Washington,* ed. Harlan and Smock, 7:268–269.

39. Ibid.

40. Thomas Goode Jones to Booker T. Washington, Sept. 10, 1903, in *The Papers of Booker T. Washington*, ed. Harlan and Smock, 7:281.

41. Stanley W. Frisch to the U.S. Attorney General, Feb. 18, 1904, The Peonage Papers, Library of Congress, Washington, DC, microfilm, reel 2.

42. Charles W. Russell to Attorney General, June 1909, The Peonage Papers, Library of Congress, microfilm, reel 2; Daniel, *The Shadow of Slavery*, 63–64.

43. Daniel, *The Shadow of Slavery*, 67.

44. See "The Case of Alonzo Bailey," *Outlook*, Jan. 21, 1911, 101–104.

45. Louis R. Harlan, *Booker T. Washington: The Wizard of Tuskegee, 1901–1915* (New York: Oxford University Press, 1983), 250; Daniel, *The Shadow of Slavery*, 70–72; Benno C. Schmidt Jr., *The Judiciary and Responsible Government, 1910–1921* (New York: MacMillan Publishing Co., 1984), 858.

46. Thomas Goode Jones to Theodore Roosevelt, Oct. 2, 1908, Roosevelt Papers, Library of Congress.

47. Theodore Roosevelt to Lyman Abbott, June 22, 1903, in *Letters of Theodore Roosevelt*, ed. Morrison, 3:551–552; Stoddard, "An Experiment in Progressivism," 94–95.

48. Fred Ball to Mr. Harr, Oct. 11, 1910, The Peonage Papers, reel 4, frames 722–740. The "Suggestions" are attached to the Ball letter. The full text of these "Suggestions" is reprinted in Appendix F.

49. Ibid., frame 729.

50. Ibid., frames 737–738.

51. *Bailey v. Alabama*, 219 U.S. 219 (1911).

52. Ibid., 244. The majority opinion was written by Justice Charles Evans Hughes, the newest member of the court.

53. *Bailey v. Alabama*, 246

54. David E. Bernstein and Ilya Somin cite *Bailey*'s connection to the Great Migrations to dispute Michael Klarman's assertion that the Supreme Court is not capable of bringing about social change. See Bernstein and Somin, "Judicial Power and Civil Rights Reconsidered," *Yale Law Journal* 114 (Dec. 2004): 612. On the decline of peonage after *Bailey* see ibid., 622. On the Great Migrations, see Nicholas Lemann, *The Promised Land: The Great Black Migration and How It Changed America* (New York: Knopf, 1991); Joe William Trotter Jr., ed., *The Great Migration in Historical Perspective* (Bloomington: Indiana University Press, 1991); James R. Grossman, *Land of Hope: Chicago, Black Southerners, and the Great Migration* (Chicago: University of Chicago Press, 1989); and Stephan Thernstrom and Abigail Thernstrom, *America in Black and White: One Nation, Indivisible* (New York: Simon and Schuster, 1997), 78–96.

55. For threats against Jones during the *Peonage Cases* see C.W. Russell to Attorney General, The Peonage Papers, reel 2.

56. Thomas Goode Jones to Theodore Roosevelt, Sept. 28, 1912, Theodore Roosevelt Papers, Library of Congress.

57. *Ex parte Riggins,* 134 F. 404 (C.C.N.D. Ala., Oct. 24, 1904).

58. For a description of the events in Huntsville, see articles on the lynching in the *Atlanta Constitution,* Sept. 8, 1904, through Sept. 22, 1904; and Ray Stannard Baker, *Following the Color Line: An Account of Negro Citizenship in the American Democracy* (New York: Doubleday, Page and Co., 1908), 191–193.

59. David D. Shelby to Thomas Goode Jones, Sept. 12, 1904, Thomas Goode Jones Papers, Alabama Department of Archives and History (hereafter cited as ADAH), Montgomery, AL, box 3, file 29.

60. Ibid. Full text of Section 5508 is in Appendix A.

61. David D. Shelby to Thomas Goode Jones, Sept. 14, 1904, Jones Papers, ADAH, box 3, file 29. Emphasis appears in the original.

62. Ibid.

63. Paul Speaks to Thomas Goode Jones, Sept. 20, 1904, Jones Papers, ADAH, box 3, file 29.

64. David D. Shelby to Thomas Goode Jones, Sept. 28, 1904, Jones Papers, ADAH, box 3, file 29.

65. *Montgomery Advertiser,* Oct. 12, 1904, 3.

66. Ibid.

67. Ibid.

68. Ibid.

69. Ibid., 11.

70. Ibid.

71. Ibid., 14.

72. Ibid., 3.

73. Newspaper account attached to Jones's letter to Theodore Roosevelt, Oct. 25, 1904, Theodore Roosevelt Papers, microfilm, series 1, film 49.

74. John H. Rogers served as judge of the U.S. District Court for the Western District of Arkansas from 1896 to 1911. In the months before Judge Trieber wrote this letter to Judge Jones, Judge Rogers sentenced convicted whitecappers to prison. In 1905, Judge Rogers unsuccessfully attempted to convince a grand jury to indict the white ringleaders of a race riot in Harrison, AR. See Jacqueline Froelich and David Zimmerman, "Total Eclipse: The Destruction of the African American Community of Harrison, Arkansas, in 1905 and 1909," *Arkansas Historical Quarterly* 58 (summer 1999): 145–148. On Rogers in general, see *In Memoriam, John Henry Rogers* (Fort Smith, AR: Calvert-McBride, 1912).

75. Jacob Trieber to Thomas Goode Jones, Oct. 14, 1904, Jones Papers, ADAH, box 3, file 29. The full text of this letter is reprinted in Appendix C.

76. Ibid.

77. Eli Shelby Hammond to Thomas Goode Jones, Oct. 19, 1904, Jones Papers, ADAH, box 3, file 29.

78. Edmund Waddill Jr. to Thomas Goode Jones, Oct. 26, 1904, Jones Papers, ADAH, box 3, file 29.

79. Ibid.

80. Miriam Leakey to Thomas Goode Jones, Nov. 12 and Nov. 20, 1904, Jones Papers, ADAH, box 3, file 30.

81. Mary Frances Berry, *Black Resistance, White Law: A History of Constitutional Racism in America* (New York: Appleton-Century-Crofts, 1971), 126.

82. Levert Clark to Thomas Goode Jones, Nov. 2, 1904, Jones Papers, ADAH, box 3, folder 30.

83. "An Ardent Admirer (White)" to Thomas Goode Jones, Oct. 12, 1904, Jones Papers, ADAH, box 3, file 29.

84. J. C. Styles to Thomas Goode Jones, Oct. 15, 1904, Jones Papers, ADAH, box 3, file 29.

85. W. R. Pettiford to Thomas Goode Jones, Oct. 17, 1904, Jones Papers, ADAH, box 3, file 29.

86. Wellington Adams to Thomas Goode Jones, Oct. 26, 1904, Jones Papers, ADAH, box 3, file 29.

87. Booker T. Washington to Thomas Goode Jones, Oct. 14, 1904, Jones Papers, ADAH, box 3, file 29

88. H. J. Redd to Thomas Goode Jones, Oct. 14, 1904, Jones Papers, ADAH, box 3, file 29.

89. A. P. Agee to Thomas Goode Jones, Oct. 26, 1904, Jones Papers, ADAH, box 3, file 29.

90. Augustus O. Bacon to Thomas Goode Jones, Nov. 11, 1904, Jones Papers, ADAH, box 3, file 30.

91. T. S. Maxey to Thomas Goode Jones, Nov. 21, 1904, Jones Papers, ADAH, box 3, file 30.

92. Thomas Goode Jones to Theodore Roosevelt, Oct. 25, 1904, Theodore Roosevelt Papers, microfilm, series 1, reel 49.

93. Thomas Goode Jones to Theodore Roosevelt, Nov. 5, 1904, Theodore Roosevelt Papers, microfilm, series 1, reel 49.

94. Harvey E. Jones to Thomas Goode Jones, Nov. 1, 1904, Jones Papers, ADAH, box 3, file 30.

95. *Ex parte Riggins*, 134 F. 404 (C.C.N.D. Ala. Oct. 24, 1904).

96. Ibid., 408.

97. Ibid., 419.

98. Ibid., 409, 422.

99. Ibid., 422. See also Thomas Goode Jones, *Has the Citizen Of The United States, In The Custody Of The State's Officers, Upon Accusation Of A Crime Against Its Laws, Any Immunity Or Right Which May Be Protected By The United States Against Mob Violence?* which was presented to the Alabama State Bar Association, July 1, 1905, and is located in the Library of Congress, Washington, DC.

100. *Riggins v. United States,* 199 U.S. 547.

101. *United States v. Powell,* 151 F. 652 (C.C.N.D. March 22, 1907).

102. Ibid. Italics added by author for emphasis.

103. Ibid., 654.

104. Ibid., 656.

105. Ibid., 656. Italics added by author for emphasis.

106. Ibid.

107. Ibid., 661.

108. Ibid.

109. Ibid.

110. Ibid.

111. Ibid., 660.

112. Ibid.

113. Ibid., 663.

114. Ibid., 664. Italics added by author for emphasis.

115. *United States v. Powell affirmed,* 212 U.S. 564 (1909). As for lynching in particular, Southern Democratic senators prevented any federal anti-lynching laws from being passed by Congress. It was not until World War II that the Civil Rights Section of the Justice Department began to involve itself in the prosecution of lynchers. It did so on the basis of Judge Jones's arguments in *Ex parte Riggins.* It was not until 1953 that the United States experienced a lynch-free year. See Robert K. Carr, *Federal Protection of Civil Rights: Quest for a Sword* (Ithaca, NY: Cornell University Press, 1947), 163–176; and W. Fitzhugh Brundage, *Lynching in the New South: Georgia and Virgina, 1880–1930* (Urbana: University of Illinois Press, 1993), 245–259.

Chapter Five: Conclusion

1. On classical legal thought and legal philosophy at this time, see William M. Wiecek, *The Lost World of Classical Legal Thought: Law and Ideology*

in America, 1886–1937 (New York: Oxford University Press, 1998); Morton J. Horwitz, *The Transformation of American Law, 1870–1960: The Crisis of Legal Orthodoxy* (New York: Oxford University Press, 1992), 3–21; Michael Klarman, *From Jim Crow to Civil Rights: The Supreme Court and the Struggle for Racial Equality* (New York: Oxford University Press, 2004), 2–6; and William W. Fisher, Morton J. Horwitz, and Thomas A. Reed, eds., *American Legal Realism* (New York: Oxford University Press, 1993), xi–xv.

   2. *U.S. v. Morris,* 125 Fed. 322–331 (District Court, E.D. Arkansas, E.D. Oct. 9, 1903).

   3. *Ex parte Riggins,* 134 F. 404.

   4. For explicit statements by Speer and Trieber regarding their use of original intent, see *Clarke v. Central Railroad and Banking Company of Georgia,* 50 F. 341; *In re Charge to Grand Jury,* 151 F. 835; *United States v. Schlierholz,* 137 Fed. 617 (1905).

   5. *U.S. v. McClellan,* 127 Fed. 973 and 975–976; and *U.S. v. Morris,* 125 Fed. 326–327.

   6. For those who question the concept of original intent, see Jack A. Rakove, *Original Meanings: Politics and Ideas in the Making of the Constitution* (New York: Knopf, 1996); and Michael Vorenberg, *Final Freedom: The Civil War, the Abolition of Slavery, and the Thirteenth Amendment* (New York: Cambridge University Press, 2001). In support of the concept of original intent, see Keith Whittington, *Constitutional Interpretation: Textual Meaning, Original Intent, and Judicial Review* (Lawrence: University of Kansas Press, 1999). On general acceptance of a broader interpretation of the amendments, see Robert J. Kaczorowski, "Congress's Power to Enforce Fourteenth Amendment Rights: Lessons from Federal Remedies the Framers Enacted," *Harvard Journal on Legislation* 42 (winter 2005): 187–280; Harold M. Hyman and William M. Wiecek, *Equal Justice under Law: Constitutional Development, 1835–1875* (New York: Harper and Row, 1982), 401–402; and Laurent B. Frantz, "Congressional Power to Enforce the Fourteenth Amendment against Private Acts," *Yale Law Journal* 73 (July 1964): 1354.

   7. See *Jones v. Alfred A. Mayer Co.,* 392 U.S. 409 (1968); and Jacobus TenBroek, *Equal under Law* (New York: Collier Books, 1965).

   8. See Alexander Tsesis, *The Thirteenth Amendment and American Freedom: A Legal History* (New York: New York University Press, 2004), 37–40, 53–57, 79–111; Kaczorowski, "Congress's Power to Enforce Fourteenth Amendment Rights," 187–280; Abel A. Bartley, "The Fourteenth Amendment: The Great Equalizer of the American People," *Akron Law Review* 36 (2003): 473–490; Baher Azmy, "Unshackling the Thirteenth Amendment: Modern Slavery and a Reconstructed Civil Rights Agenda," *Fordham Law Review* 71 (Dec. 2002): 981–1061.

9. *Jamison v. Wimbish,* 130 Fed. 352.

10. *In re Birdsong,* 39 Fed. 598.

11. Recent biographers of Chief Justice John Marshall and Justice John M. Harlan have emphasized the influence that the American Revolution and the Civil War had on those individuals, respectively, and their actions as judges. The Civil War and its aftermath in the South, likewise, had an enormous affect on Trieber, Speer, and Jones and their judicial careers. See R. Kent Newmyer, *John Marshall and the Heroic Age of the Supreme Court* (Baton Rouge: Louisiana State University Press, 2001), 2; and Linda Przybyzewski, *The Republic According to John Marshall Harlan* (Chapel Hill: University of North Carolina Press, 1999), 12.

12. *Official Proceedings of the Constitutional Convention of the State of Alabama, May21st, 1901, to Sept. 3rd, 1901* (Wetumpka, AL: Wetumpka Printing Co., 1940), vol. 4, 4303.

13. *Argument of Emory Speer, United States Attorney, in the Case of the United States versus Jasper Yarbrough* (Atlanta: W. H. Scott, 1883), 57–58, located in Special Collections Department, Robert W. Woodruff Library, Emory University, Atlanta, GA.

14. *United States v. McClellan,* National Archives, Southeast Region, East Point, GA, Record Group 21, District Court, Northern District of Georgia, Case #10165 and 10166. Speer's sentence.

15. The only instance in which Judge Trieber faced the issue of racial disfranchisement came in the case of *Knight v. Shelton,* 134 Fed. 423 (1905), which dealt with the Arkansas poll tax. Trieber ruled that the poll tax was unconstitutional, but only because it did not meet the state constitutional requirement of being ratified by a majority of all those who cast votes in the 1893 election, not just a majority of those who voted on that particular question. Nevertheless, because of his ruling, Arkansas voters did not have to pay a poll tax to vote in federal elections until 1909, when a second referendum on the issue was held and it received the requisite number of votes. See John William Graves, "Negro Disfranchisement in Arkansas," *Arkansas Historical Quarterly* 26 (autumn 1967): 217–220.

16. Jacob Trieber to Henry King, Aug. 8, 1900, Letters of Jacob Trieber, 1898–1903, Letterpress book, sec. 1, shelf 2, book 41, Arkansas History Commission, Little Rock, AR.

17. See Jacob Trieber to Powell Clayton, Oct. 7, 1898, Letters of Jacob Trieber, 1898–1903, Letterpress book, sec. 1, shelf 2, book 41, Arkansas History Commission.

18. Jacob Trieber to Major Charles Gordon Newman, Nov. 21, 1898, Letters of Jacob Trieber, 1898–1903, Letterpress book, section 1, shelf 2, book 41, Arkansas History Commission.

19. Gerald H. Heaney, "Jacob Trieber: Lawyer, Politician, Judge," *University of Arkansas at Little Rock Law Journal* 8 (1985–1986): 431. Original found in the *Arkansas Gazette*, Aug. 29, 1898; Swamp Democrats were those Democrats from delta counties of eastern Arkansas.

20. Jacob Trieber to Theodore Roosevelt, Feb. 27, 1905, Theodore Roosevelt Papers, Library of Congress, microfilm, series 1, reel 53. It may be significant to note that all three judges greatly respected and admired President Roosevelt. Speer and Trieber followed him out of the Republican Party in 1912, and Jones considered him a close friend and claimed to have voted for him, despite his Democratic credentials.

21. Jacob Trieber to W. A. Webber, June 12, 1901, quoted in Heaney, "Jacob Trieber," 440–441.

22. Ibid., 34.

23. *Official Proceedings of the Constitutional Convention of the State of Alabama, May 21st, 1901 to September 3rd, 1901* (Wetumpka, AL: Wetumpka Printing Co., 1940), 4:4304.

24. While attempting to explain Trieber's actions on the bench, Jeannie Whayne points to his embrace of paternalism, as demonstrated by his membership in the secretive and exclusive XV Club. Whayne asserts that while many in that prestigious club no doubt opposed his call for federal intervention, a significant number agreed with Trieber that both the South and blacks would be better off in the care of elites like themselves. Whayne, *A New Plantation South: Land, Labor, and Federal Favor in Twentieth-Century Arkansas* (Charlottesville: University Press of Virginia, 1996), 53–54.

25. W. Fitzhugh Brundage noted that businessmen made up a significant portion of the small number of white southerners who denounced lynching at the turn of the century, primarily out of their economic interests.

26. Heaney, "Jacob Trieber," 463–464.

27. Mary Ann Hawkins, "'He Drew the Lightning': Emory Speer, Federal Judge in Georgia, 1885–1918," (MA thesis, Georgia State University, 1984), 41.

28. Paul M. Gaston, *The New South Creed: A Study in Southern Mythmaking* (New York: Alfred A. Knopf, 1970).

29. Jacob Trieber to Thomas Goode Jones, Oct. 14, 1904, Thomas Goode Jones Papers, Alabama Department of Archives and History, Montgomery, AL, box 3, file 29.

30. Thomas Goode Jones to Theodore Roosevelt, Aug. 3, 1903, Theodore Roosevelt Papers, microfilm, series 1, reel 35.

31. Thomas Goode Jones to Grover Cleveland, Oct. 2, 1901, Theodore Roosevelt Papers, microfilm, series 1, reel 20. Cleveland forwarded the letter to Roosevelt.

Bibliography

Primary Sources

Argument of Emory Speer, United States Attorney, in the case of the United States versus Jasper Yarbrough. Atlanta: W. H. Scott, 1883. Special Collections Department, Robert W. Woodruff Library, Emory University, Atlanta, GA.

Jones, Thomas Goode. Papers. Alabama Department of Archives and History, Montgomery, AL.

The Peonage Papers, Library of Congress, Washington, DC.

Roosevelt, Theodore. Papers. Manuscript Division, Library of Congress, Washington, DC.

Source-Chronological Files, Office of the United States Attorney General, Record Group 60, National Archives, Washington, DC.

Trieber, Jacob. Collection. Arkansas History Commission, Little Rock, AR.

United States Department of Justice Files. Record Group 60, National Archives, Washington, DC.

United States Department of Justice Files. Year Files. 1902–1903. National Archives, Washington, DC.

United States District Court Records. National Archives Regional Branch, Southeast Region, East Point, GA.

United States District Court Records. National Archives Regional Branch, Southwest Region, Fort Worth, TX.

United States District Court Records. Western District of Arkansas, 1844–1906. Special Collections, Mullins Library, University of Arkansas, Fayetteville, AR.

Washington, Booker T. Papers. Manuscript Division, Library of Congress, Washington, DC.

Books

Andrews, Carol Rice, Paul M. Pruitt Jr., and David I. Durham. *Gilded Age Legal Ethics: Essays on Thomas Goode Jones' 1887 Code and the Regulation of the Profession.* Tuscaloosa: Occasional Publications of the Bounds Law Library, 2003.

Bailey, Mark W. *Guardians of the Moral Order: The Legal Philosophy of the Supreme Court, 1860–1910.* DeKalb: Northern Illinois Press, 2004.

Baker, Ray Stannard. *Following the Color Line: An Account of American Negro*

Citizenship in the Progressive Era. New York: Doubleday, Page, & Co., 1908.

Bass, Jack. *Taming the Storm: The Life and Times of Judge Frank M. Johnson and the South's Fight over Civil Rights*. New York: Doubleday, 1993.

Belknap, Michal. *Federal Law and Southern Order: Racial Violence and Constitutional Conflict in the Post-Brown South*. Athens: University of Georgia Press, 1987.

Benedict, Michael Les. *A Compromise of Principle: Congressional Republicans and Reconstruction, 1863–1869*. New York: Norton, 1974.

———. *Preserving the Constitution: Essays on Politics and the Constitution in the Reconstruction Era*. New York: Fordham University Press, 2006.

Berger, Raoul. *Government by Judiciary: The Transformation of the Fourteenth Amendment*. Cambridge, MA: Harvard University Press, 1977; repr., Indianapolis, IN: Liberty Fund, 1997.

Bernstein, David E. *Only One Place of Redress: African Americans, Labor Regulations, and the Courts from Reconstruction to the New Deal*. Durham, NC: Duke University Press, 2001.

Berry, Mary Frances. *Black Resistance, White Law: A History of Constitutional Racism in America*. New York: Appleton-Century-Crofts, 1971.

Bickel, Alexander M., and Benno C. Schmidt Jr. *The Judiciary and Responsible Government, 1910–1921*. New York: Macmillan Publishing Co., 1984.

Bodenhamer, David J., and James W. Ely Jr. *Ambivalent Legacy: A Legal History of the South*. Jackson: University Press of Mississippi, 1984.

Boles, John B., and Evelyn Thomas Nolen, eds. *Interpreting Southern History: Historiographical Essays in Honor of Sanford W. Higginbotham*. Baton Rouge: Louisiana State University Press, 1987.

Brandwein, Pamela. *Reconstructing Reconstruction: The Supreme Court and the Production of Historical Truth*. Durham, NC: Duke University Press, 1999.

Brown, Richard Maxwell. *Strain of Violence: Historical Studies of American Violence and Vigilantism*. New York: Oxford University Press, 1975.

Brundage, W. Fitzhugh. *Lynching in the New South: Georgia and Virginia, 1880–1930*. Urbana: University of Illinois Press, 1993.

Cardozo, Benjamin N. *The Nature of the Judicial Process*. New Haven: Yale University Press, 1921.

Carr, Robert K. *Federal Protection of Civil Rights: Quest for a Sword*. Ithaca, NY: Cornell University Press, 1947.

Chadbourne, James H. *Lynching and the Law*. Chapel Hill. University of North Carolina Press, 1933.

Cohen, William. *At Freedom's Edge: Black Mobility and the Southern White Quest for Racial Control, 1861–1915*. Baton Rouge: Louisiana State University Press, 1991.

Cortner, Richard C. *A Mob Intent on Death: The NAACP and the Arkansas Riot Cases.* Middletown, CT: Wesleyan University Press, 1988.

Cresswell, Stephen. *Mormons and Cowboys, Moonshiners and Klansmen: Federal Law Enforcement in the South and West, 1870–1893.* Tuscaloosa: University of Alabama Press, 1991.

Cummings, Homer, and Carl McFarland. *Federal Justice: Chapters in the History of Justice and the Federal Executive.* New York: Macmillan, 1937.

Curriden, Mark, and Leroy Phillips Jr. *Contempt of Court: The Turn-of-the-Century Lynching that Launched a Hundred Years of Federalism.* New York: Farrar, Straus and Girouz, 1999; repr., New York: Random House, 2001.

Curtin, Mary Ellen. *Black Prisoners and Their World, Alabama, 1865–1900.* Charlottesville: University Press of Virginia, 2000.

Cutler, James Elbert. *Lynch-Law: An Investigation into the History of Lynching in the United States.* New York: Longman, Green and Co., 1905.

Dabney, Virginius. *Liberalism in the South.* Chapel Hill: University of North Carolina Press, 1932; repr., New York: AMS Press, 1970.

Daniel, Pete. *The Shadow of Slavery: Peonage in the South, 1901–1969.* Urbana: University of Illinois Press, 1972.

DeSantis, Vincent P. *Republicans Face the Southern Question: The New Departure Years, 1877–1897.* Baltimore: Johns Hopkins University Press, 1959.

Dittmer, John. *Black Georgia in the Progressive Era, 1900–1920.* Urbana: University of Illinois Press, 1977.

Dorsen, Norman, Paul Bender, Burt Neubrone, and Sylvia Law. *Emerson, Haber, and Dorsen's Political and Civil Rights in the United States.* 4th ed. Vol. 2, *1952.* Boston: Little, Brown and Company, 1979.

Dray, Philip. *At the Hands of Persons Unknown: The Lynching of Black America.* New York: Random House, 2002.

Eidsmoe, John A. *Warrior, Statesman, Jurist for the South: The Life, Legacy, and Law of Thomas Goode Jones.* Harrisonburg, VA: Sprinkle Publications, 2003.

Fairman, Charles. *Reconstruction and Reunion, 1864–88.* Parts 1 and 2. Vols. 4 and 6 of *The Oliver Wendell Holmes Devise: History of the Supreme Court of the United States,* ed. Paul A. Freund and Stanley N. Katz. New York: Macmillan, 1971 and 1987.

Fisher, William W., Morton J. Horwitz, and Thomas A. Reed, eds. *American Legal Realism.* New York: Oxford University Press, 1993.

Foner, Eric. *Reconstruction: America's Unfinished Revolution, 1863–1877.* New York: Harper and Row, 1988.

Frederickson, George M. *The Black Image in the White Mind: The Debate on Afro-American Character and Destiny, 1817–1914.* New York: Harper and Row, 1971.

Freyer, Tony A., ed. *Defending Constitutional Rights: Frank M. Johnson*. Athens: University of Georgia Press, 2001.

Freyer, Tony A., and Timothy Dixon. *Democracy and Judicial Independence: A History of the Federal Courts of Alabama, 1820–1994*. Brooklyn, NY: Carlson Publishing, 1995.

Gaston, Paul M. *The New South Creed: A Study in Southern Mythmaking*. New York: Alfred A. Knopf, 1970.

Gatewood, Willard B., Jr. *Theodore Roosevelt and the Art of Controversy: Episodes of the White House Years*. Baton Rouge: Louisiana State University Press, 1970.

Gillette, William. *The Right to Vote: Politics and the Passage of the Fifteenth Amendment*. Baltimore: Johns Hopkins University Press, 1965.

Goldman, Robert M. *"A Free Ballot and a Fair Count": The Department of Justice and the Enforcement of Voting Rights in the South, 1877–1893*. New York: Garland Publishing, 1990.

————. *Reconstruction and Black Suffrage: Losing the Vote in Reese and Cruikshank*. Lawrence: University Press of Kansas, 2001.

Goodwyn, Lawrence. *Democratic Promise: The Populist Moment in America*. New York: Oxford University Press, 1976.

Grantham, Dewey. *Southern Progressivism: The Reconciliation of Progress and Tradition*. Knoxville: University of Tennessee Press, 1983.

Graves, John William. *Town and Country: Race Relations in an Urban-Rural Context, Arkansas, 1865–1905*. Fayetteville: University of Arkansas Press, 1990.

Griffin, Kathryn. *Judge Learned Hand and the Role of the Federal Judiciary*. Norman: University of Oklahoma Press, 1973.

Hackney, Sheldon. *Populism to Progressivism in Alabama*. Princeton: Princeton University Press, 1969.

Hall, Kermit L., ed. *The Oxford Companion to the Supreme Court of the United States*. New York: Oxford University Press, 1992.

Hall, Kermit L., and James W. Ely Jr. *An Uncertain Tradition: Constitutionalism and the History of the South*. Athens: University of Georgia Press, 1989.

Hamilton, Charles V. *The Bench and the Ballot: Southern Federal Judges and Black Votes*. New York: Oxford University Press, 1973.

Harlan, Louis R. *Booker T. Washington: The Making of a Black Leader, 1856–1901*. New York: Oxford University Press, 1972.

————. *Booker T. Washington: The Wizard of Tuskegee, 1901–1915*. New York: Oxford University Press, 1983.

Harlan, Louis R., and Raymond W. Smock, eds. *The Booker T. Washington Papers*. 14 vols. Urbana: University of Illinois Press, 1972.

Harris, Robert J. *The Quest for Equality: The Constitution, Congress, and the Supreme Court*. Baton Rouge: Louisiana State University, 1960.

Higgs, Robert. *Competition and Coercion: Blacks in the American Economy, 1865–1914*. New York: Cambridge University Press, 1977.

Hirshson, Stanley P. *Farewell to the Bloody Shirt: Northern Republicans and the Southern Negro, 1877–1893*. Bloomington: Indiana University Press, 1962.

Holmes, William F. *The White Chief: James Kimble Vardaman*. Baton Rouge: Louisiana State University Press, 1970.

Horwitz, Morton J. *The Transformation of American Law, 1870–1960: The Crisis of Legal Orthodoxy*. New York: Oxford University Press, 1992.

Huebner, Timothy S. *The Southern Judicial Tradition: State Judges and Sectional Distinctiveness, 1790–1890*. Athens: University of Georgia Press, 1999.

Hyman, Harold M., and William M. Wiecek. *Equal Justice under Law: Constitutional Development, 1835–1875*. New York: Harper and Row, 1982.

In Memoriam, John Henry Rogers: United States District Judge, Eighth Circuit, Western District of Arkansas, 1845–1911. Fort Smith, AR: Calvert-McBridge Co., 1912.

Johnson, John W., ed. *Historic U.S. Court Cases, 1690–1990: An Encyclopedia*. New York: Garland Publishing, 1992.

Kaczorowski, Robert J. *The Politics of Judicial Interpretation: The Federal Courts, Department of Justice and Civil Rights, 1866–1876*. Dobbs Ferry, NY: Oceana Publications, 1985.

Kelly, Alfred H., Winfred Harbison, and Herman Belz. *The American Constitution: Its Origins and Development*. 6th ed. 1948, repr., New York: W. W. Norton, 1983.

Klarman, Michael J. *From Jim Crow to Civil Rights: The Supreme Court and the Struggle for Racial Equality*. New York: Oxford University Press, 2004.

Konvitz, Milton R. *The Constitution and Civil Rights*. New York: Columbia University Press, 1947.

Labbe, Ronald M., and Jonathan Lurie. *The Slaughterhouse Cases: Regulation, Reconstruction, and the Fourteenth Amendment*. Lawrence: University Press of Kansas, 2003.

Litwack, Leon F. *Trouble in Mind: Black Southerners in the Age of Jim Crow*. New York: Alfred A. Knopf, 1998.

Lively, Donald E. *The Constitution and Race*. New York: Praeger, 1992.

Logan, Rayford W. *The Betrayal of the Negro: From Rutherford B. Hays to Woodrow Wilson*. New York: Collier Books, 1965.

———. *The Negro in American Life and Thought: The Nadir, 1877–1901*. New York: Dial Press, 1954.

Magrath, C. Peter. *Morrison R. Waite: The Triumph of Character*. New York: Macmillan, 1963.

Maltz, Earl M. *The Fourteenth Amendment and the Law of the Constitution*.

Durham, NC: Carolina Academic Press, 2003.

Mancini, Matthew J. *One Dies, Get Another: Convict Leasing in the American South, 1866–1928.* Columbia: University of South Carolina Press, 1996.

Morgan, H. Wayne. *From Hayes to McKinley: National Party Politics, 1877–1896.* Syracuse, NY: Syracuse University Press, 1969.

Morison, Elting E., ed. *The Letters of Theodore Roosevelt.* Cambridge, MA: Harvard University Press, 1954.

Morris, Edmund. *Theodore Rex.* New York: Random House, 2001.

Newmyer, R. Kent. *John Marshall and the Heroic Age of the Supreme Court.* Baton Rouge: Louisiana State University Press, 2001.

Nieman, Donald G. *Promises to Keep: African-Americans and the Constitutional Order.* New York: Oxford University Press, 1991.

Niswonger, Richard L. *Arkansas Democratic Politics, 1896–1920.* Fayetteville: University of Arkansas Press, 1990.

Novak, Daniel A. *The Wheel of Servitude: Black Forced Labor after Slavery.* Lexington: University Press of Kentucky, 1978.

Oshinsky, David M. *"Worse than Slavery": Parchman Farm and the Ordeal of Jim Crow Justice.* New York: Free Press, 1996.

Pfeifer, Michael J. *Rough Justice: Lynching and American Society, 1874–1947.* Urbana: University of Illinois Press, 2004.

Przybyszewski, Linda. *The Republic According to John Marshall Harlan.* Chapel Hill: University of North Carolina Press, 1999.

Rabinowitz, Howard. *Race Relations in the Urban South, 1865–1890.* New York: Oxford University Press, 1978.

Rosenberg, Gerald N. *The Hollow Hope: Can Courts Bring About Social Change?* Chicago: University of Chicago Press, 1991.

Ross, Michael A. *Justice of Shattered Dreams: Samuel Freeman Miller and the Supreme Court during the Civil War Era.* Baton Rouge: Louisiana State University Press, 2003.

Saunders, Robert, Jr. *John Archibald Campbell, Southern Moderate, 1811–1889.* Tuscaloosa: University of Alabama Press, 1997.

Scaturro, Frank J. *The Supreme Court's Retreat from Reconstruction: A Distortion of Constitutional Jurisprudence.* Westport, CT: Greenwood Press, 2000.

Schultz, David A., ed. *Leveraging the Law: Using the Courts to Achieve Social Change.* New York: Peter Lang, 1998.

Shapiro, Herbert. *White Violence and Black Response: From Reconstruction to Montgomery.* Amherst: University of Massachusetts Press, 1988.

Smock, Raymond W., ed. *Booker T. Washington in Perspective: Essays of Louis R. Harlan.* Jackson: University Press of Mississippi, 1988.

Sosna, Morton. *In Search of the Silent South: Southern Liberals and the Race Issue.* New York: Columbia University Press, 1977.

Stockley, Grif. *Blood in Their Eyes: The Elaine Race Massacres of 1919.* Fayetteville: University of Arkansas Press, 2001.

TenBroek, Jacobus. *Equal under Law.* New York: Collier Books, 1965.

Tindall, George Brown. *South Carolina Negroes, 1877–1900.* Columbia: University of South Carolina Press, 1952.

Tolnay, Stewart E., and E. M. Beck. *A Festival of Violence: An Analysis of Southern Lynchings, 1882–1930.* Urbana: University of Illinois Press, 1995.

Trelease, Allen W. *White Terror: The Ku Klux Klan Conspiracy and Southern Reconstruction.* New York: Harper and Row, 1971.

Tsesis, Alexander. *The Thirteenth Amendment and American Freedom: A Legal History.* New York: New York University Press, 2004.

Tucker, David M. *Arkansas: A People and Their Reputation.* Memphis, TN: Memphis State University, 1985.

Vandiver, Margaret. *Lethal Punishment: Lynching and Legal Executions in the South.* New Brunswick, NJ: Rutgers University Press, 2006.

Vorenburg, Michael. *Final Freedom: The Civil War, the Abolition of Slavery, and the Thirteenth Amendment.* New York: Cambridge University Press, 2001.

Waldrep, Christopher. *The Many Faces of Judge Lynch: Extralegal Violence and Punishment in America.* New York: Palgrave Macmillan, 2002.

———. *Night Riders: Defending Community in the Black Patch, 1890–1915.* Durham: Duke University Press, 1993.

Waldrep, Christopher, and Donald G. Nieman, eds. *Race, Crime, and Justice in the Nineteenth-Century South.* Athens: University of Georgia Press, 2001.

Waskow, Arthur I. *From Race Riot to Sit-In, 1919 and the 1960s.* Garden City, NY: Doubleday and Company, 1966.

Webb, Samuel L., and Margaret E. Armbrester, eds. *Alabama Governors: A Political History of the State.* Tuscaloosa: University of Alabama Press, 2001.

Whayne, Jeannie M. *A New Plantation South: Land, Labor, and Federal Favor in Twentieth-Century Arkansas.* Charlottesville: University Press of Virginia, 1996.

Whayne, Jeannie M., and Willard B. Gatewood, eds. *The Arkansas Delta: Land of Paradox.* Fayetteville: University of Arkansas Press, 1993.

Whittington, Keith E. *Constitutional Interpretation: Textual Meaning, Original Intent, and Judicial Review.* Lawrence: University of Kansas Press, 1999.

Wiecek, William M. *The Lost World of Classical Legal Thought: Law and Ideology in America, 1886–1937.* New York: Oxford University Press, 1998.

———. *The Supreme Court in American Life.* Baltimore: The Johns Hopkins University Press, 1988.

Wiener, Jonathan M. *Social Origins of the New South: Alabama, 1860–1885.* Baton Rouge: Louisiana State University Press, 1978.

Williams, Lou Falkner. *The Great South Carolina Ku Klux Klan Trials, 1871–1872.* Athens: University of Georgia Press, 1996.

Williamson, Joel. *The Crucible of Race: Black-White Relations in the American South since Emancipation.* New York: Oxford University Press, 1984.

Woodman, Harold D. *New South—New Law: The Legal Foundations of Credit and Labor Relations in the Postbellum Agricultural South.* Baton Rouge: Louisiana State University Press, 1995.

Woodward, C. Vann. *Origins of the New South, 1877–1913.* Baton Rouge: Louisiana State University Press, 1951.

——— ——. *The Strange Career of Jim Crow.* Rev. ed. New York: Oxford University Press, 1957.

Wright, George C. *Racial Violence in Kentucky, 1865–1940: Lynchings, Mob Rule, and "Legal Lynchings."* Baton Rouge: Louisiana State University Press, 1990.

Wyatt-Brown, Bertram. *Southern Honor: Ethics and Behavior in the Old South.* New York: Oxford University Press, 1982.

Wynes, Charles E., ed. *Forgotten Voices: Dissenting Southerners in an Age of Conformity.* Baton Rouge: Louisiana State University Press, 1967.

Zangrando, Robert L. *The NAACP Crusade against Lynching, 1909–1950.* Philadelphia: Temple University Press, 1980.

Articles/Chapters

Alexander, Hooper. "Race Riots and Lynch Law: The Cause and the Cure." *Outlook* 85 (February 1907): 259–268.

Aucoin, Brent J. "Thomas Goode Jones and African American Civil Rights in the New South." *Historian* 60 (winter 1998): 257–271.

Azmy, Baher. "Unshackling the Thirteenth Amendment: Modern Slavery and a Reconstructed Civil Rights Agenda." *Fordham Law Review* 71 (December 2002): 981–1061.

Bartley, Abel A. "The Fourteenth Amendment: The Great Equalizer of the American People." *Akron Law Review* 36 (2003): 473–490.

Bell, Derrick A., Jr. "The Racial Imperative in American Law." In *The Age of Segregation: Race Relations in the South, 1890–1945,* ed. Robert Haws Jackson, 3–28. Jackson: University Press of Mississippi, 1978.

Benedict, Michael Les. "Preserving Federalism: Reconstruction and the Waite Court." *Supreme Court Review* (1978): 39–79.

———. "Preserving the Constitution: The Conservative Basis of Radical Reconstruction." *Journal of American History* 61 (June 1974): 65–90.

Bernstein, David E., and Ilya Somin. "Judicial Power and Civil Rights Reconsidered." *Yale Law Journal* 114 (December 2004): 592–656.

Bootle, William Augustus. "Historical Connections: Henry Kent McCay, Emory Speer, and Alexander A. Lawrence, Sr." *Journal of Southern Legal History* 3 (1994): 327–334.

Brodie, Sydney. "The Federally-Secured Right to be Free from Bondage." *Georgetown Law Journal* 40 (March 1952): 367–398.

Brown, Richard Maxwell. "The American Vigilante Tradition." In *Violence in America: Historical and Comparative Perspectives,* ed. Hugh Davis Graham and Ted Robert Gurr, 144–218. Beverly Hill, CA: Sage Publications, 1979.

Brundage, W. Fitzhugh. "The Darien 'Insurrection' of 1899: Black Protest during the Nadir of Race Relations." *Georgia Historical Quarterly* 74 (1990): 234–253.

Capeci, Dominic J., Jr., and Jack C. Knight. "Reckoning with Violence: W.E.B. DuBois and the 1906 Atlanta Race Riot." *Journal of Southern History* 62 (November 1996): 727–766.

Cardyn, Lisa. "Sexualized Racism/Gendered Violence: Outraging the Body Politic in the Reconstruction South." *Michigan Law Review* 100 (February 2002): 675–867.

"Case of Alonzo Bailey." *Outlook* (January 1911): 101–103.

Claude, Richard. "Constitutional Voting Rights and Early U.S. Supreme Court Doctrine." *Journal of Negro History* 51 (April 1966): 114–124.

Cohen, William. "Negro Involuntary Servitude in the South, 1865–1940: A Preliminary Analysis." *Journal of Southern History* 42 (February 1976): 31–60.

Cresswell, Stephen. "Enforcing the Enforcement Acts: The Department of Justice in Northern Mississippi, 1870–1890." *Journal of Southern History* 53 (August 1987): 421–440.

Crosby, Michael H. "Twentieth Century Slavery Prosecutions: The Sharpening Sword." *Criminal Justice Journal* 8 (1985–1986): 47–88.

Crum, Benjamin P. "The Alabama Code of Legal Ethics." *American Lawyer* 2 (July 1941): 245–246.

Curtis, Michael Kent. "John A. Bingham and the Story of American Liberty: The Lost Cause Meets the 'Lost Clause.'" *Akron Law Review* 36 (2003): 617–668.

Daniel, Pete. "The Metamorphosis of Slavery, 1865–1900." *Journal of American History* 66 (June 1979): 88–99.

DuBose, John W. "A Historian's Tribute to Thomas Goode Jones." *Alabama Lawyer* 14 (1953): 46–68.

Dukes, Marshall Burke. "The Investigation of the Behavior of Judge Emory Speer: Lack of Judicial Temperament Does Not Impeachment Make." *Journal of Southern Legal History* 6 (1998): 1–54.

Eidsmoe, John A. "Warrior, Statesman, Jurist for the South: The Life, Legacy, and Law of Thomas Goode Jones." *Jones Law Review* 5 (2001): 51–225.

Farnum, George R. "Thomas Goode Jones, Warrior, Jurist, and Apostle of Unity." *American Bar Association Journal* (December 1943): 719–721.

Feldman, Glenn. "Lynching in Alabama, 1889–1921." *Alabama Review* (April 1995): 114–141.

Fisher, William W., III. "Texts and Contexts: The Application to American Legal History of the Methodologies of Intellectual History." *Stanford Law Review* 49 (May 1997): 1065–1110.

Frantz, Laurent B. "Congressional Power to Enforce the Fourteenth Amendment against Private Acts." *Yale Law Journal* 73 (July 1964): 1353–1384.

Froelich, Jacqueline, and David Zimmerman. "Total Eclipse: The Destruction of the African American Community of Harrison, Arkansas, in 1905 and 1909." *Arkansas Historical Quarterly* 58 (summer 1999): 131–159.

Gatewood, Willard B., Jr. "Theodore Roosevelt and Arkansas, 1901–1912." *Arkansas Historical Quarterly* 32 (spring 1973): 3–24.

Gillman, Howard. "What's Law Got to Do with It? Judicial Behavioralists Test the 'Legal Model' of Judicial Decision Making." *Law and Social Inquiry* 26 (spring 2001): 465–504.

Gingras, Lambert. "Congressional Misunderstanding and the Ratifiers' Understanding: The Case of the Fourteenth Amendment." *American Journal of Legal History* 40 (January 1996): 41–71.

Goldman, Robert M. "No 'Right' to Vote: The Reconstruction Election Cases." In *Historic U.S. Court Cases, 1690–1990: An Encyclopedia,* ed. John W. Johnson, 363–366. New York: Garland Publishing, 1992.

Graves, John William. "Negro Disfranchisement in Arkansas." *Arkansas Historical Quarterly* 26 (autumn 1967): 199–225.

Harlan, Louis R. "The Secret Life of Booker T. Washington." *Journal of Southern History* 37 (August 1971): 393–416.

Heaney, Gerald. "Jacob Trieber: Lawyer, Politician, Judge." *University of Arkansas at Little Rock Law Review* 8 (1985–1986): 421–478.

Holmes, William F. "Labor Agents and the Georgia Exodus, 1899–1900." *South Atlantic Quarterly* 79 (1980): 436–448.

———. "Moonshiners and Whitecaps in Alabama, 1893." *Alabama Review* 34 (January 1981): 31–49.

———. "Whitecapping: Agrarian Violence in Mississippi, 1902–1906." *Journal of Southern History* 35 (May 1969): 165–185.

Huff, William Henry. "Peonage or Debt Slavery in the Land of the Free." *National Bar Journal* 3 (1945): 43–49.

Huq, Aziz Z. "Peonage and Contractual Liberty." *Columbia Law Review* 101 (March 2001): 351–391.

"Important Court Decision." *Voice of the Negro* 3 (February 1906): 88.

"John H. Rogers." *Proceedings of the 14th Annual Session of the Bar Association of Arkansas* (1911): 21–22.

Johnson, G. G. "Southern Paternalism toward Negroes after Emancipation." *Journal of Southern History* 23 (1957): 483–509.

Jones, Walter B. "History of the Alabama Lawyers' Code of Ethics." *Alabama Lawyer* 17 (January 1956): 18–24.

"Judge Jacob Trieber." *Proceedings of the 31st Annual Session of the Bar Association of Arkansas* (1928): 131–132.

Kaczorowski, Robert J. "Congress's Power to Enforce Fourteenth Amendment Rights: Lessons from Federal Remedies the Framers Enacted." *Harvard Journal on Legislation* 42 (winter 2005): 187–283.

———. "Searching for the Intent of the Framers of the Fourteenth Amendment." *Connecticut Law Review* 5 (winter 1972–73): 368–398.

———. "The Supreme Court and Congress's Power to Enforce Constitutional Rights: An Overlooked Moral Anomaly." *Fordham Law Review* 73 (October 2004): 153–243.

———. "To Begin the Nation Anew: Congress, Citizenship, and Civil Rights after the Civil War." *American Historical Review* 92 (February 1987): 45–68.

Kennedy, Randall. "Race Relations Law and the Tradition of Celebration: The Case of Professor Schmidt." *Columbia Law Review* 86 (December 1986): 1622–1661.

Kens, Paul. "Whose Intent and Which Purpose? The Origins of the Fourteenth Amendment." *Reviews in American History* (March 1992): 59–64.

Lemmon, Sarah M. "Transportation Segregation in the Federal Courts since 1865." *Journal of Negro History* 38 (April 1953): 174–193.

Lurie, Jonathan. "Civil Rights or Last Rites?" In *Historic U.S. Court Cases, 1690–1990: An Encyclopedia,* ed. John W. Johnson, 367–372. New York: Garland Publishing, 1992.

Mack, Kenneth W. "Law, Society, Identity, and the Making of the Jim Crow South: Travel and Segregation on Tennessee Railroads, 1875–1905." *Law and Social Inquiry* 24 (spring 1999): 377–404.

Matthews, John M. "Dissenters and Reformers: Some Southern Liberals between the World Wars." In *Developing Dixie: Modernization in a Traditional Society,* ed. Winfred B. Moore Jr., Joseph F. Tripp, and Lyon G. Tyler Jr., 167–178. New York: Greenwood Press, 1988.

McFeely, William S. "Amos T. Akerman: The Lawyer and Racial Justice." In *Region, Race, and Reconstruction: Essays in Honor of C. Vann Woodward,* ed. J. Morgan Kousser and James M. McPherson, 395–415. New York: Oxford University Press, 1982.

McLaughlin, Glory. "A 'Mixture of Race and Reform': The Memory of the Civil War in the Alabama Legal Mind." *Alabama Law Review* (fall 2004): 285–309.

McMillan, Malcolm Cook. "Thomas Goode Jones, 1844–1914, Warrior, Statesman, and Jurist." *Alabama Lawyer* 17 (1956): 376–381.

Moore, James Tice. "Redeemers Reconsidered: Change and Continuity in the Democratic South, 1870–1900." *Journal of Southern History* 44 (August 1978): 357–378.

Nieman, Donald G. "The Fourteenth Amendment Receives Its First Judicial Construction." In *Historic U.S. Court Cases, 1690–1990: An Encyclopedia,* ed. John W. Johnson, 252–260. (New York: Garland Publishing, 1992).

Norrell, Robert J. "Law in a White Man's Democracy: A History of the Alabama State Judiciary." *Cumberland Law Review* (2001): 135–163.

Palmer, Robert C. "The Parameters of Constitutional Reconstruction: Slaughter-House, Cruikshank, and the Fourteenth Amendment." *University of Illinois Law Review* (1984): 739–770.

"Peonage Cases." *Harvard Law Review* 17 (1903): 121–122.

Pruitt, Paul M., Jr. "The Life and Times of Legal Education in Alabama, 1819–1897: Bar Admissions, Law Schools, and the Profession." *Alabama Law Review* 49 (1997): 281–312.

———. "Thomas Goode Jones." In *Alabama Governors: A Political History of the State,* ed. Samuel L. Webb and Margaret E. Armbrester, 116–121. Tuscaloosa: University of Alabama Press, 2001.

Przybyszewski, Linda. "Judicial Conservatism and Protestant Faith: The Case of Justice David J. Brewer." *Journal of American History* 91 (September 2004): 471–496.

Rable, George C. "The South and the Politics of the Anti-lynching Legislation, 1920–1940." *Journal of Southern History* 51 (May 1985): 201–220.

Riegel, Stephen J. "The Persistent Career of Jim Crow: Lower Federal Courts and the 'Separate but Equal' Doctrine, 1865–1896." *American Journal of Legal History* 28 (January 1984): 17–40.

Roback, Jennifer. "Southern Labor Law in the Jim Crow Era: Exploitative or Competitive?" *University of Chicago Law Review* 51 (fall 1984): 1161–1192.

Rodabaugh, Karl Louis. "The Alliance in Politics: The Alabama Gubernatorial Election of 1890." *Alabama Historical Quarterly* 36 (1974): 54–80.

———. "'Kolbites' versus Bourbons: The Alabama Gubernatorial Election of 1892." *Alabama Historical Quarterly* (winter 1975): 275–321.

Rogers, O. A., Jr. "The Elaine Race Riots of 1919." *Arkansas Historical Quarterly* 19 (summer 1960): 142–150.

Rotnem, Victor W. "The Federal Civil Right 'Not to Be Lynched.'" *Washington University Law Quarterly* 28 (February 1943): 57–73.

Rust, Barbara. "The Right to Vote: The Enforcement Acts and Southern Courts" *Prologue* 21 (1989): 231–237.

Schlanger, Margo. "Beyond the Hero Judge: Institutional Reform Litigation as Litigation." *Michigan Law Review* 97 (May 1999): 1994–2036.

Schmidt, Benno C., Jr. "Juries, Jurisdiction, and Race Discrimination: The Lost Promise of *Strauder v. West Virginia.*" *Texas Law Review* 61 (May 1983): 1401–1499.

————. "Principle and Prejudice: The Supreme Court and Race in the Progressive Era. Part 2: The Peonage Cases." *Columbia Law Review* 82 (1982): 422–496.

Stephenson, D. Grier, Jr. "The Supreme Court, the Franchise, and the Fifteenth Amendment: The First Sixty Years." *UMKC Law Review* 57 (fall 1988): 47–66.

Sullivan, Barry. "Historical Reconstruction, Reconstruction History, and the Proper Scope of Section 1981." *Yale Law Journal* 98 (1989): 541–564.

Summersell, Charles. "The Alabama Governor's Race in 1892." *Alabama Review* 8 (January 1955): 5–35.

Surrency, Edwin C. "The Appointment of Federal Judges in Alabama." *American Journal of Legal History* 1 (April 1957): 148–154.

Swinney, Everrete. "Enforcing the Fifteenth Amendment, 1870–1877." *Journal of Southern History* 28 (1974): 202–218.

Terrel, Mary C. "Peonage in the United States." *Nineteenth Century* 72 (1907): 306–322.

Tsesis, Alexander. "Furthering American Freedom: Civil Rights and the Thirteenth Amendment." *Boston College Law Review* 45 (March 2004): 307–389.

Vines, Kenneth N. "Federal District Judges and Race Relations Cases in the South." *Journal of Politics* 26 (May 1964): 337–357.

Ward, Herbert. "Peonage in America." *Cosmopolitan Magazine* 39 (1905): 423–430.

Whayne, Jeannie. "Low Villains and Wickedness in High Places: Race and Class in the Elaine Race Riots." *Arkansas Historical Quarterly* 58 (autumn 1999): 285–313.

Woodman, Harold D. "The New History Views the Postbellum South." *Journal of Southern History* 43 (November 1977): 523–544.

————. "Post–Civil War Southern Agriculture and the Law." *Agricultural History* 53 (January 1979): 319–337.

Judicial Cases

Bailey v. State. 158 Ala. 18 (1908).

Bailey v. Alabama. 211 U.S. 452 (1908).

Bailey v. State. 161 Ala. 75 (1909).

Bailey v. Alabama. 219 U.S. 219 (1911).

Boyle v. St. Louis & S.F.R. Co. 222 Fed. 539 (1915).
Chicago R.I.&P. Railway Co. v. Ludwig. 156 Fed. 152 (1907).
Civil Rights Cases. 109 U.S. 3 (1883).
Clyatt v. United States. 197 U.S. 207 (1905).
Ex parte Riggins. 134 Fed. 304 (1907).
Ex Parte Yarbrough. 110 U.S. 653 (1884).
Hodges v. United States. 203 U.S. 1 (1906).
In re Arkansas Rate Cases. 168 Fed. 720 (1909).
In re Arkansas Rate Cases. 187 Fed. 290 (1911).
James v. Bowman. 190 U.S. 127 (1903).
Jones v. Alfred H. Mayer Co. 392 U.S. 409 (1968).
Knight v. Shelton. 134 Fed. 423 (1905).
Peonage Cases. 123 Fed. 671 (1903).
Peonage Cases. 136 Fed. 707 (1905).
Slaughter-House Cases. 83 U.S. (16 Wallace) 36 (1873).
United States v. Cruikshank. 92 U.S. 542 (1875).
United States v. Harris. 106 U.S. 629 (1883).
United States v. Morris. 125 Fed. 322 (1903).
United States v. Powell. 151 Fed. 648 (1907).
United States v. Reese. 92 U.S. 214 (1876).
United States v. Reynolds. 235 U.S. 133 (1914).
United States v. Shauver. 214 Fed. 156 (1914).
United States v. Williams. 341 U.S. 84 (1951).
Wimbish v. Jamison. 199 U.S. 599 (1904).

Unpublished Material

Aucoin, Brent. "Thomas Goode Jones, Redeemer and Reformer: The Racial Policies of a Conservative Democrat in Pursuit of a 'New' South, 1874–1914." MA thesis, Miami University, 1993.

Cresswell, Stephen. "Resistance and Enforcement: The United States Department of Justice, 1870–1893." PhD diss., University of Virginia, 1986.

Cummings, William. "Community, Violence, and the Nature of Change: Whitecapping in Sevier County, Tennessee, during the 1890s." MA thesis, University of Tennessee, 1988.

Davis, Hugh Charles. "An Analysis of the Rationale of R epresentative Conservative Alabamians, 1874–1914." PhD diss., Vanderbilt University, 1964.

Frost, Owen Ellis. "Theodore Roosevelt and the South, 1900–1912." MS thesis, Alabama Polytechnic Institute (Auburn University), 1949.

Hamilton, Howard Devon. "The Legislative and Judicial History of the Thirteenth Amendment." PhD diss., University of Illinois, 1950.

Hawkings, Mary Ann. "'He Drew the Lightning': Emory Speer, Federal Judge in Georgia, 1885–1918." MA thesis, Georgia State University, 1984.

Huebner, Timothy S. "The Southern Tradition: Southern Appellate Judges and American Legal Culture in the Nineteenth Century." PhD diss., University of Florida, 1993.

Huggins, Carolyn Ruth. "Bourbonism and Radicalism in Alabama: The Gubernatorial Administration of Thomas Goode Jones, 1890–1894." MA thesis, Auburn University, 1968.

Jones, Thomas Goode. "Has the Citizen of the United States, in the Custody of the State's Officers, Upon Accusation of Crime Against Its Laws, Any Immunity or Right Which May Be Protected by the United States Against Mob Violence?" Paper read before the Alabama State Bar Association, 1904, Library of Congress.

Stoddard, Sara Elizabeth Oswald. "An Experiment in Progressivism: Alabama's Crusade against Peonage, 1900–1915." MA thesis, Auburn University, 1979.

Index

Abbott, Lyman, 57
Akerman, Alexander, 105
Alabama, 2, 20, 26, 30, 45, 52–79, 84, 88,
    110, 123, 124; and Reconstruction, 54;
    1901 Constitutional Convention, 55,
    84, 88; and debt peonage, 55–63;
    Democrats, 64; and disfranchisement,
    54; and lynching, 64–72
Alabama Labor Law (1901), 57, 62
Alfred Mayer Company, 34
American Bar Association code of ethics,
    54
anti-peonage law (1867), 45, 47, 56, 106
Arkansas, 2, 5, 12, 16–35, 69, 74, 86, 88,
    93–95, 97; and debt peonage, 18–20;
    Republicans, 17, 86
Arkansas Gazette: and peonage in Arkansas,
    19–20; and whitecapping, 21, 27–30
Armstrong, William, 19
Arthur, Chester A., 37–38
Ashley County, Arkansas, 19
Atlanta Constitution, 37, 39
Atlantic Monthly, 6

Bacon, Augustus O., 71
Bailey, Alonzo, 62, 117–26. See also Bailey v.
    Alabama
Bailey v. Alabama, 62–64, 79, 117–26; and
    Theodore Roosevelt, 62; and Supreme
    Court, 63
Ball, Fred, 63
Banks County, Georgia, 38–39, 42
Bassett, John Spencer, 6
Berry, Mary Francis, 33
Bickel, Alexander, 44
Birdsong, Nat, 51
Bradley County, Arkansas, 32

Bradley, Joseph P., 9, 23–25, 81, 108
Brewer, David J., 31; and Clyatt opinion, 32
Brewster, Benjamin, 44
Brown, J. F., 30
Brown, Joseph E., 37
Brundage, W. Fitzhugh, 6
Bryson, Sallie, 38
Bryson, Warren, 38
Bush, Cad, 39

Campbell, John A., 7–8
Cardozo, Benjamin, 12
chain gangs, 3; and Fourteenth
    Amendment, 50; in Georgia, 48–51; and
    Judge Speer, 48–51
Civil Rights Act of 1866, 8; declared
    unconstitutional, 31; in Jones v Alfred
    Mayer Co. decision, 34; and whitecap-
    ping in Arkansas, 21, 24–25, 30. See also
    Section 1978
Civil Rights Act of 1870, 9, 11, 21. See also
    Section 5508 and Section 5510
Civil Rights Act of 1875, 9
Civil Rights Cases, 9, 23, 31, 40, 43, 82, 108
Clampitt, William R., 29
Clarke, James P., 27
classical legal thought, 81. See also legal
    formalism
Clayton, Powell, 17, 86
Cleveland, Grover, 37
Clyatt v. United States, 32
Cosby, Barancas, 60–62
Cosby, George, 60–62
Colfax Riot (Grant Parish Massacre), 10
contract-labor laws, 3. See also debt peonage
convict leasing system, 3, in Alabama, 55
Coosa County, Alabama, 60–61

Court of Appeals, U.S. (Fifth Circuit), 26, 64
Crawley, William, 45–47
Crisis, 47–48
Cross County, Arkansas, 21, 29–30

Daniel, Pete, 60
Daniels, Josephus, 6
David, Matilda, 39
Davis, Henry, 19
Davis, Jeff, 5, 27
Day, William R., 31
debt peonage, 3, 4, 6, 13, 110–11; in
    Alabama, 28, 55–63; in Arkansas, 18–20;
    in *Clyatt* case, 32; and Fourteenth
    Amendment, 117–18, 120; in Georgia,
    45–48, 106–7; history of, 56; and Judge
    Speer, 45–48, 105–15; and Thirteenth
    Amendment, 18, 45, 118–20
Democratic Party, 27, 33, 38, 39, 44; and
    contract labor, 3; in Alabama, 64; in
    Georgia, 38; and Judge Jones, 54–56; in
    the post-bellum South, 86; and Recon-
    struction, 2; and white supremacy, 2, 33,
    54, 86
disenfranchisement, 5, 86–87, considered in
    Alabama, 54
DuBois, William Edward Burghardt, 47–48

Elmore, John A., 53
ethics code, 54

Fifteenth Amendment, 2, 6, 10, 23, 43, 44,
    74, 78, 82
Fortune, T. Thomas, 61
Fourteenth Amendment, 2, 6–8, 9, 23–24,
    63, 108, 112; and the chain gang, 50;
    and debt peonage, 117–18, 120; and
    lynching, 66–67, 73–79, 82; original
    intent of, 82–83

Garfield, James, 38
Gaston, Paul, 88
Georgia, 2, 4, 12, 37–51,69 ,98, 113, 115;
    and debt peonage, 45–48, 105–7;
    Democrats, 38; lynching in, 70–71;
    Republicans, 38

Going, L. C., 27, 29
Gordon, John B., 53
Grady, Henry, 37

Hammond, Eli Shelby, 70
Harlan, John Marshall, 11, *Hodges* dissent,
    31–32
Heflin, J. Thomas, 55, 60
Hill, Benjamin H., 38
Hill, Robert, 19
Hodges, Reuben: convicted of whitecapping,
    29, 30. *See also Hodges v. United States*
Hodges v. United States, 31–34, 78; and
    Marshall dissent, 31–32; overruled by
    Supreme Court, 34, 74
Holmes, Oliver Wendell, 63
Huebner, Timothy, 6
Hunt, Ward, 10
Huntsville, Alabama: lynching of Horace
    Maples, 64; and Judge Jones, 64–72
Hyman, Harold, 33

Jackson, Thomas J. "Stonewall", 53
James v. Bowman, 44
Jamison, Henry, 48
Jamison v. Wimbish, 48–51, 83
Jones v. Alfred H. Mayer Co., 33–34, 83
Jones, Joseph Lee, 33–34
Jones, Thomas Goode, 2, 6, 11, 30, 52–79
    81; appointed to federal bench, 53;
    background, 53; and *Bailey* case, 62–64,
    117–26; on change in federalism
    brought about by Civil War, 77–78;
    compared to Judge Trieber on peonage,
    20; and Klarman thesis, 13–14; and legal
    formalism, 12; and lynching, 55; and
    Maples lynching, 26–27, 64–72; motive
    for pro-black rulings, 15, 81–90; opposi-
    tion to convict-leasing, 55; opposition
    to disenfranchisement, 54; opposition to
    race-based funding of public schools,
    54; and *The Peonage Cases,* 45, 55–62,
    110; political career, 54; and race rela-
    tions in the South, 68; at state
    Constitutional Convention, 55; and
    U.S. v. Powell, 74–79

Kentucky, 9
King, William Rufus, 37
Klarman, Michael J., 12–14
Knox, Philander C., 55, 57
Kolb, Reuben, 54
Ku Klux Klan, 4, in Georgia, 42, 45
Ku Klux Klan Act (1871), 9

Leakey, Miriam, 70
Lee, Robert E., 6, 84
legal formalism, 11, 81; and judges, 12
legal realists, 83
Lewis, J. H., 37
Liberman, Samuel H., 34
Lincoln County, Arkansas, 19
Lively, Donald, 8
Lowndes County, Georgia, 45, 106
Louisiana, 7, 10, 11, 24, 124
Lurton, Horace H., 63
lynching, 5–6, 8, 12, 13, 26, 27, 89, 97; in
    Alabama, 53, 55, 64–65; and Fourteenth
    Amendment, 66–67, 73–79, 82; and the
    federal government, 65; in Georgia, 70;
    and Judge Jones, 64-74, 77, 79, 82; and
    Section 5508, 64; and Thirteenth
    Amendment, 66, 68, 70, 72, 74, 82

Macon, Georgia, 48–51
Maples, Horace: lynching of 26, 64–65; and
    Judge Jones, 26–27, 64–72
Maxey, T. S., 71
McClellan, Thomas, 45–47, 105–15
McElwee, John, 19
McKay, H. K., 42
McKinley, William, 17–18
McRee, Edward, 45, 105–6
Melton, Samuel, 44
Miller, Samuel, 7–8, 43, 81, 109
Mississippi, 4–5, 113
Missouri, 17, 33

National Afro-American Council, 58
National Association for the Advancement
    of Colored People, 2, 19, 47
Newman, William, 47
New Mexico, 56, 106

New South; defined, 14; and the judges, 15,
    84–90; and Henry Grady, 37; New
    South Creed, 14
New York Times, 39, 42
North Carolina, 6
Novak, Daniel, 4

paternalism, 11, 14, 46, 84–90
Peck, Elijah Woley, 53
peonage. See debt peonage
Peonage Cases, 56–62, 123, 125; and Judge
    Jones, 45, 55-62, 110
Phillips County, Arkansas, 17, 20
Plessy v. Ferguson, 9, 12, 33
Poinsett County, Arkansas, 21, 25, 29
Powell, Robert, 74
Prigg v. Pennsylvania, 25
Przybyszewski, Linda, 11
Pugh, Joseph, 19
Pugh, Thomas, 19
Pulaski County, Arkansas, 32

radical racism, 14–15, 89
Reconstruction, 3, 4, 6, 8–11, 13, 15, 18,
    32, 33, 53, 72, 77, 78, 81–84, 90, 108; in
    Arkansas, 17; and Democrats, 2; and
    Republicans, 2; and Judge Speer, 38
Reese, William S., Jr., 57
Remmel, H. L., 86
Republican Party, 6, 18, 33, 51, 53, 54, 86;
    in Arkansas, 17, 86; in Georgia, 38; and
    Reconstruction, 2
Rice, Samuel F., 53–54
Riggins, Ex parte, 72–74, 78, 81; and
    Supreme Court, 74, 76–77
Riggins, Thomas, 72–74
Roosevelt, Theodore, 47, 51, 55, 64, 71, 86,
    89, 101, appoints Judge Jones to bench,
    53; and Bailey case, 62; praises Jones for
    anti-peonage efforts, 57–58
Rogers, John H., 12, 30, 69, 98
Roulhac, Thomas, 26–27, 65
Russell, Charles W., 62

Sanders, Berry, 38–39
Sanders, Maria, 38–39

Sanders, Minyard, 39
Section 1978 (Revised Statutes of 1874), 21–23, 26, 32, text of, 91
Section 5508 (Revised Statutes of 1874), 21–23, 26, 32, 93; and lynching, 64; text of, 91; and Yarbrough case, 39, 43
Section 5510 (Revised Statutes of 1874), 21, text of, 92
Section 5520 (Revised Statutes of 1874), 43
Shapiro, Herbert, 4
sharecropping, 3
Shelby, David D., 26, 64–65
Sherman, William Tecumseh, 37
Slaughterhouse Cases, 6–8, 9, 11, 42, 82
Sledd, Andrew, 6
South Carolina, 5, 37, 45; and "Red Shirts," 44
Southern Watchman, 38
Speer, Emory, 2, 6, 11, 36–51 69, 81, 98; and abuse of black prisoners, 51; appointed as federal judge, 37; background, 37; and chain gang, 48–51; death, 51; and debt peonage, 45–48, 105–15; and Klarman thesis, 13–14; and legal formalism, 12; motive for pro-black rulings, 15, 81–90; nearly impeached, 51; political career, 38; on race relations in the South, 40–41, 46; and Reconstruction, 38; and "Red Shirts" in South Carolina, 44; and Yarbrough case, 40–42, 76
Stephenson, Marshall L., 17
Stewart, Potter, 34–35
Story, Joseph, 25
Sumter Sun, 54
Supreme Court, U.S., 1; and *Bailey* decision, 63; and chain gang, 50–51; embraces broad interpretation of Thirteenth Amendment in 1968, 34; and *Hodges* case, 74, 79; and judicial counterrevolution, 6–11, 90; narrow interpretation of Reconstruction amendments, 23, 32–33, 76–77, 79, 90; Republican majority on, 2; and *Riggins* case, 74, 76–77; uphold *Yarbrough* decision, 42
Taft, William Howard, 35, 51

Tallapoosa County, Alabama, 60–61
TenBroek, Jacobus, 83
Tennessee, 8, 70
Texas, 19, 32, 71
Thirteenth Amendment, 2, 4, 6–7, 107–15, broad interpretation of 9, 18, 34–35; and debt peonage, 18, 45, 118–20; and lynching, 66, 68, 70, 72, 74, 82; original intent of, 82–83; and Supreme Court, 34; text of, 107; and whitecapping, 21–26, 28, 31–32
Tillman, Ben, 5
Tompkins, Henry B., 42–43
Trieber, Jacob, 2, 6, 11, 15, 16–35, 57, 65, 68, 72, 79, 81; as an active Republican, 17–18; background, 17–18; and broad interpretation of Reconstruction amendments, 18; corresponds with Judge Jones on lynching, 69–70, 97–99; death, 35; and definition of slavery, 22; and Elaine Race Riot, 20; first Jew appointed as U.S. district judge, 17; and Klarman thesis, 13–14; and legal formalism, 12; motive for pro-black rulings, 15, 81–90; overruled by Supreme Court in *Hodges* case, 31–33; and peonage, 18–20; and race relations in the South, 69; text of charge to the jury in whitecapping case, 93–95; and whitecapping, 21–30
Turner, Fletcher, 59–60

U.S. v. Cruikshank, 10–11, 23, 24, 42–43, 69
U.S. v. Harris, 8–9, 25, 108
U.S. v. Hodges, see *Hodges v. United States*
U.S. v. McClellan and Crawley, 45–47, 81, text of opinion, 105–115
U.S. v. Morris, et al, 23–27, 28, 34, 57, 65, 68, 72, 81
U.S. v. Powell, 74–79
U.S. v. Reese, 9–10, 43, 124

Vardaman, James K., 5
Villard, Oswald Garrison, 57
Virginia, Ex parte, 82
Voice of the Negro, 11, 47–48

voting rights, 2, 5, 9–10, 18–19, 23, 38, 43,
  63, 76, 86. *See also* disenfranchisement

Waddill, Edmund, Jr., 70
Walker, Abram J., 53
Ware County, Georgia, 45, 105
Washington, Booker T., 6, 55, 60; and *Bailey*
  case, 62; and peonage pardons, 61; praises
  Judge Jones for efforts against debt
  peonage, 57–59; praises Jones for *Riggins*
  charge, 71; recommended appointment
  of Jones, 53, 64
Whayne, Jeannie M., 33
Whipple, W. G., 21, 30
White, Walter, 19
whitecapping, 4–5, in Arkansas, 21–32; in
  Georgia, 38; and Thirteenth Amend-

ment, 2126, 28, 31–32; and Judge
  Trieber, 21–30, 93–95
white supremacy, 1, 2, 5, 14, 15, 27, 28, 35;
  and Democrats, 2, 33, 54, 86; in South
  Carolina, 44
Wiecek, William, 33
Williams, John A., 18
Wimberley, Minter, 48
Wynes, Charles, 6

Yancey, William Lowndes, 53
Yarbrough family, 39, 42
Yarbrough, Ex parte, 23, 42–44, 76, 85, 109;
  and Section 5508, 39, 43; and Judge
  Speer, 40–42, 76; and Supreme Court,
  42

Brent J. Aucoin is an associate professor of history at Southeastern College at Wake Forest, a school of the Southeastern Baptist Theological Seminary. He has also taught as an assistant professor of history at Williams Baptist College in Arkansas.